William Spaid
Epiphany 1988

Baptismal Moments; Baptismal Meanings

Baptismal Moments; Baptismal Meanings

Daniel B. Stevick

THE CHURCH HYMNAL CORPORATION, NEW YORK

The Church Hymnal Corporation
800 Second Avenue
New York, NY 10017

10 9 8 7 6 5 4 3 2 1

to Leo

Table of Contents

Introduction,1987

In 1973 the Liturgical Commission was ready to send out for consideration by the Episcopal Church, *Prayer Book Studies 26,* "Holy Baptism together with A Form for the Affirmation of Baptismal Vows with the Laying-On of Hands by the Bishop also called Confirmation." It could be argued that the orders for Holy Baptism and for Confirmation as proposed in 1973 and adopted in *The Book of Common Prayer* 1979 are the most changed of any Prayer Book rites since 1552. Contrarily, it could be argued that the changes are less important than are the continuities between the new rites and the Prayer Book tradition and the early liturgical sources to which it has always appealed. In any case this work of the Drafting Committee, concurred in by the Standing Liturgical Commission, could hardly have been distributed assuming that its intentions would be self-evident. A substantial introductory essay seemed desirable.

I was asked to prepare such a work. Although the general argument was my own, the lines of exposition reflected long months of discussion by an able and devoted Committee. The "Author's Preface" from 1973 is printed here to record the circumstances that brought the work into being and to recall some of the author's specific indebtednesses and fond memories.

The 1973 "Supplement" had an extensive distribution in the Church. It was widely read and—making allowances for readers being kind to an author—widely appreciated. During several months in 1973 and 1974 in which I traveled, speaking to diocesan and other groups about Christian Initiation and the proposed rites, it was quite extraordinary to see how carefully many persons had read the "Supplement" to Prayer Book Studies 26 and what perceptive questions they raised.

In the following pages I shall suggest that the changes of 1973–79 can be understood in the context of: (1) a new cultural situation that requires the church to see itself and its task in new ways; (2) important work in early and medieval sources for our knowledge of the development of Christian initiatory rites, many of which were unavailable to the liturgists of the 16th century, and some of which were quite new to the scholars responsible for the 1928 Prayer Book; (3) recent reinvestigation of the intentions of the first English Prayer Books; and (4) a long history of Anglican discussion and dissatisfaction, scholarly and pastoral.

The rites of Christian Initiation that were adopted in the Proposed Book of 1976 and in the Prayer Book of 1979 were somewhat altered from *Prayer Book Studies 26* of 1973. The "Supplement" thus became outdated. It not only referred to a rite which differed from the Prayer Book text, but as an explanatory account its "tense" was wrong. A rationale was needed after 1976 and 1979, not for a proposed rite, but for the authorized rite of the Episcopal Church. Yet the "Supplement" remained the only work of any length that was specifically addressed to these new rites—rites which were important for the Episcopal Church and were being followed with interest by other churches as well. A number of discriminating people remarked that they wished the "Supplement" might still be available. But it had sold out, and it could not serve a new purpose without revision and updating.

Since 1973 a number of things have happened that alter the situation for which the "Supplement" might have a second life. Some of them are touched upon in the following pages, but just as a record of how rapidly things move in liturgy these days, some of these events of the past fifteen years might be noted:

The rite in *Prayer Book Studies 26* had gone through a number of versions, as drafts were circulated and comments received. The process of change did not stop with the Liturgical Commission's publication of *Prayer Book Studies 26*. As the rite left the hands of the Committee and the Liturgical Commission and moved toward adoption, the words at the "sealing" (*BCP,* p. 308) were altered; someone must have thought they were improved. The single form of "The Laying-On of Hands" by the bishop, which in *Prayer Book Studies 26* had functioned for all of the forms of the renewal of baptismal promises, was broken down into the categories of Confirmation, Reception, and Reaffirmation (*BCP,* pp. 309f. and 418f.). And a rubric (second rubric, p. 412), was added to the directions for the rites—added without the churchwide discussion that so important a provision should have had. With these substantive changes, but with most of its structure and wording intact, the rite was adopted by actions of the General Conventions of 1976 and 1979. It is by now no longer a form of printed words offered for examination and approval, but a living vehicle by which the Church ministers the rites of Christian Initiation. It carries with it more than a decade of pastoral experience by congregations, parish clergy, and bishops.

The very important "Catechumenate" was made available when *The Book of Occasional Services* was authorized, also by the 1979 Convention. This original and usable text (*BOS,* pages 112–125) provides for the special requirements of preparing adults for Baptism, while at the same time its location in a separate document keeps in the text of the Prayer Book a single rite which is suitable for infants, adults, or a combination of the two.

Since the appearance of *Prayer Book Studies 26* and the Prayer Book, there has been a small literature of comment on the Episcopal Church's rites for Christian Initiation:

■ Marion Hatchett, whose own research on Cranmer and the first English Prayer Books had so advanced Anglican thinking on the liturgics of Christian Initiation, wrote an important article supporting the proposed texts in "The Rite of 'Confirmation' in the Book of Common Prayer and in Authorized Services 1973," in *Anglican Theological Review,* 1974.

■ The same year, Leonel Mitchell, who had been a member of the Drafting Committee where his fund of learning put everyone much in his debt, gave a sympathetic explanation of the proposed rites for an ecumenical readership in "Revision of the Rites of Christian Initiation in the American Episcopal Church," in *Studia Liturgica.*

■ For the Fall 1974 number of *Nashotah Review,* Louis Weil wrote "Christian Initiation: A Theological and Pastoral Commentary on the Proposed Rites." This article was published later as a booklet by Associated Parishes. Although it is only sixteen pages long, it is much in little.

■ In 1975 the late Urban T. Holmes wrote *Confirmation: The Celebration of Maturity in Christ.* In this book Dean Holmes was not writing specifically on the rites of *Authorized Services,* 1973 (although his second chapter is informative on the liturgics of Confirmation); rather, he sought to explain Confirmation in ways that were in keeping with the rites as they were developing in the drafting process—a process with which this author was associated. Holmes felt that the liturgical texts had grown out of pastoral insights and that their reception in the church required theological and pastoral rethinking. New Prayer Book rites could not commend themselves without modes of thought appropriate to their reconsidered shape and function.

■ In 1978 a Roman Catholic scholar, Frank C. Quinn, completed his careful comparative study for a dissertation at Notre Dame, "Contemporary Liturgical Revision: The Revised Rites of Confirmation in the Roman Catholic Church and in the American Episcopal Church." The historical work in this thesis is a mine of information and insight.

■ Dr. Mitchell returned to the subject in 1978 in another *ATR* article defending the rites of the Proposed Book against what he took to be uninformed criticisms, "The Theology of Christian Initiation and the Proposed Book of Common Prayer."

■ For a symposium volume, *Prayer Book Renewal,* edited by H. Barry Evans and published in 1978, Bishop Frederick B. Wolf contributed a chapter, "Christian Initiation." Bishop Wolf brought to this essay not only his own wisdom and experience but also his work with the Drafting Committee.

■ In an issue of *Studia Liturgica* devoted to articles on Christian Initiation, Louis Weil, thinking, quite rightly, that a survey of thought and practice in the Anglican Communion by R.C.D. Jasper had been provincially British and had given inadequate attention to the work done in the Episcopal Church, made a brief, well-stated rejoinder, "Christian Initiation in the Anglican Communion: A Response," *SL,* 1977.

■ The splendid work in The Church's Teaching Series on the liturgical system of the Episcopal Church, *Liturgy for Living,* by Charles Price and Louis Weil, 1979, explains the Prayer Book rites of Christian Initiation with informed sympathy.

■ In 1982 A. Theodore Eastman (now the Bishop of Maryland) published his fine work, *The Baptizing Community: Christian Initiation and the Local Congregation.* This is a book about Christian Initiation which assumes and explains the Prayer Book rites, concerned that what they make possible be understood and carried out. It is the best work that has ever been done in the Episcopal Church (and certainly one of the best in any church) on making Baptism an integral, foundational part of parish life.

■ In a symposium volume, *Confirmation Re-Examined,* edited by the late Kendig B. Cully and published in 1982, several contributions deal specifically with the Prayer Book rites. The brief opening chapter, "Confirmation in the Episcopal Church and in the Church of England," by Reginald Fuller, contains valuable historical material and out-of-the-way information on English developments. L.L. Mitchell's entry, "Christian Initiation, Rites of Passage, and Confirmation," clarifies a great deal that might be confusing to persons who approach the new rites and find them different from those in earlier Prayer Books. I contributed a rather closely written chapter, "The Liturgics of Confirmation," which gives an account of the liturgical history and pastoral intentions of the rites of the 1979 Prayer Book. This symposium as a whole lacks internal coherence; in fact, it seems to contain internal contradictions. But it exhibits the differences current in the Episcopal Church over what to make of Christian Initiation and the new Prayer Book rites.

■ The pages on the rites of initiation in Marion Hatchett's indispensable *Commentary on the American Prayer Book,* 1980, are clear and packed with information.

■ In 1984 Charles Price wrote "Rites of Initiation," an "Occasional Paper" distributed by the Standing Liturgical Commission. It sets forth briefly and cogently the intention of the rites of Baptism and Confirmation of the Prayer Book (although it is at least tolerant of other opinions).

■ The best account now in print of the handling of the rites of initiation in the Prayer Book is the third chapter, "The New Rite of Confirmation in the Episcopal Church," in *The Rite of Confirmation: Anointing with the Spirit,* published in 1985 by Gerard Austin of Catholic University. This author is well informed on what has been done in the Episcopal Church, and he regards this work as of ecumenical importance.

■ Dr. Mitchell's *Praying Shapes Believing: A Theological Commentary on the Book of Common Prayer,* published in 1985, contains a chapter of forty pages on "Christian Initiation." It is a solid exposition, largely letting the Prayer Book explain itself.

■ Most recently, Dr. Mitchell has written on "The Place of Baptismal Anointing in Christian Initiation," in *ATR,* 1986.

While thinking in terms of authors and titles, it might be mentioned that several of the now essential books on Christian Initiation have only appeared since 1973. The discussion of the subject is not where it was then. One might mention H.M. Riley's *Christian Initiation* (1974), a careful comparative study of the baptismal lectures from the fourth century; the late Alexander Schmemann's eloquent theological account of the Eastern rites, *Of Water and the Spirit* (1974); the papers from an important conference held at Notre Dame University, published in the symposium *Made, Not Born: New Perspectives on Christian Initiation and the Catechumenate* (1976); J.D.C. Fisher's learned and concise *Confirmation Then and Now* (1978); Aidan Kavanagh's well-argued and well-written work, *The Shape of Baptism: The Rite of Christian Initiation* (1978), giving fresh insight on the tradition and on the relevance of the RCIA; and the fine general book, *Baptism: Christ's Act in the Church* (1982), by the Methodist liturgist Laurence Stookey. Mention was made above of the late Urban T. Holmes's presentation of Confirmation in a developmental context, *Confirmation: The Celebration of Maturity in Christ* (1975); of Bp. Eastman's *The Baptizing Community* (1982) and of Gerard Austin's *The Rite of Confirmation: Anointing with the Spirit* (1985), but they should be noted among the now essential titles. (This list does not include the rather substantial recent literature on early Communion; it will be cited in a later chapter.) In the present revision I have made no effort to bring this post-1973 literature in fully. To do so would create a new and a much longer book. But this (no doubt incomplete) listing of important work done since 1973 indicates that the subject of Christian Initiation continues to attract good scholarship and good writing.

The work for *Prayer Book Studies 18* and *26* was begun without the kind of ecumenical consensus about Christian Initiation that had informed and supported changes in the Eucharist since the early stages of revision. Commissions in several churches were working on the matter at about the same time. There was substantial agreement about what the problems were, and a common reading of the past. But the way forward was not clear. The Liturgical Commission of the Episcopal Church, whose rhythms were determined by meetings of General Convention, was on a schedule that put it slightly ahead of most of the others. As the work of the Episcopal Church became known, the general direction it had taken seems to have been influential. The design of new rites for Christian Initiation in the *Lutheran Book of Worship* (1978); in the baptismal texts issued by the Methodist Church ("We Gather Together," 1980), in *Holy Baptism and Service for the Renewal of Baptism* (1985), a liturgical resource for Presbyterian churches; and in *The Book of Alternative Services* (1985) of the Anglican Church of haps others as well) all seem to take a direction pioneered in the Episcopal Church's work of the early 1970s.

Undoubtedly the most important single publication on the subject since 1973 is the Roman Catholic Church's *Rite of Christian Initiation of Adults,* which was issued in the United States in its English text in 1974. Following the Vatican Council (1963–65), the Congregation of Rites was authorized to prepare new liturgical texts. As these were issued in Latin, the various language communities cast them into the several vernaculars, and they became available to the church. A "Rite for the Baptism of Children" was published rather quickly, in 1970. It is a good revision of the rite it replaced. The "Rite of Christian Initiation of Adults"—usually referred to as the RCIA—took longer to prepare. (The Committee which worked on it was led by the eminent liturgist Balthasar Fischer, of Trier.) The rite fills a substantial book, containing a full catechumenate and a number of revolutionary provisions. In structure it is generally modeled on the baptismal practices of the early church— practices which seem to be functional for the church in a post-Christian society as they were when the church devised such rites to shape its common life as a group of convinced believers in a pre-Christian society. The rite soon caught the imagination of persons who interpreted persuasively its significance for community, worship, and mission. What would it do for a parish if the catechumenate were a regular part of its life? if the parish were a community obviously structured for the making of new Christians? Conferences, literature, and parish programs have sought to give substance to the possibilities opened by these old yet new initiatory practices. Mention will be made of the RCIA and its influence in the following chapters, for the thinking and the pastoral work of all the churches in the West now has to take account of this remarkable document and the awakening it has occasioned.

There have been some influential ecumenical statements on Baptism in the past few years: *One Baptism, One Eucharist and a Mutually Recognized Ministry,* Faith and Order Paper No. 73, was issued in 1975, summarizing many years of discussion. It was followed by the *Baptism, Eucharist and Ministry* (often spoken of as BEM) statement, Faith and Order Paper No. 111, in 1982—a broadly based agreed statement which has stirred productive discussion. Some liturgical texts illustrating both the historical tradition and an emerging consensus have been gathered in M. Thurian and G. Wainwright (eds.), *Baptism and Eucharist: Ecumenical Convergence in Celebration,* 1983. The material on Baptism was prepared by Max Thurian of the Taize Community. Any denominational discussion of Christian Initiation today that fails to take account of this ecumenical work is inexcusably provincial.

The quantity and importance of this new material—plus the changes in my own thinking and experience over fourteen years—has meant that this revision is in many respects a different and larger book than was the 1973 "Supplement."

Perhaps I should add what may be clear enough. Although the Standing Liturgical Commission published the 1973 edition of this work and gave approval to its argument, this revision has been carried out independently.

Daniel B. Stevick
Cambridge, Massachusetts

Author's Preface, 1973

The services in *Prayer Book Studies 26,* unlike those in previous booklets of the series, are commented upon in a signed essay. That being the case, perhaps the author may step out from the wings for a prefatory note and some acknowledgments.

This essay was originally written at the request of the Chairman of the Drafting Committee on Christian Initiation, the Rev. Bonnell Spencer, O.H.C. It was felt that a rather full explanation was called for at this point to give an overview of some of the issues that confront the doctrine and administration of Christian Initiation in today's Church. The resulting draft was too long (and doubtless too idiosyncratic) to allow the Liturgical Commission to make it its own, and issue it under its own signature, as some other introductory material has been issued. The Commission, after a careful reading, has commended it as an introduction to the thinking that produced the rites in *Prayer Book Studies 26* and as a study guide to current discussion of Christian Initiation. But it is not the Commission's official account of the rites being proposed.

Anglican rites have characteristically stood as vehicles of the liturgical actions of the Church without any official, binding, definitive rationale. The tradition of liturgies and the tradition of explanation of liturgies have been distinct. The two interact, of course, and especially so at times when liturgies are undergoing change. But the two are not identical. If the initiation rites of *Prayer Book Studies 26* commend themselves to the Church, they may well be seen in other contexts, and may receive other and better explanations than the one which accompanies their publication. If this essay can contribute to the depth and sophistication with which Christian Initiation is discussed, it will have done its task.

Anyone familiar with any of the kinds of material dealt with here will recognize how much more might be said at every point. Little in the essay is original, and nothing is argued exhaustively. Yet it seemed important to bring together theological, historical, pastoral, and strategic considerations. The interdisciplinary character of this account may suggest the many-sidedness of the issues of Christian Initiation in the concrete life of the church.

As this study went through its revisions, useful suggestions were made by members of the Drafting Committee on Christian Initiation and by members of the Liturgical Commission. Special mention should be made of two committee members, the Rev. Dr. Leonel L. Mitchell and the Rev. Dr. Thomas J. Talley, who gave generous help at many points in the writing, but whose learning and care in statement were particularly valuable in the historical material. The general outline and argument and all of the remaining defects are my own.

—Daniel B. Stevick

Introductory

The rites of Christian Initiation have classically been three: Baptism, Confirmation, and first Communion. These rites are closely bound up with one another, with the Gospel itself, with the shared life of the Church, and with individual Christian identity. Yet, important though they are, these classic actions have not been constant. Over the centuries, they have been variously interpreted, variously combined, and variously administered. They have had fully as complicated a history as has the Eucharist, and one that has been given less attention.

The Episcopal Church's pattern for becoming a Christian, not greatly different from the pattern of many other Western churches, has been a two-stage rite. At birth a child of the Christian community is baptized. The baptized child is regarded as a member of the Church and is nurtured as such. The child is granted a significant, if still partial, share in the Church's life. At a later time, after he or she has developed a capacity for understanding and has received some teaching, the child is confirmed by the bishop and admitted to Communion. This has been the basic pattern for which the liturgical texts were written and around which clergy, parents, teachers, and children have understood their roles. This pattern has been adapted as necessary to suit the different circumstances of persons who come to Christian faith as adults, or who come as baptized Christians to the Episcopal Church from another obedience.

In recent generations, dissatisfaction has been expressed in Anglicanism and in many other parts of the ecclesiastical world with the accustomed rites of becoming a Christian. The issues raised are of several kinds. Liturgical and theological clarity are obscured when rites closely united in meaning are observed in two widely separated stages. As the historical record is more adequately filled out, it is clear that rites largely shaped in the late Middle Ages and the 16th century cannot, with respect to certain important features, be identified with customs of the early Christian centuries—a disquieting consideration for a Communion which has taken the New Testament and the early Church as its norm for teaching and practice. Further, the two-stage pattern seems to assume, for its best operation, social conditions and ways of personal development which cannot be taken for granted today.

Rather generally it is felt that the sign of Christian membership has become a thing of reduced significance. Rites that should stand for an original and powerful apprehension of the reality of God have become perfunctory and casual. Some reform movements have sought to make the existing ritual patterns workable. Of course, pastoral diligence is always desirable, but uneasiness has increasingly come to focus on the adequacy of the accustomed ritual pattern itself.

We are now in a period of deep cultural change. History—and, as the community of faith would see it, the Lord of history—is asking for serious rethinking of the Church's own identity and its relation to its society. A kind of death and resurrection—a process with which the Church should be familiar and which it should not fear—is taking place. Institutional and ritual forms are feeling the pressure of new demands. Old truths are being repossessed; continuities are being freshly emphasized; essential and nonessential elements of the liturgical inheritance are being disentangled. New adaptations, recognizing unprecedented factors present in today's world, are being tried. It would be strange if something as basic to Christian community and life as Baptism were unaffected by such upheavals. And of course it is not. In many churches and in many parts of Anglicanism, modifications of traditional rites of initiation are being discussed, proposed, and introduced.

In the following essay the work on Christian Initiation which was done in the Episcopal Church and came to expression in *The Book of Common Prayer*, 1979, is in mind from the start. But that work was broadly based. It involved fresh examination of historical material and some reconceiving of theological and pastoral issues. Hence this work provides a general introduction to some current ecumenical thinking about Christian Initiation.

Specifically, this presentation begins with a brief chapter of theological affirmations concerning Christian Initiation, for responsible practice must commend itself by its rootage in the basic meanings of the Gospel and of this sacrament of the Gospel. The historical sketch which follows emphasizes the variety in the practice of Christian Initiation, and the account narrows on the specific history which has given the Episcopal Church its initiatory customs. A brief analysis of the contemporary situation of the Christian community in Western culture identifies some systemic factors which are raising problems for inherited initiatory practices and understandings. Some of the specific issues which gather around infant Baptism, and around adolescent Confirmation and first Communion are then examined, for there is important modern insight concerning all three and the relationship among them. The fact that we have three words for the inherited initiatory moments can suggest three ritual events of approximately equal importance, each with a distinct meaning. The process of becoming a Christian, in its theological, ritual, and human sides, may in fact be much more complex and more interesting than the naming and describing of three liturgical events would suggest. Finally, some directions for change are indicated, leading to a running commentary on the rites in *The Book of Common Prayer*, 1979—rites which, like similar rites in some other churches today, are a challenge to ecclesiology and pastoral practice. A bibliography suggests resources for further inquiry.

Some Basic
Theological
Meanings

Baptism is a sacrament of beginnings, of newness, of grace, of a fresh start within history and in the depths of individual life. It is the beginning of life in Christ and his people. It is the sign of the new life which is always coming into being within the old but ever young Church. It is the Christian Gospel in action, declaring and effecting the new age in Christ. Baptism is the ritual side of the mysterious way by which world passes over into church and church reaches into the world.

This newness has its source in Jesus Christ. Baptism signifies and conveys that one great redemptive reality which centers in him. His coming in fulfillment of the long-laid divine purpose, his life of obedience and self-giving, his death (which is called his "baptism" in Lk. 12:50; Mk. 10:38*f*) and resurrection, were not only his own individual achievement. In them he was a representative, inclusive figure—the one person for all people. He graciously identified himself with the "many." He is the inauguration of a new humanity, the "firstfruits" of the race renewed after the intention of the Creator. The New Testament presents Christ's work as having universal, even cosmic significance. It is, so to speak, the world's true washing, the birth of a new creation, the overcoming of darkness by light, the breaking of the powers of bondage. It promises the final renovation of all things. Through Christ the new age of righteousness and life has dawned within the old age of sin and dying.

The new reality which has come in Christ calls into being a community of response. Indeed, the Christ-reality is neither known nor apprehended apart from the Church-reality. The Church is set in history as sign of the new thing which has come to be in Christ, and which is coming to be. It is an organic bonding of lives that share in one another, as together they share in the life of their common Lord. It is the communion united with God in Christ and available for witness and service to the world.

But the collective life of the Church begins in individuals. "What was once done for us must be enacted in us."[1] Baptism is the sacramental link between the individual and the redemption which Christ has secured for all. It is a death and resurrection which brings a repenting and believing person within that transformed life whose manifestation is the Church. An ecumenical statement a few years ago said: "The Baptism of Jesus meant that the one righteous One took upon himself the sin of the many and became one with them. Our Baptism means that we, the many, are incorporated into him and become one with him and in him."[2] Baptism reproduces within the believer the redemptive death and resurrection of Jesus. It is the step by which a person leaves the old age—its style and power—and enters the new. For the person who enters, the step is radical—a step likened to cleansing something hopelessly stained, or to passing out of the death-in-life into which we are born and into the true life which one enters by being reborn.

The meanings of Baptism, such as washing, death and resurrection, new birth, child of God, reclothing, awakening, marking with a sign, enlightenment, are obviously expressed in metaphoric speech. No other kind of language is available for ultimate meanings. Images are drawn from the deepest reaches of human experience; they are, at the same time, our principal terms for capturing the disclosure of God. The encounter of God and ourselves, in its certainty and its mystery, creates and renews great basic images; the images can evoke and inform the recognition of God. Although these images suggest and do not explain, they nevertheless have meaning and convey meaning. They give the

2

mind work to do. They reach toward discursive, reasoned-out explanation. But they always exceed such meanings as confessing, inquiring believers can supply.[3]

It is apparent that the church's account of Baptism does not use peripheral symbols. The terms in which the church speaks of Baptism are a selection of the central body of terms in which it speaks of the saving Mystery in which its own life is constituted. From the side of the action of God, Baptism signifies and imparts the outreaching love of the Father, restoring persons to the intention of the Creator. It unites persons with Christ the Redeemer, and places them within the redemption-bearing community, his Body. It is the seal in the Holy Spirit of the new life, present and to come. From the side of the human response, Baptism enacts and shapes the entry on the life of faith, obedience, and expectation. It is the sacrament of conversion, expressing a new mind, a redirection, the rejection of the tyranny of sin and the commitment to righteousness. It is the inauguration of a life renewed and set free.

But what Baptism pledges and begins is not fully accomplished in this life. The power of the old age persists. Sin and failure mark the record of the baptized community. The baptismal life is a conflict between the transformation begun by God's gift and the weakness and hardness of heart that remain a present reality. But Baptism reaches forward. It is a sacrament of inaugurated eschatology. In the midst of sin and death it speaks of that which lies beyond the dominion of sin and death and is held in the purpose of God. Meanwhile, "we wait" (Rom. 8:23).

All of Christian life—its beginning and its end, now and forever—is related by this sacramental sign to the life of God in a bond that endures.

No liturgical form and no pastoral practice can capture so large a meaning. The best rites can only hint at deep unseen, unverifiable, inexpressible realities. They speak of life hid with Christ in God (Col. 3:3). Yet Christ has been pleased to minister himself, graciously and fully, through liturgies and customs that seem thin, prosy, and inadequate. Emergency conditions have sometimes restricted to a minimum the words and actions of baptisms which are nevertheless acknowledged to be true actions of divine grace and human faith. Yet, even though under necessity very little may be enough, the Church cannot legitimately ask, when it fashions its rites, how little can safely be done. On the highest theological grounds, a great Gospel requires the Church to give serious attention to devising the best forms of liturgy it can—forms that at one level are clear, elemental, and enactable, and on another level suggest some of the splendor that permeates the act of becoming a Christian.

CHAPTER II

A Sketch of Historical Development

Baptism witnesses to the continuity of the Christian community. By this initiatory action the church carries its past into each generation. In order to form a responsible judgment of what may be required in any present moment, it is necessary to have some awareness of that past. The accustomed rites of Christian Initiation have a long history—a record impressive both for its continuity and for its variety.

A. The New Testament

The Church has been a baptizing community from its beginning. The first Christian sermon is reported to have closed with the plea "Repent and be baptized every one of you in the name of Jesus Christ for the forgiveness of sins, and you shall receive the gift of the Holy Spirit" (Acts 2:38). Christian Baptism probably, but not quite certainly, found a model in Jewish proselyte baptism, and it obviously stood in continuity with the anticipatory ministry of John the Baptist. Indeed, it drew on some of the deepest and oldest religious instincts of the race. But it claimed a crucial originality. It was, on the Church's account of the matter, a rite grounded in the authority over heaven and earth given to the risen, living Christ (Matthew 28:18–20). It was Baptism in his Name and into his life-through-death (Acts 2:38; Romans 6:3–5).

The references to Baptism, which are frequent in the New Testament, tell us more about meanings of the rite than about the manner of its enactment. It signifies union with Christ's death and resurrection (Romans 6:3*f.*). It is a washing by which one is reborn (Titus 3:5, metaphors mix freely). By it the Spirit brings individuals into the One Body (1 Corinthians 12:12*f.*)—a community whose oneness transcends divisions of ethnicity or sex (Galatians 3:27*f.*). It calls one to awaken to the light of Christ (Ephesians 5:14, probably a fragment of a baptismal hymn). The baptized have put off their old clothing and put on new (Galatians 3:27; Colossians 3:10, 12–14); having "put on Christ," they are committed to a new mode of life. If Baptism can be spoken of as a sign because it bears rich meaning, it is an effective sign, conveying what it signifies. It is "for the forgiveness of sins" (Acts 2:38); it "saves" (1 Peter 3:21).

The narratives of baptisms in the Book of Acts are notoriously difficult. Acts emphasizes that the Church was a preaching movement and that Baptism was a convert's response to the word and a witness to faith, "They that received his word were baptized" (Acts 2:41). Baptism, as one writer puts it, "might be called an embodiment of the *kerygma*."[1] Sometimes—by no means always—both a water-moment and a Spirit-moment are described. But they are not always in the same sequence:

Sometimes evidence of the Holy Spirit came before or at Baptism. When the Spirit had taken such initiative, the act of Baptism was the Church's obedient response. The account of Peter at the house of Cornelius (Acts 10) is the clearest instance of this pattern. As Peter spoke, the Holy Spirit fell on the hearers, and Peter asked "Can any one forbid water for baptizing these people who have received the Holy Spirit just as we have?" (Acts 10:47). In the narrative of Acts, this incident is crucial, for it represents the carrying of the Christian mission (despite Peter's initial scruples) to the gentiles. This missionary breakthrough is validated by a new Pentecost—as is suggested by the speaking in tongues and by the words "These people who have received the Holy Spirit *just as we have*."[2]

Sometimes, however, a manifestation of the Spirit followed Baptism. The mission of Peter and John to Samaria (Acts 8:4–8, 14–17) illustrates this pattern. The believers had "only been baptized in the name of the Lord Jesus." But when the apostles came and laid their hands on them "they received the Holy Spirit." The narrative in this instance also seems to be told with missionary advance primarily in mind. Samaria was schismatic Jewish territory. The apostles "at Jerusalem" sent Peter and John, who "came down" to Samaria (Acts 8:14*f.*), evidently to unite the new group of Christians with the parent community.[3]

In some instances, however (8:36, 38; 16:15 & 33; and 18:8 will illustrate), the evidence of the Spirit and the ministry of the apostles are not mentioned at all. The term "Baptism" —the washing, the bath— stands alone.

Readers have gone to this earliest historical account seeking the authoritative sacramental practice of the apostolic era. But that is not what the document is about. The Book of Acts tells of missionary expansion, and the diverse initiatory patterns seem to show that the Spirit-led church, as it spread and diversified, yet remained one.

The New Testament contains no clear indication of a probationary period for converts prior to their Baptism. As soon as there was evidence of belief, water (apparently quite common water) was sought, and the convert was baptized. (Acts 8:36–38 and 16:31–33 are two examples.) The new reality had manifested itself, and its sign need not be delayed. The early church had teachers, perhaps some of them receiving some type of payment for their work (Galatians 6:6). But the teaching was not of those preparing for baptism, but of the already baptized.

If we ask whether or not "infant Baptism" was the practice of the primitive church we probably ask the wrong question. The New Testament does not speak of "infant Baptism," but there are strong suggestions of what might be termed "family Baptism."[4] Apparently Christian thinking followed Jewish thinking in regarding a household as a unity. When the head of the household became a Christian, it was inconceivable that all the members of the household would not enter the new life in Christ together. (In Jewish practice, children were included with their parents in proselyte baptism.) The faith of only one of the parents was enough to bring the children within the new relationship (1 Corinthians 7:14). Since the early church was a vital, missionary community, the accounts that it left of baptisms tell, as missionary narratives do, of adult converts. The place of children was derivative.

B. The Early Church

Within a short time, the rites of Christian Initiation took on greater formalization and complexity. Some basic baptismal meanings came to be ritually enacted. New features were added as pastoral and evangelistic strategy seemed to require.

As the church moved into a predominantly gentile society, it developed a period of teaching, probation, and limited membership, known as the catechumenate, prior to Baptism. This catechumenate may have had roots in the first century, and by the third century, it was well established. The way of life of one who sought to become a Christian was scrutinized. Catechumens might have to change their employment, for in the ancient world many kinds of work involved some acquiescence in idolatry or immoral practices. The catechumens received instruction from catechists, who might be clerical or lay. They would (as Christians in training) share in the community's works of charity. And they attended the Sunday Eucharist, but only for the service of readings and preaching. This probationary period could extend for as long as three years.

Baptisms took place at Easter; hence the rites would be enacted against an interpreting background of Jesus' death and resurrection and of Exodus motifs from the Old Testament. Baptism was an entry into the great Paschal Mystery which gathered up the central redemptive themes of the faith. Through Baptism into Christ, enslavement to the tyranny of sin was broken. The true Passover had been sacrificed. A baptized person had come through the Red Sea into a new pilgrimage, united to a new covenant people, moving toward a promised land of which sacramental life, the bread in the wilderness, was a foretaste.

The initiatory rite was quietly dramatic. After days of final preparation and an all night vigil of instruction and prayer, those to be baptized were brought before daybreak on Easter morning to the water. The water might be outdoors, or within a house. Moving water was preferred. The candidates would lay aside all clothing and jewelry and be led into the water. There, each one, sometimes turning to the West, would renounce all pagan loyalties—"Satan, his works and his pomp." He or she would then turn to the East and be asked three questions, corresponding to the three sections of what came to be the Apostles' Creed: "Do you believe in God, the Father Almighty?...In Jesus Christ, his only Son, Our Lord?...In the Holy Spirit, the Church, and the life everlasting?" After each reply of "I believe," the candidate would be baptized. Often this part of the rite would be led by presbyters. (Deaconesses or women attendants also took part. While the church insisted on nudity at baptism, it was also concerned for modesty and the avoidance of scandal.) Children who could not answer for themselves were baptized with their families, and others answered for them. The newly baptized persons emerged from the water and (in many parts of the church) were anointed, usually over the entire body. They reclothed themselves (later in the era they received white garments). They were then conducted to the eucharistic assembly, where, for the first time, they shared in the kiss of peace and the people's prayers, made their own offering of bread and wine, and received the Body and Blood of Christ.

The ritual actions that often came between Baptism and the receiving of Communion varied from region to region. The important Syrian Church had no postbaptismal anointing, and scholars differ as to what the anointing it put prior to Baptism signified.[5] (The rites of Antioch in the fourth century, described by John Chrysostom, have no anointing following Baptism, and it is in the water that the Holy Spirit descends on the baptized "through the words and hands of the priest.") In different regions of the church the newly baptized persons received a signing with the cross, a laying on of hands, a second anointing by the bishop, or even in some places foot washing.

The initiatory rites were elaborated in the course of time. When, beginning in the third century, baptisteries were built at major churches, they were often domed structures, with an octagonal or round floor plan, located apart from the eucharistic room and used once a year. At daybreak on Easter, the candidates would pass down three steps (symbolic of Jesus' three days in the tomb) into a pool, which was decorated with mosaics, and be immersed three times in flowing water. As they stepped out of the water, again by three steps, and were reclothed, they would pass to the eucharistic room by way of the bishop who would seal each one.

Enrolling as a catechumen became a rather full ceremony. In some places austerities and exorcisms to expel evil spirits were preparatory rituals. During the catechumenate the terms of the Creed (which were no longer secret) were imparted to the learners, and at the moment of Baptism the brief "formula of baptism," which had at first been peculiar to the Syrian Church, replaced the interrogatory use of the Creed. The water was blessed in a lengthy, poetic prayer. Instructions on the meaning of the Creed and the sacraments were given by the bishop in the days after Easter.[6] The bishop, in effect, said to the newly baptized: "Remember what was done to you; I will tell you its meaning." The early church was persuaded that for explanation to be effective, something should have happened that was so rich and powerful that it required explanation.

The early liturgies of initiation gave form to actual inward processes of leaving paganism and entering the community in Christ. The words of the rites, the expressive ceremonies, and the interpretive explanations would all have been remembered by the adults who had experienced them as parts of one decisive event—a watershed in each one's own experience, a putting away of one way of life and an entry on another.

Perhaps it is obvious that this process, insofar as it is effective, works itself out of a job. In a population center, after all of the adults have either themselves been through these initiatory rites or else are the children of those who have been through them, the catechumenate ends. The practice of Baptism will undergo changes. It is impossible to say at what point most baptisms came to be of children born to Christian parents. Doubtless the Church moved into this "second generation" situation at different times in different places. But "in the great centers of the West there were probably few adults left to be baptized by the year 500."[7]

Two theological tendencies were at work in the early church that had differing effects on baptismal practice. One was the rather moralistic view that Baptism cleansed only from sins committed prior to Baptism. Baptism was thought of as an absolution, largely retroactive in efficacy—hence, as many people saw it, the later its administration, the better. This teaching removed the urgency from infant Baptism. In fact, fear of postbaptismal sin led, in the third century and following, to the postponement of Baptism even in instances of persons born to devout parents.[8] Many statements from the period contain exhortations to adults who had postponed Baptism until late in life to postpone it no longer.

The other tendency, which proved more powerful and lasting, was the growing definition of original sin. Augustine, the greatest theological mind of the early Western church, influenced by his own twice-born experience and by his conflict with Pelagius, became convinced that guilt is inherited by all persons by their descent from Adam. He sought in this matter to follow St. Paul, but he depended on the Latin Bible which contained a misleading translation of Romans 5:12—a text which Augustine cited repeatedly in this matter. In his account of redemption in Christ, Paul describes the entry of sin, and with it death, as an existing condition which can be represented by the name of Adam— one person standing for all people. Then Paul says that death spread to the race "because all sin" (the Greek is *eph ho pantes hemarton*). Paul meant: "... because (as a matter of record) all (as they had opportunity and competence) sinned (consented to the Adamic condition)." Paul is not being deterministic. He has a deep awareness of the collective weight of human sin, but he is contrasting the old solidarity (Adam) with the greater new solidarity (Christ). Both consist of a preexisting condition brought about by one for many; but that condition is entered upon as we make an original deed our own, as we participate in it. But the Latin text on which Augustine depended gave a fatalistic sound to the argument. It read *in quo omnes peccaverunt,* or "in whom all sinned," by which Augustine understood: "In whom (in solidarity with Adam, the primal parent) all (as a matter of inherited condition) sinned." When he concluded that all are born guilty, Augustine thought that he was following a teaching of Paul's. In addition to this biblical authority, it is evident that Augustine argued, at least in part, from church practice to doctrine. He reasoned that since Baptism is, by general Christian consent, taken to be for the forgiveness of sins, and since the Church, as a matter of long practice, administers Baptism (including its exorcisms) to infants, therefore infants must, in some sense, have sinned. The analysis of sin was (for Augustine as for Paul) the reverse side of an affirmation of redemption. Baptism is an effective sign, and infants are beneficiaries of grace through the Church.[9]

Augustine's doctrine that Baptism cleansed from inherited guilt reinforced the practice of baptizing children as early as possible. Until fairly modern times, this teaching (often reduced to little more than a superstition) formed at least one important background factor in the common rationale in the West for the practice of infant Baptism.

The change to infant Baptism brought no changes in the liturgies. Forms that had brought adult converts into the church continued to be used, but for a markedly different function. The service of making a catechumen was moved to the church door as a preamble to Baptism proper. Responses, renunciations, and commitments were made entirely by others in the name of the child. The liturgical forms were compressed into a rite that lasted only a few minutes. Yet the same words and actions were used, and the same theological account of their meaning was given, as when the initiatory process had occupied an adult convert for months or years.

C. Adaptation I: The Delegation of Ministries

The Christian movement began in the centers of population, and bishops were located in cities. But as churches took responsibility for evangelizing outlying areas, congregations, with resident presbyters, grew up which were dependent on the urban center and its chief pastor but which were at some distance from the see city. Increasingly, the full sacramental life that had been exercised by or under the presidency of the bishop came to be claimed and exercised by presbyters in local parishes. The continuation of initiatory rites in which bishops, priests, and deacons took part together became particularly difficult.

Outside the immediate sphere of influence of the Church of Rome, the initiatory rite in its unity was left as the prerogative of the local priest. This pattern is known today largely as the practice of the Eastern churches, but it was for a time also the practice of large portions of the West. The right to administer Christian Initiation in its entirety was exercised by presbyters in Spain and in parts of France and in northern Italy.

The prevalence in the West of presbyteral administration of both Baptism and the postbaptismal rites is not as widely recognized as it should be. But evidence is abundant. A brief selection may suggest the character of the material.

For Spain, the important text, the *Liber Ordinum,* gives directions concerning the newly baptized infant: "The priest anoints him with chrism, making the sign of the cross on his forehead alone.... Then he lays his hand upon him."[10] The Council of Elvira (305 CE) legislated that persons baptized by a layman (Canon 38), or a deacon (Canon 77), should be brought to a bishop to be confirmed. Persons baptized by a presbyter are not mentioned as being under a similar requirement.[11] A scholar who has recently surveyed the evidence summarizes his findings for seventh century Spain of presbyteral "perfecting":

> *I can only conclude that there were episcopal baptisms, baptisms administered by presbyters (and* chorepiscopi?*) at the command of, sometimes in the absence of, the bishop, and presbyteral baptisms* per se; *that oil was used, sometimes twice, sometimes perhaps together with the water poured; that... the minister's hand was imposed and the sign of the cross often (but not necessarily) traced on the forehead... I can only think that any baptism by any minister, given regularly and attested, was accepted as complete and sufficient.*[12]

For Gaul, the *Missale Gothicum,* a Gallican sacramentary from about 700 CE, contains, in the priest's rite of Baptism, a direction and prayer for the postbaptismal anointing. This anointing, which is spoken of as "the garment of immortality," is part of a baptismal rite which is taken to be complete. Other evidence is consistent with this document. L.L. Mitchell summarizes: "None of the Gallican sacramentaries includes a rite of episcopal confirmation, nor have we any evidence requiring us to assume that such a rite was customarily added to the extant baptismal rites, nor that the administration of the single Gallican postbaptismal anointing was confined to bishops."[13]

For northern Italy, the evidence contains a rite (in the Ambrosian *Manual*) with a postbaptismal anointing by a priest, while the bishop is present, and a rite (described by Beroldus in the 12th century) with a postbaptismal episcopal anointing. Evidently the two should be taken as equivalent.[14]

By allowing the presbyter, when necessary, to be the minister of all parts of Christian Initiation, the actions of water baptism, anointing (or other form of postbaptismal rite), and first Communion remained parts of a single event. There were changes from the customs of antiquity. All these actions, which were developed initially for use with prepared adults, came to be administered to infants. Even though the unity of the rite was preserved, its link with the Paschal season was eventually lost; baptisms came to depend on when a child was born, not on when (in ritual time) Christ had died and risen.[15] The bishop (today in the East generally the Patriarch) participated only as the minister who blesses the chrism.

This pattern of initiation was an adaptation, made to deal with social and ecclesiastical developments. It once commended itself as a good adaptation throughout many parts of the Christian community, East and West. It has persisted as the initiatory way of the East. It provides an alternative pattern by which to examine the very different line of development of which the Western churches are heir.

D. Adaptation II: The Division of the Rite

In much of the West, by a gradual process, another pattern came to prevail. The initiatory rite was broken up. Its parts came to be observed at different times and by different ministers. Actions which had been moments within a unified ritual became, in effect, separate services.

Even in the pre-Constantinian church, disciplinary conflicts over schismatic baptism had suggested an independent identity for an episcopal laying-on of hands. Differing provincial customs had grown up in North Africa and in Rome for the reconciliation to the church of those who had been baptized in schismatic groups. Cyprian, arguing from local African tradition and from his own theology of the church, held that persons baptized in schism had not been truly baptized at all; when they sought to identify with the catholic Church, the whole initiatory ritual needed to be repeated. But the Roman community upheld a different practice. True Baptism belonged to the Name, not to the administering group. But Baptism could only become efficacious within the true catholic community. By Roman custom, schismatics, on their reconciliation, did not have their Baptism repeated, provided it had been formally correct. The bishop's laying on of hands, however, was used as a gesture of unity and pardon. This practice gave one step of the baptismal rites a meaning apart from the rest.

The Church of Rome was especially conservative in keeping the bishop's prerogative as the minister of a required baptismal anointing. Dioceses in central Italy were small, and most people could visit the bishop's church easily. Many persons were brought into the Christian community at initiation ceremonies held at Easter and Pentecost, presided over by the bishop. Where the local priest became the usual minister of water Baptism and the presbyteral anointing, the rite of initiation was regarded as incomplete without the bishop's anointing. As soon as the baptized child and the bishop could be brought together, the bishop "perfected" the Baptism. For many centuries, in the vicinity of Rome, this pattern seems to have worked well. Most persons received episcopal chrismation, and not much time elapsed between the two initiatory acts.

In time, the Roman practice was extended more widely in the West, but not without difficulty. A few items in this development (most of them the subject of complicated scholarly discussion) can be noted.

Jerome wrote (c.379 CE) that "it is the custom of the church that the bishop should rush about to those who have been baptized by presbyters and deacons far from the larger cities, to invoke the Holy Spirit upon them by the laying on of hands."[16] When one discounts Jerome's sarcastic tone, the passage is a valuable early reference to bishops travelling to administer their own part of Christian Initiation to those who lacked it. Characteristically Jerome argued that the bishop is the minister of this laying on of hands, not by a law of necessity, but as a matter of order and dignity.

In a letter to Decentius of Gubbio (416 CE), Pope Innocent I decreed that consignation of baptized infants should be only by the bishop, for this specific ministry belongs only to those in "the highest rank of the pontificate." A presbyter might anoint the baptized with chrism (blessed by the bishop) whether the bishop were present or not, but only the bishop might sign the baptized on the forehead.[17]

Gregory the Great wrote an illuminating sequence of letters in 593 CE to the troublesome Archbishop of Sardinia. In the first, Gregory said that presbyters might anoint newly baptized persons on the breast, but anointing on the forehead is reserved for the bishop. This regulation evidently went against long-standing local custom and caused offense. In a later letter, Gregory, with his usual statesmanship, allowed presbyters (where a bishop could not be present) to anoint the forehead of persons newly baptized.[18]

At the end of the era of the Church Fathers, the Roman custom of a second postbaptismal anointing, reserved to the bishop, was a minority practice in the Christian world. The letters of Gregory indicate that it was not even insisted on throughout the Roman province. In the city of Rome, however, its use allowed the rites of initiation to be observed as a ritual unity, with the bishop (whose personal participation had become exceptional elsewhere) taking his part as the minister of the second postbaptismal anointing.

The tendency to regional differences in liturgical practice, which has been indicated by this rapid examination of some of the early evidence for Christian Initiation, continued during the disintegration of western Europe following the collapse of the Roman Empire. The imposition of something like unity required central leadership. The eighth century reforms under Charlemagne sought greater standardization of practice in the West. Service books of the highest authority were obtained from Rome, and new texts partially drawn from them were introduced into Gaul and Germany, and ultimately more widely throughout Europe. Episcopal Confirmation, which appeared in these Roman texts, became part of the expected system in places that had not known it.

In northern Europe, dioceses were large, travel was difficult, and bishops were not always resident. Bishops could not visit congregations readily, and few people could come to the see city. In some places "baptismal churches" were designated in decentralized areas of the diocese, and Christian Initiation might be administered there at appointed seasons by authorized ministers. But the Roman pattern, reserving the second postbaptismal chrismation for the bishop, represented an ideal for which adequate conditions did not exist. As a result, where Confirmation was not actually neglected, the events of the initiatory rite grew apart. Not all bishops were diligent about confirming, and not all parents were diligent about having children confirmed. Moreover, Confirmation, unlike Baptism, was not regarded as necessary for salvation. As a result, when Confirmation was observed, it came at a stage of life somewhat later than infancy.

Legislation in the next few centuries seems designed to place Confirmation as close to Baptism as possible. But such laws witness to problems of neglect and delay. An English canon from 960 CE gives a sense of the period: "We teach that each priest perform Baptism as soon as it is required. And then let him enjoin his parish that each infant be baptized within thirty-seven days, and that no one too long remain unbishoped."[19] A widely promulgated rule required parents to bring children for Confirmation whenever the bishop came within seven miles. Under prevailing conditions of communication and travel, such a rule can hardly have been very effective. In local regulations, Confirmation was required at various ages, ranging from one to seven years.[20]

By the 13th century, seven years was coming to be regarded as a minimum, rather than a maximum age. With this acceptance of a separation in time, some expectation grew up that instruction of at least a rudimentary sort would have taken place before Confirmation.[21]

In the Middle Ages many persons were baptized and became communicants, Confirmation having been bypassed. In 1282 Archbishop Peckham issued a canon (best remembered because, through the Sarum *Manual,* it became the "confirmation rubric" in the Prayer Books) requiring that Confirmation be the prerequisite to receiving Communion. His aim was to rescue Confirmation from the "damnable negligence" into which it had fallen. Yet the rite continued to be administered carelessly. One scholar summarizes, "Gradually but inevitably, Confirmation in the West became the privilege of the few rather than the obligation of the many."[22]

As the divided rite became the usual practice, theologians provided it with an attractive rationale. St. Thomas taught that baptism made one a member of Christ and the Church and gave the Holy Spirit. Confirmation he described (using as authoritative some phrases introduced into the tradition and perpetuated by his predecessors) as an "increase of grace" (*augmentium gratiae*), strengthening (*robur*) with gifts of the Spirit appropriate to spiritual combat (*confirmamur ad pugnam*).[23] This two-stage initiation he related to observed stages of human development. Infants live largely for themselves; but as they grow, they come to live in and toward the world. Baptism is the church's way of meeting birth. Confirmation belongs to growth, to advancement to spiritual perfection (more a category of salvation than of chronological age), and to struggle with spiritual enemies. "Confirmation is to Baptism as growth to birth." Thus, the practice of the late Middle Ages (which was not known to be the development that, in fact, it was) became the basis for the characteristic Western doctrine of Confirmation.

E. The Churches of the Reformation

The major Reformers assumed and defended the practice of infant Baptism. Indeed, the continuity of baptismal teaching and practice at the Reformation is remarkable for a time of much discontinuity. Luther was thankful that Baptism had, over the centuries, remained relatively uncorrupted.[24] The churches of the Reformation adapted the baptismal rites to correspond more closely than they had with the actualities of infant Baptism, which was the universal practice.[25]

Luther's conception of Baptism was highly personalized. His Baptism spoke to him, or God spoke to him through his Baptism, assuring him of forgiveness and pledging divine power forever on the side of the believer. Calvin stressed the community of faith; Baptism brought one into the society of believers. For both of these reformers Baptism was a sign that effected what it signified.

Lutherans and Calvinists had no similar attachment to Confirmation. In both traditions, the rite as it had been practiced in Catholicism was attacked with wonderful rhetorical vigor.[26] Since it lacked clear New Testament warrant, it was regarded as an invented sacrament. Since it was administered by the bishop, it was regarded as pretending to a superiority over Baptism. The Reformed tradition had a general distaste for the involvement in Christian worship of material things—at least material things not clearly warranted in scripture. In the case of Confirmation, the offense was the chrism.

Yet the Reformers felt the pastoral and theological need for what John Calvin called "a catechetical exercise, in which children or youths [would] deliver an account of their faith in the presence of the Church."[27] Concern for adult ratification ("true confirmation") as the complement of infant Baptism lay deep in the Reformed impulse. It can be traced to Wycliffe and to the Bohemian Brethren, followers of Jan Huss. Luther himself provided no liturgical text for Confirmation, though within his own lifetime some of his followers did.[28] Catechisms were written, and the clergy added teaching to their accepted duties. Confirmation, administered by local presbyters, became the occasion on which instructed young Christians, who had been baptized in infancy, made public witness to the faith and accepted the duties and privileges of adult church membership. The conscious elements of catechesis and commitment which in the early church had gathered around Baptism and which had been lost in the Middle Ages, were restored in the churches of the Reformation—but gathered now around an adolescent rite of Confirmation and First Communion.

From the 16th century, some varieties of Protestant thought and practice rejected infant Baptism. They could not credit the application of meanings formed around the primitive church's baptism of converts to a rite in which there was no conversion or personal expression of faith on the part of the one being baptized. Children of Christian parents were only baptized when, having reached years of accountability, they were able to present themselves and be received into the Church "on profession of faith." This conviction concerning Baptism brought into being groups of Christians which did not recognize the Baptism of others—a shocking tear in the fabric of a society bound together by this sign of a common faith. These groups formed, not churches of ethnic continuity, but "believers' churches."[29] The idea of religious toleration grew slowly, and it was difficult in the 16th century to distinguish religious separatism from sedition. These churches were not accepted as simply Christian bodies with different doctrines and uses; they were shamefully persecuted.

F. Anglicanism

The English Church at the Reformation kept the two-stage medieval pattern of Christian Initiation: Baptism, administered at the time of birth, by the local priest; Confirmation, at a later life stage, administered by the bishop.[30] Only those who had been confirmed were to be admitted to Communion. For his liturgies, Cranmer adapted the Latin rites of the Sarum *Manual,* but he worked into his text and rubrics many features from Reformed and Lutheran sources from the Continent. As was the case with the Eucharist, substantial differences are apparent in the structure and actions of the rites of Baptism and Confirmation of the first two Prayer Books.

The 1549 Prayer Book: The 1549 Baptism service opened at the church door. (A rubric commended that Baptism be on a Sunday or other holy day when a congregation would be present.) Following a preface and a lengthy prayer, the child was given the sign of the cross upon the forehead "...in token that thou shalt not be ashamed to confess thy faith in Christ crucified." After another prayer, there was an exorcism, commanding the unclean spirit to "come out and depart from these infants." A Gospel passage about Jesus and the children was read, followed by an exhortation which led to the Lord's Prayer and the creed (the "giving" of the creed). This service at the church door concluded with a prayer for the increase of faith and the gift of the Holy Spirit.

The service moved into the church, where, at the font, there was another exhortation followed by renunciations and promises (which included the creed in interrogatory form—the "return" of the creed) by the godparents in behalf of the child. The Baptism, in the triune name (by dipping the child three times in the water) came next, followed by giving the chrysom, a white garment. The priest then anointed the infant upon the forehead using a formula that spoke of "the unction of the Holy Spirit." The rite concluded with a vigorous exhortation concerning postbaptismal instruction and conduct.

What was meant by the postbaptismal anointing? In the Sarum *Manual* the priest, after the Baptism, had anointed the child on the head, using words concerning Christ and salvation: "...regenerated thee by water and the Holy Ghost,...given thee remission of all thy sins,...the chrism of salvation." But the medieval rite at this point did not speak of the gift or presence of the Spirit. The "unction of the Holy Spirit" phrase in the 1549 Prayer Book and the anointing on the forehead, previously the bishop's act, indicate Cranmer's deliberate introduction of Confirmation by a presbyter within the Baptism action itself.

But however complete the Baptism rite was thought to be, this Prayer Book contained a service of Confirmation, introduced by a very full set of rubrics setting forth the pastoral or catechetical intent of the rite. Confirmation was meant to provide children who had come to "years of discretion" with a ritual occasion in which they might ratify the promises of Baptism "with their own mouth, and with their own consent, openly before the Church." (The phrase "years of discretion" was not uniformly understood, but it was evidently regarded in the 16th century as meaning around ten or twelve years of age.)[31] To be eligible, a child should be able to say the creed, the Lord's Prayer, and the ten commandments, and to answer questions from the catechism. The action was taken to impart gifts of the Spirit suitable to adult life.

The rite which followed these lengthy explanations was quite brief. It began with a prayer by the bishop for the sevenfold gifts of the Spirit. Then God was asked to "sign" the confirmands "and mark them to be thine for ever," and to "confirm and strength [sic] them with the inward unction of thy Holy Ghost." The bishop did not anoint the child, but made the sign of the cross on the forehead of each, and laying his hands upon the confirmand said, "N. I sign thee with the sign of the cross and lay my hand upon thee, in the name of the Father and of the Son and of the Holy Ghost." The rite concluded with a prayer and blessing.

One may note that the purpose stated in the opening rubrics is not really carried out in the rite itself. No baptismal promises are actually renewed. (Although the bishop might ask the confirmands questions from the catechism.) Rather, the heart of the rite is the bishop's post-baptismal blessing, full of a sense of the Holy Spirit. The central formulae are performative: The bishop asks God to "confirm, sign and mark" the confirmand, while the bishop lays his hand on each and gives the sign of the cross, saying "I sign thee." Even though, as we have noted, a presbyteral anointing was retained and heightened in the 1549 Baptism rite, the bishop's central action at Confirmation is no longer anointing, as it had been in the medieval services. Cranmer may have been responding to the Reformed conviction that material things should not be used in worship, unless they were things specifically required by scripture. In any case, anointing was replaced by the laying on of hands —a gesture which in the New Testament speaks of such things as bonding, blessing, commissioning, and healing. From the time of this Prayer Book, the laying on of hands was regarded, in Anglican custom and liturgical books, as an adequate outward and visible sign for the bishop's ministry of Confirmation.

The 1552 Prayer Book: The 1552 rite introduced many differences. The service at the church door was dropped. (Most features in it were duplicated in the later portion of the service), and everything took place in the church at the font. After a brief address, the priest led a quite full prayer, followed by the Gospel from Mark 10 about Jesus and the children. An exhortation commented on the Gospel reading and led to another prayer. Renunciations and promises, including the creed, followed. A series of short prayers led to a prayer over the water. (It is not a consecration of the font; it speaks of divine action in the persons to be baptized, but not on the water.) Then the Baptism was performed. The requirement of "trine immersion" was dropped in favor of dipping the child in the water—"so it be discreetly and warily done."

Then, in Cranmer's second model, the priest signed the child on the forehead with the cross, "in token that hereafter he shall not be ashamed to confess the faith of Christ crucified, and manfully to fight under his banner against sin, the world and the devil, and to continue Christ's faithful soldier and servant until his life's end." This act of signing on the forehead had been the bishop's act at Confirmation in the previous book, and these words had formed part of the service at the door. In 1552 they were combined in this location immediately after the Baptism itself, where the sign of the cross seems to have taken the place of the postbaptismal anointing. The chrysom was dropped here, and the exorcism had been omitted earlier in the rite.

The words that Cranmer brought into this postbaptismal position in 1552 are images—confessing the faith, fighting as a soldier under Christ's banner—which in the late Middle Ages had come to describe Confirmation. The consignation had also been a part of post-baptismal rites in the early church, and the signing on the forehead had generally been reserved for the bishop. (In 1549 the signing on the forehead—with laying on of hands, and without anointing—had been the bishop's action at Confirmation.) These first two Prayer Books seem to represent (each in its own way) 16th century attempts to restore the unity of the initiatory ritual. In both Prayer Books, immediately after the water baptism, the minister performs an action and speaks some words deriving from the rite which in the West had come to be called Confirmation.[32]

The Confirmation service in 1552 continued from 1549 the rubrics explaining its intention. At the heart of the brief rite itself, the bishop's prayer for the gifts of the Holy Spirit is changed from "Send down from heaven...upon them," to "strengthen them... with the Holy Ghost." It reads less like a fresh imparting of the Holy Spirit than like a new vitality in a presence already assured in Baptism. The bishop's words at the central action took a similar direction. Laying his hand upon each child, he asked God, in what is clearly a prayer, that the child might "daily increase in thy Holy Spirit more and more."

All of the baptismal rites of the first Prayer Books were for children. Neither the texts nor the rubrics of 1549 or 1552 envisioned anything else. But in the Prayer Book revision of 1662 a service of adult Baptism, adapted from the infant Baptism rite, was provided for the first time. Since the disruptions of the 17th century, many people, through neglect, necessity, or conscientious scruple, had not been baptized in infancy.

The 1662 revision also brought the personal "ratification" of baptismal vows out of the explanatory rubric where it had been lodged and into the action of the Confirmation rite itself. The bishop asked the confirmands:

> *Do ye here in the presence of God, and of this congregation, renew the solemn promise and vow, that was made in your Name at your Baptism; ratifying and confirming the same in your own persons, and acknowledging your selves bound to believe and to do all those things which your Godfathers and Godmothers then undertook for you?"*
>
> *[text and spelling from 1662]*

Regrettably, occasion was not taken to provide for adults by a single rite which combined Baptism and the laying on of hands without the repetition of vows. The revisers "provided an office [for adults] which contained only the smallest number of changes from the infant rite, and then required that the adult so baptised should as speedily as possible be confirmed by a rite which had in view those baptised in infancy."[33] The Prayer Book tradition has struggled with this inadequacy ever since.

Since the First Prayer Books: The practice of the Church of England has been uneven since the 17th century. Parish clergy administered Baptism quite faithfully. Although some 17th- and 18th-century bishops did their best as ministers of Confirmation, the numbers of people were large, travel was difficult, there were no assisting bishops, and little theological urgency had attached itself to the observance. Episcopal visitations for confirming do not loom large in the biographies of bishops, nor in the records of parish life. When bishops confirmed, little was done to personalize the rite; large groups were sometimes confirmed *en masse.* Many Bishops carried out their duties carelessly. The low point in Confirmation practice seems to have come in the late 18th century.[34]

Both the Evangelical Movement and the Oxford Movement took Confirmation seriously; Evangelicals because it stressed teaching and inward experience; Tractarians because it represented an ancient ministry of the bishop and emphasized preparation for the Holy Eucharist. In the 19th century there were several rancorous controversies about baptismal regeneration. The important constructive ideas of F.D. Maurice on the meaning of Baptism gained a following. Maurice spoke of Baptism as a sign of the universal Headship of Christ; thus Baptism has something to say about one's humanity, not just about one's religious profession. Standards of practice were also addressed. The model for the modern, deeply pastoral parochial visit of the bishop to confirm a well-prepared class seems to have been provided by the 19th-century Bishop of Oxford, Samuel Wilberforce.[35]

In the Episcopal Church in the colonial period, there were no bishops, and except for persons who had received Confirmation in England, members were admitted to Communion without being confirmed—under these circumstances, desire for Confirmation sufficed. For a time after the episcopate had been secured, dioceses were entire states, and bishops were rectors of large parishes. Episcopal visitations for confirmation were infrequent.

When John Henry Hobart became Bishop of New York (effectively from 1811 on), he undertook, as part of his energetic pastoral episcopate, the ministry of Confirmation. The records of his visitations and Confirmations are an impressive indication of his sacramental conception of his office. Those who came to the Episcopal Church did so by Confirmation; and those who were Episcopalians, many of whom had not been confirmed, were expected to receive this episcopal blessing. Confirmation thus was made an important part of Episcopalian self-definition. More than any other single figure, Hobart set the model for modern practice of Confirmation in the Episcopal Church.[36]

As, in the early 19th century, the Church expanded westward under missionary bishops, the pastoral oversight of a Father in God came to be part of the earliest experience of most congregations. The comfortable doctrine of the ubiquity of bishops was made possible by modern means of transportation.

This historical sketch will have suggested that modern initiatory customs and understandings have had a long and varied history. The "one Baptism" has been adapted widely over the centuries as changing situations have seemed to require.

Adaptation is clearly inevitable. The basic elements of Baptism are simple and hence flexible; and the cultures and situations into which Baptism has been carried are diverse. Much adaptation has been carried out by persons with a strong pastoral sense that the initiatory words and actions as they stood did not suit the people and place at hand. Through adaptation the rite is made accessible.

But the process of adaptation can be looked at critically. It is striking how often the forms of Christian Initiation have been shaped by extrinsic forces. Augustine derived his theology from current church custom, and defended it by a faulty reading of St. Paul. The Roman view that the bishop should retain the right to confirm prevailed in the West by a process that had little to do with the merits of the practice. The size of dioceses in northern Europe brought nontheological and nonliturgical problems to the administration of Christian Initiation. St. Thomas worked out his doctrine of Confirmation to explain the practice of confirming at a moment of life subsequent to Baptism—a practice which he had no way of knowing was a somewhat accidental Western development. The rites of the 16th-century Reformation and Counter-Reformation were shaped without essential historical data as to how initiatory rites and practices had developed.

Pragmatic, disciplinary, and polemic considerations have dominated the history of Christian Initiation. Few new departures have stemmed from a fresh insight into the meaning of becoming a Christian. Rites of Christian Initiation for today ought to have behind them an appreciative and critical review of the historical process which has brought us where we are. But we do not need another improvisation now. We need, within our specific historic situation, a renewed apprehension of the meaning of this basic sacrament of redemption, community, faith, and life. Liturgical integrity requires, above all else, rites fashioned under the informing criterion of the Gospel they enact.

CHAPTER III

The Situation Now: The Breakdown of "Christendom"

The situation in which we are living seems to call for ritual events as signs of social continuity in the midst of change and as means of interpreting ourselves to ourselves under the threat of meaninglessness. Ritual, to be effective, needs to have a measure of givenness. It does not necessarily have to be exempt from change, but it surely should not be something we devise to suit our moment. It will then tell us what we already know. But with respect to Christian Initiation, the present situation raises urgent questions about familiar, traditional actions and meanings. Customs, teachings and rituals which once commended themselves as self-validating, functional, and life-supporting, no longer seem fully convincing. It is worth asking why the Anglican pattern of initiation rites, largely unchanged for four centuries, is under question in the mid-20th century.

A pervasive factor is the altered relation between the Christian community and Western society. Ritual must provide focus points for life as we actually experience it. When the Church is fairly well adjusted to the structure and ways of a society—and this adjustment may contain many sustained tensions—the Church's practice and its expectations for its members seem believable and livable. One's inner awareness confirms institutional pattern and doctrine.

But when changes throw the Church's relation to its society out of adjustment, old rites and ways can seem arbitrary—forms to be gone through, but with their meaning deeply qualified. In a period of change, there is certain to be a great deal of widely felt frustration, individual and shared. The individual believer holds dual membership—deriving something from and owing something to both Christ and culture. This duality must be containable so that one can grow to stable, coherent selfhood. Change in the relation of Christ and culture puts the individual under stress. In the collective life too, a large, diversified community, groping toward a new adjustment, can seldom be graceful and confident. Things which used to work, and teachings which once were persuasive are felt to be problematic. Something has gone wrong. It is easy to turn the confusion inward and blame oneself. The long-trusted system could not have let one down. Cheerleader-like, one says that with effort we could make it work again.

Christian Initiation has been the way in which, at least since the 16th century, the Church has sought to interpret the two crises of being born and of growing up. To a great extent the Christian churches, in their somewhat official or established position, have provided the culture with rites of passage—rites of marriage and burial, as well as of birth and puberty. Being born and growing up are physiological, biological events. But their meaning is socially determined. They are looked at and handled differently in different parts of the world, and their meaning within any society may undergo change. In our time we are going through a deep, pervasive upheaval which is shaking the social conditions to which the forms of religious life have related. At the same time, the Christian community is seeking, out of its internal resources, a more independent basis for its life and mission. If it has become over-identified with a cultural moment, it can only be true to itself by criticizing, by its own Gospel, that over-identification.

These changes are often described as the breakdown of "Christendom." The term refers to the body of positive accommodations between Christianity and the organized life of Western culture that has prevailed, with changing forms but with important continuities, from the fourth century through late antiquity, the Middle Ages, and the Renaissance.

Societies were taken to be Christian people. (This understanding was always partially delusional. It was able to ignore the presence of Jewish and other religious minorities as well as of persons alienated from religion altogether. It had neither philosophy nor structures to contain religious pluralism.) Some favored status, official or informal, was accorded to Christian leaders and institutions. Throughout the society, there was wide acceptance, even among persons whose own faith was nominal or nonexistent, of the Christian myth, teachings, forms of piety, and ethics. Christianity pervaded the imaginative forms and modes of discourse of the society. It was not necessarily a unifying force; but if groups quarreled, they all argued the issues and each explained why it was right and the other wrong in ways informed by Christian categories. Groups were moved by deep spiritual forces that used Christian sanctions. Even when persons rejected faith, it was the pervasive Christian faith they rejected. Much of the artistic and intellectual heritage of the Mediterranean world and of Western Europe and North America carries the stamp of Christendom. One dare not idealize "ages of faith." There was ignorance, cruelty, and social oppression in the period— much of it supported by religion. This "Constantinian" relationship had great strengths and great weaknesses. Christian culture is too complex, and we are too close to it, for a just evaluation of it to be possible.

But the important fact with respect to it is that, at least within the last three centuries, this "Constantinian" arrangement has been crumbling. The West is by now deeply secularized. Major decisions, individual and social, are made without reference to Christian revelation, faith, or ethical sanctions. Other authorities, other presiding myths, other motivations, other criteria, now move and control. When it comes to God, the modern world "has no need of that hypothesis." The modern West is post-Constantinian. The religion that may have been close to the cultural center now stands as a privatized thing at the margin.

The disintegration of Christendom is uneven. In some places it is very far advanced. In other places, aspects of the old relationship may still be important spiritual and social realities. In many places, however, its residual forms seem like empty houses in which no one is living. Judgments in such matters may well differ. But forms of Christendom, where they endure at all, can only be accepted at face value at the risk of underestimating the actual de-Christianization of Western society.

In this situation, the church is seeking a new sense of itself and its mission. But the search is difficult, for the searchers are within a bewildering process which they cannot stop in order to conduct a dispassionate examination. One is daily making commitments in complex and in many ways unprecedented situations—situations in which one wishes for time and information that one is not given. It is like trying to say where one is and to judge what is moving and what is not when one is riding a carousel.

There are many ways of misjudging the task—particularly in the United States, where, by statistical measure, religion remains vigorous, and yet, paradoxically, secularism is pervasive. American society has periodic fits of religiosity, and public expressions of private piety are commonly required. But glitzy, materialistic, militaristic, exploitive, fiercely competitive standards prevail—at a terrible cost to personhood and community. Some groups seem intent on halting retreat by preserving what they take to be tokens of Christendom and a privileged place for religious observance—prayer at public functions, designation of America as a Christian nation, and the like. There is some historical fallacy and political naivete in such efforts. They take such public signs to mean more than they do. Meanwhile the actual capitulation of religion itself to secularity goes unidentified. (One notes that groups that want to challenge the teaching of evolution in public education are very often themselves deeply compromised by implicit social Darwinism, of which they are quite unaware. The measures churches use for judging their own success often are essentially secular measures.) Religious groups, some of which would be thought conservative and some liberal, have quietly absorbed secular standards of valuation so as to have become inoffensive sanctifiers of society as it is—so identified with it that they can neither judge nor redeem. One dare not underestimate the power of modern secular society. It seldom throws believers to the lions, but it may do something worse: it keeps them in harmless places of modest honor, in return for which they provide structures of justification for collective self-interest.

One should not speak as though "secular" meant "bad" or "wrong." Lines of hearing and speaking need to be kept open between the church and the "saeculum," for, however little it understands itself so, and however much it orders itself away from God, it is God's world.

During many generations past, the Church has corrected its own limited understandings of itself and of the ways of God through discoveries and insights from science, humanistic scholarship, social studies, political critique, and through creative work in the arts. Deep expressions of human tragedy and glory, which have been lost in the timid unreality of the churches, have come from the visual arts, music, poetry, novel, and drama. God who has something to say to the world through the church has something also to say to the church through the world, and there are secular prophets through whom it can be said. The contemporary situation does not set up a relationship of unrelieved hostility between the church and its society so much as it brings into consciousness a relationship that is highly complex and in change. This church/world boundary is fluid and not fully clear. When one seeks to describe it or to locate oneself with reference to it, possibilities for self-deception abound. The relationship requires discriminating attention.

The Church, where it wishes to retain ecclesial integrity (rather than to accept a domesticated place as a chaplaincy to prevailing values) is forced to raise its consciousness. Life in society and life in the Church are not parts of an experienced continuum. Being a good member of the society does not necessarily support being a good Christian. Being a good Christian may set one against society at crucial points. Individual and collective decisions are constantly demanded. A Christian identity is a more specifically religious, and a less conventionally social, thing. Karl Rahner proposes that in the modern situation—he calls it the *diaspora*—"Christianity ceases to be a religion of growth and becomes a religion of choice."[1]

Christian Baptism is a border rite. It marks the boundary between Church and not-Church. A change in the relationship between Church and society is certain to change the function of baptismal rites, as it is certain to change the experience patterns to which those rites must refer. In one situation, Christian Initiation may express the continuity between being a socialized person and being a Christian; the baptismal registers of the parishes may virtually be the vital statistics of the society. But in another situation, Christian Initiation may express discontinuity. To be marked with the sign of the cross may make one a marked person. At one moment the Church may want to identify closely with and to interpenetrate its culture; at another, it may be compelled to be sharply distinct.[2] These situational factors put pressure on the theology, practice, and forms of Baptism.

To a great extent, the liturgical forms and the supporting concepts of Christian Initiation in the Prayer Book tradition trace to the ages of Christendom—a situation to which they were well suited. A writer commented a few years ago:

> The initiation practice and liturgical forms of Anglicanism are among those products of a world-view, and an understanding of the Church's role in that world, which have forgotten we have here no fixed camp and no abiding city.[3]

If that accommodation to a past era is to be questioned, the questioning can arise from an appeal to origins. The sacraments of Christian Initiation derive from the Gospel. They were themselves born from a situation of *kairos*—a death and resurrection. They admit one to a community of pilgrims and strangers. Like the Gospel, they can remain true to themselves, while yet adapting in a variety of cultural conditions. In each adaptation, they should represent the richness of the message of Christ—but perhaps with changing accents. Always the Gospel is life-affirming. But in our time, when the culture is deceived about life, Baptism (in its liturgies and its associated pastoral processes) may be required to rediscover its character as "a revolutionary manifesto that subverts many of the values on which we have sold ourselves in the past few years."[4]

The historical sketch in the previous chapter will have suggested the faithful creativity of the early church in working out effective ritual for the serious process of becoming a Christian—ritual that had to separate persons from one social context in one order of reality and bring them into another.[5] Familiarity with the early church's ways of Baptism is of more than antiquarian interest. If we are moving into a post-Constantinian situation, we are likely to be misled if we attempt to perpetuate within it structures of common life that were created for and were functional in an era that is ending.

But what model do we have for Christian Initiation in a post-Christian society? To answer quickly, we have the model of the church before the rise of Christendom. It was working in a hostile or at least an impercipient society. Its task was to shape an elite community of believers strong enough to hold against eclectic Hellenistic society—a community that knew its own calling so well that it might be effective upon society by distinguishing itself from that society. There are factors in the world-church today that reproduce the conditions of the epoch prior to the rise of a Christian culture more closely than they do the conditions of the centuries of Christendom that have fallen in between. In a sense, the early church is not a past community that is of interest to historians. Rather, it is our contemporary. We can learn from it, for it was doing something strikingly like what we are being called to do.

At the same time that this change is taking place in the past centers of Christian culture, the theology and practice of Christian Initiation are influenced in some measure by "the coming of the third church." In Third World lands, the Christian community is growing rapidly. It is clear that by the year 2000 the bulk of the world's Christian population will be in Latin America, Africa, and Asia.[6] Much of this new growth is through adult converts. In bringing these converts into the faith, the "younger churches" are reinventing the catechumenate. Lay catechists fill roles of leadership, especially where trained clergy are in short supply. The churches are facing problems of postbaptismal discipline. Initiatory structures that were functional when the early church was an evangelizing community are functional again.[7]

What is happening in the post-Christian West has a curious historical affinity with what is taking place in the Eastern and Southern worlds. If we are moving into a post-Christian society in North America, we may find a model for Christian Initiation in the practice of churches that once were and are now at work in pre- or non-Christian societies. We will most certainly be misled if we try to perpetuate, in the demise of cultural Christendom, the initiatory practices that were shaped for the maintenance of a Christian society. Our situation may make us close neighbors with the Third World churches and contemporaries with the early church.[8]

There is a general recognition in our time that the breakdown of an old set of cultural accommodations is an opportunity at least as much as it may be a loss. Old assumptions are being shaken; innovation is required. But the death of the old, and the coming to birth of the new, is a kind of *kairos*—a moment in which God moves in history to challenge, demand, call, and open fresh possibility. It was remarked earlier that many of the customs and rites and frames of understanding which are associated with Baptism and Confirmation as they have been practiced for many generations trace to developments that took place in the long centuries of Christendom—an era that is passing or has passed. No one can endure a time of convulsive social change without some deep, underlying continuities. A time of *kairos* is a time of testing, so that the things which cannot be shaken may remain. But it is a time for discrimination. There is danger in carrying baptismal assumptions, practices, and understandings, from Christendom into a post-Christian era, without questioning and reevaluation.

CHAPTER IV

Persistent Issues:
1. Infant Baptism

This essay began with the observation that the rites of Christian Initiation are classically three: Baptism, Confirmation, and First Communion. These three ritual events have, for many centuries, been observed throughout much of the West at distinct times and officiated at by different ministers. But they are separated moments of an original unity. Despite their long-standing division in the West, they remain so interrelated that serious question about any one of them affects thinking about the other two. The reconsideration on which the new rites of the past decade and a half have been based has had to take account of each of the three and the relation among them.

The situation of the Church in its culture, as sketched in the foregoing section, has posed urgent questions for all parts of the initiatory complex. In other church/culture settings, moments that were separated in time may yet have provided an individual Christian with a sense of personal meaning and continuity because of the religious forces which unified the society. One's birth and one's coming of age were within a fairly coherent reality-sense. Or so we surmise. Did the ritual events deliver the intended meaning for most Christians of past generations? It cannot be shown that they did, nor can one be sure that they did not. Empirical study would be useful, even though difficult. But if the faith community's ways of interpreting and supporting birth and growth were connected and effective in the past, the ebbing tide of faith has left infant Baptism and adolescent Confirmation and First Communion privatized, isolated, and open to question. The following three chapters of this essay will consider the questions which have for some time been raised concerning each of the separated events of Christian Initiation.

One of the basic questions which has been freshly raised is the old question: "Who is a proper subject for Christian baptism?" The answers that had been accepted for generations no longer pass without examination.

The Situation

Any investigation within the Episcopal Church of who should be candidates for Baptism has to take account of the situation of churches in American society. But most of the fundamental patterns of Christian Initiation in American churches show signs of their derivation from 16th-century Europe. The question of who shall be baptized takes a somewhat different form on each side of the Atlantic, and it arises with different urgency. Little critical thinking on infant Baptism has originated in the Episcopal Church. The topic, by contrast, has been quite preoccupying in the Church of England and in many of the churches of Europe, where social consequences of long histories as state churches are evident.

The leaders of the English Reformation, formed as they were in the late medieval period and working under powerful Tudor monarchs, assumed that to be a citizen and to be a Christian were both normal parts of one's English inheritance. The English Church and the English Commonwealth were the same society, called by different names and seen from different perspectives. The Prayer Book contained no service of adult Baptism from 1549 until 1662. The liturgy assumed that children would grow to religious understanding and competence much as they did to physical, linguistic, and social competences. This assumption was shared, of course, by much of continental Reformed, Lutheran and

Catholic thought; it was an extension of medieval Christendom.

The intention to shape England as a Christian nation unified by a single Church may have represented a great dream, but it never worked. Religious pluralism was a fact of English society from Tudor times. It was slowly recognized in law and in social privilege from the 17th through the 19th centuries. Yet the traditional place which the Church has held in English society continues to be reflected in staggering problems over Christian Initiation. It remains a widespread practice to have children baptized "C. of E.," even though little will be done about these baptisms later. It is a kind of claim that many parents feel they can make on the Church, which many incumbents do not believe they have a right to refuse. The result of years of such practice is that something like 55 percent of the English population is baptized in the Church of England, while only about 6 percent of those eligible make Easter Communions.[1] Such statistics indicate the seriousness of the problem which has come to be known as "indiscriminate baptism."[2] More than one attitude toward it is possible for conscientious clergy. Yet many have become persuaded that for the Church to continue to encourage this widespread but doubtful practice cheapens one of the Gospel sacraments and lowers regard for the Church.

Similar questions are being raised in other European countries in which similar disproportion prevails and other state churches are asking what their pastoral responsibility is. Such debates have a long history, but their emergence in modern times with new urgency has a fairly specific origin. During the terrible testing in the 1930s and '40s the folk-churches of central Europe had to a dismaying extent been taken in by an ideology of land and people and blood. In the light of this capitulation, probing theological minds turned to another ecclesiology. Since the state churches had been made vulnerable by their identification with the society, the true church was seen as a confessing church, defined by its loyalty to Jesus Christ in life and in death. Such a break with past church-and-folk solidarities suggested, to rigorous minds, a revision of baptismal polity. Several of the great theologians of Europe criticised infant Baptism. Karl Barth, at the height of his influence, wrote *The Teaching of the Church Regarding Baptism* (1948), which spoke of infant Baptism as "a clouded sacrament," and proposed that Baptism be considered a sign to be performed by a believer.[3] There were agreements with and rejoinders to Barth's understanding of Baptism, but the issue was alive in European theological discussion as it had not been since the Reformation.

The American situation is not the same as the British or the European. All American churches are voluntary associations. None receives state support, and none is meant to have any legal disadvantage. Belonging to any particular church or to none at all tends to be a willed or chosen thing in most parts of American society. Yet factors derived from the Old World inheritance apply in the social role and the self-identity of many American churches. Some religious groups have long histories as carriers of ethnic identity; some bear frontier experience into their modern, urban collective selfhood. The Episcopal Church, perhaps trading on its Englishness, has stood for some social status in many communities. People who turn to it for little else have turned to it for functions which represent socially accepted rites of passage. It would be difficult and doubtless unprofitable to inquire whether the Episcopal Church has a higher proportion of loosely attached members than most other churches. But the factor is large enough so that Episcopalian clergy often wonder about their duty. When they are approached by a family remotely connected with the parish but seeking Baptism for a child, they ask how they can avoid adding to the number of nominal members, and whether they would be doing the child, the family, or the Church any good by consenting to the Baptism unless the parents accept some commitment and responsibility.

The Arguments

Such considerations deal with how infant Baptism can be responsibly administered. But questions have increasingly been raised as to whether or not it is possible to practice infant Baptism responsibly at all.

In the individualism of the modern world and especially of American society, many adults ask how much they can honestly promise in the name of an infant in so personal a matter as ultimate religious faith and loyalty. There are also indications that young persons, for their part, are not inclined to regard themselves as bound by commitments that were made, however solemnly, by their parents in their name without their consent. The Church is something from which they are free to sign off since, as they see it, they never signed on in the first place.

Further, the theology of infant Baptism is less secure than is sometimes realized. The most common rationale seems to be that the inclusion of infants within the baptized community witnesses to God's initiative. God loves us when we are helpless; grace acts toward us prior to anything we have done or could have done; God places us within the divine family apart from any achievement of our own. This is a powerful theological idea, stating something that one would want to affirm about God in behalf of a Christian child. But is it an aspect of the Christian message that is inherent in the rite of Baptism? Although it was anticipated by Augustine, the motif of prevenience is a new theological account of infant Baptism; it was not used for this purpose prior to the modern era. It gives a rationale more directly derived from the Christian Good News than was the anxiety over sin (largely based in bad news) which gave urgency to infant Baptism until recent generations. But it might be argued that it is, no less than the idea of inherited guilt, an *ex post facto* theological account which grew up to support an existing church practice.

Despite such arguments as these, there are still good reasons for infant Baptism.[4] They might be suggested here in merest summary as reasons based in God's grace, reasons based in the constitution of the family, and reasons based in the shared life of the Church:

- Children of a devout family stand in vital relation with God from the time they are born. (Perhaps from before!) Baptism is a witness to the actuality of God's presence, love and judgment in the lives of such children, as it reaches them in care and acceptance through their parents in the Church. They can be children of God before they have words by which to grasp or to express the relation. Baptism attests this divine involvement in each life from its very start.

- On the human side, infant Baptism expresses the deep continuity of human generations. What parents regard as of ultimate value for life for their children, they do not, because they cannot, withhold until their children can make up their own minds in the matter. The faith by which the parents live will be imparted to their children. Devout parents do, in fact, make renunciations and pledges in behalf of their children. Baptism is a sign of the inclusion of a child in a vital community of shared faith and covenant obligation. The family is thus a divinely ordained unit in creation and in redemption.

- The impossibility of articulate faith on the part of the one being baptized does not mean that infant Baptism is devoid of faith. It is an occasion full of faith; a child (whose inner life will be largely vicarious in character through many formative years) is carried on the living faith of that complex of interrelated persons, the Church. Every effort to make infant Baptism more a family-in-the-Church occasion speaking of redemption and less a family-in-the-community occasion speaking of respectability, has helped to bring out the inherent evangelical seriousness of the rite.

Yet such reasons as these are not likely to commend themselves to everyone. Even among faithful Christian parents in the churches which have traditionally practiced infant Baptism, it may not seem appropriate to bring children to Baptism. Where the arguments for infant Baptism seem less than fully compelling, other possibilities are likely to be explored. Baptisms which in the past might have been perfunctorily sought will not be done, and baptisms that might have been conscientiously done will be conscientiously postponed.

Many parts of the Christian community have been wrestling with this issue for some time. Several Church of England, Roman Catholic, Lutheran, Congregationalist, and Methodist studies (more in Britain than in the United States) have questioned infant Baptism. They judge it to have been so abused as to be beyond reclamation. Some writers propose a service of naming, blessing, and admission to the catechumenate for infants. Baptism would be a later and a different thing.[5] Others, agonized clergy among them, suggest a moratorium on infant Baptism —a suggestion they are ready to back by not bringing their own children to Baptism, even though they think of their own families as among those in which the practice might be justified. They are willing to protest in this drastic way what seems to them the debasement of one of the Church's sacraments. Such questioning and such proposals are part of the ecumenical conversation on the meaning of initiatory rites in a post-Christian society.

The factors which have raised this issue urgently elsewhere are also present within the Episcopal Church—although somewhat concealed. As the churches of the West move beyond what has been described above as "Christendom," it cannot be assumed that influences from a Christianized society will be an ally to fill out the promise of infant Baptism or to compensate for lax administration. It may seem necessary to stress adult decision. In a sense, infant Baptism is a test and a challenge to the adult community. A congregation of generally nominal Christians is simply incompetent to practice infant Baptism. It is not observing for itself, at its own level of maturity, the promises that it is asked to affirm in behalf of a child.[6]

Yet few people who speak realistically of these issues seem to want or expect a wholesale abandonment of infant Baptism. A shift to the obvious alternative—the Baptism on an adult basis of children of practicing Christian parents—would solve little, for the churches which practice "believers' Baptism" are experiencing with their own children many of the same questions over the right age for Baptism that other churches have over the right age for Confirmation.[7] The principle of believers' Baptism is clear enough: One is to receive Baptism only upon a free, adult profession of faith. But when does one become competent to make such a profession? Where believers' Baptism is the prevailing pattern in a community, the interior decision it requires becomes quite predictable. The inward experience of children tends to follow the suggestion of the social structures in which they grow up. And where conversion leading to Baptism is expected of children or young people, the appropriate experience occurs at about the anticipated age. It remains so much under the control of the elder generation and the community pattern which an impressionable individual internalizes that it is only questionably adult in character.

The point is not that one of these patterns—infant Baptism or believers' Baptism—is good, and the other wrongheaded. Rather, the point is that the handling of children in the faith is an inherently difficult question, and one on which the earliest Christian writings (all of them rather "first generation" in character) give no help. Although there is some inferential evidence, there is no clear record in our earliest sources that children born to converts after they themselves became Christians were baptized in infancy. But there is even less indication that such children were regarded as outside the baptized life until they reached some unspecified "age of accountability."

Both systems draw on concepts that cannot be found in the earliest Christian documents. Each system seems to look best as critic of the abuses of the other. Each tends toward decadence when it is alone and unchallenged.

There are almost classic lines of argument:

■ Those who require articulate faith on the part of anyone who is to be baptized often think of infant Baptism, in which such faith is missing, as "magic"—an irreverent human attempt to control the divine. But with at least equal truth, believer's Baptism can be thought to confine the relation to God to purely conscious processes, to forms of words; it seems to baptize persons into a conversion experience. In its effort to avoid the appearance of managing God, it winks at manipulating people.

■ In order to avoid any appearance of controlling the divine, those who practice believers' Baptism have customarily spoken of baptism as an "ordinance," not a sacrament. They understand it as a human act of witness to divine action—not as itself divine action. Thus it belongs to the economy of obedience, not to the economy of redemption; it is not something that one does in the course of becoming a Christian, but something which someone who has become a Christian does as a sign for others. Such doctrine raises barriers to mutual recognition of Baptism. Two parties are using the same word, but the things they mean by it are to a marked extent incompatible. But is this sharp distinction between what God does for and in us and what we do in response to God true to the nature of biblical faith. The mystery of which Baptism speaks is the mystery of "I, yet not I, but Christ in me."[8] In the profoundest aspects of the divine-human relation, subjectivity and objectivity cannot be separated.[9] Some baptistic theologians (particularly in Europe) now freely speak of Baptism as "for the forgiveness of sins," as an enacted word of God.[10] Such modification of simplistic formulations makes real dialogue on sacramental issues possible; one can conceive of theological statements and structures that could contain two modes of practice.[11]

42

■ Those who defend believers' Baptism are shocked at evidence of careless admission to Baptism in other churches and at the resultant proportion of nominal members. Is that any way to form a vital, effective, committed church? Their practice of admitting to Baptism only persons who come on the basis of adult conviction should produce a church of converted believers—sometimes spoken of (with some confusion of categories) as "a regenerate church membership." A community so formed is often contrasted with the "mixed community" of a church made up of those whose true faith is not ascertained before they are admitted. But if a baptistic congregation that has been continuously in existence for several generations will look honestly at its register of baptisms, it will report disappointments, pastoral tears, failed promise, lapses and losses, just as others do. The formation of the perfect church is not within human power. The human fact of "mixture" should be foundational in any realistic ecclesiology. Some notions of membership may err on the side of inclusiveness, and some may be more restrictive. Each can be defended; each can be abused. The deceptive note is the contention that believers' Baptism eliminates the problem.

■ Groups which practice believers' Baptism have difficulty giving a theological account of the place of the child in the church. Baptistic parents cherish their children in Christ and teach them to pray. But they cannot include these children within the church as baptized Christians. Children are a theological anomaly.[12] Of course, an effective (and equally *ad hominem*) reply can be made by citing the sentimentality concerning children that often surrounds the baptism of infants. Moreover, it is not clear that those who practice infant Baptism have followed the theology of childhood very far themselves. The presence of baptized children in the church is not just incidental to the church's life and self-understanding. Rather it holds up the child as being in some sense model and judge for the adult members. An Anglican writer has said, "Both children and adults belong to God's kingdom *in the manner of childhood,* i.e., theirs is the kingdom by virtue of a grace not given by adulthood."[13] Infant Baptism makes possible a developed theology of childhood, but the task remains largely unfulfilled.

■ Believers' Baptism usually correlates with an individualistic, sectarian ecclesiology. The church is regarded as a contractual community —"a voluntary association of baptized believers."[14] By contrast, the practice of including children within the baptized community respects the mystery of the interpenetration of human lives with one another and with God, and it thus encourages an organic view of the Church, a view faithful to the ecclesiology of the New Testament. Such emphasis on social continuity assumes that influences in the family, church, and community will shape persons into conscious faith, as in fact they often still do. But this ritual pattern is ill prepared to adjust when such influences are ineffective or nonexistent, as in fact they often are. Where Baptism has come to focus predominantly on children, adult decision and commitment have been inadequately incorporated into the theology, catechetics, and liturgy of becoming a Christian.

Such arguments—sometimes friendly, sometimes acrimonious— can go on along these lines without either side really persuading the other. Yet in recent years it has seemed possible to articulate either side in such a way as to hear and respect the thing the other stands for. One can say a great deal in behalf of adult Baptism without having to say that infant Baptism is not really Baptism at all. One can defend and practice infant Baptism while recognizing some of the problems of doctrine and practice it involves. These two lines of theological construction have been worked out for many generations by separate churches with incompatible understandings of Christian Initiation. But they are now becoming differing emphases contained within some churches and some interchurch conversations.[15]

When one weighs conflicting baptismal doctrines and practices, the discussion in the previous chapter is pertinent. The matter is coming to attention in today's church and new possibilities are opening at least in part because the relation of the church and society is differently perceived. The two systems for Christian Initiation may not be equally convincing in all situations. Either might be better suited to a different relation between the Church and its social setting. A Lutheran theologian, Robert Jenson, has argued cogently:

Since infant Baptism inevitably ties the church more closely to the culture, the Church should baptize infants when it is attempting to penetrate a culture in the post-missionary situation, and become more reluctant to do so when it is attempting to re-establish its transcendence of culture after capitulating to it.[16]

Jenson's point is serious, but it should not be taken in a simplistic way. Probably no other society has had as much experience as has the American society of large baptistic populations—amounting to such forms of ecclesiastical life being virtually the established church in parts of the United States. It cannot be shown that such churches are more successful than others in avoiding captivation by an unprophetic "culture Christianity." Nonetheless, believers' Baptism, as a theology and practice of membership, is a sign of a church based in individual transformation; while infant Baptism is more likely to be a sign of a church shaped by social continuity. At times the church may need to think of itself through one of these models, at times through the other.

Recent New Factors

In recent years, a number of things have been happening in the Episcopal Church and in other churches as well to heighten the seriousness and ecclesial character of both infant Baptism and adult Baptism. Notice may be taken of some of them:

As to signs of change which apply largely, but not exclusively to *infant Baptism*: Not so many years ago, throughout the Episcopal Church, most baptisms were done at times other than at a congregational service, with only family and friends attending. Then in the early 1950s a minor revolution was brought about, largely through the awareness (articulated by some prophetic persons who were doing background thinking for Christian education) that the church is a redeemed and redemption-bearing community. It was emphasized at the time that the church, by the quality of its corporate life, imparts (or else inhibits) a gospel of divine acceptance. Baptism is the chief sign in the collective life of that acceptance and of the involvement of persons with one another in mutual caring, giving, judging, and forgiving. But church-goers could go for years without being part of a Baptism. The sign was, by common practice, removed from its natural context in the gathered community. As a consequence of such self-criticism, baptisms in much of the Episcopal Church came to be held at a congregational service, in plain view of all, the baptized children attending, and the congregation taking a vocal part. Few liturgical customs have changed with such rapidity—and all without rites or rubrics or canons directing the process.

Now that the rite of the 1979 Prayer Book is the church's text for Holy Baptism, its character seems to be bringing about further changes. Previous texts were sufficiently stiff, distanced, and nonparticipatory that it was a matter of pastoral labor to bring out the redemptive seriousness of the act. Little in the rite itself resisted its use for private baptisms. One does not want to caricature the past (which is one's own past) nor to ignore the spiritually significant, liturgically splendid, and humanly gripping baptisms that took place under previous rites, but when parents called the church saying that they wanted a child baptized (often they said "christened" —sometimes they said "done"), the action which they sought and which the church provided could be quite perfunctory.

There seems to be only anecdotal evidence in the matter, but clergy do report that the new rite is having a sobering effect on persons who might (on the basis of past experience, for which neither they nor the church should necessarily be faulted) seek baptisms on a somewhat casual basis. When the content of the Prayer Book rite is discussed, persons who are not familiar with recent church life are taken by surprise. The setting of Holy Baptism in a "chief" service of a Sunday, beginning with scripture and preaching, and culminating in the Eucharist; the participation of the congregation; the searching character of the promises—all these factors require a family to consider whether what the church offers is what it wants. (People have been known to make comments such as, "Why, it's just like going to church!") The point of the rite and of pastoral instruction is not to say a hasty "no" to parents seeking to have a child baptized—"Forbid them not." Indiscriminate Baptism is not corrected by indiscriminate rigorism. Nevertheless, some selectivity seems to be arising out of the process itself. It is not uncommon for parents to hesitate after hearing what Baptism is taken to be these days.

But frequently that is not the end of the matter. The parents are now in an exploratory dialogue with the church. The first visit familiarized them with a view of Baptism as an act of divine acceptance and gentleness and of human intentionality beyond their previous conceptions. It indicated that by Baptism one is joined to a vital community of faith and service. The sacrament speaks of life transformed by divine good news. It expresses a gospel which, without compromising its evangelical realism, attracts and invites. After a time, those parents ask for a further visit, saying, in effect: "We appreciate your seriousness when you spoke with us before. We were not ready then to go ahead with the sort of thing of which you told us. But we have had time to think, and now we would like to work toward it."

In addition to changes that arise from the present baptismal rite, parishes are undertaking a study of Baptism, often leading to the adoption of a considered policy which supports and interprets the Prayer Book rite. The stir of interest in matters of Christian Initiation is contagious; diocesan structures can help; good material is in hand. Bishop Eastman has remarked:

> It is the life-saving, life-changing nature of baptism that makes it the fundamental sacrament of the Christian community. Without it the church does not exist. When it is devalued, discounted, put off to the side, the church is essentially weak. When baptism is seen as utterly basic and central, the church comes to life.... Parishes with a high doctrine of baptism and a vigorous approach to the process of initiation will be vital centers of Christian life and witness.[17]

Parishes have been educating themselves so that the conscientious execution of the church's rites of initiation is backed by congregations and vestries, and is not thought of as a peculiarity of the parson. The varied tasks of teaching and support are carried out by gifted persons of the congregation. Some standards are accepted, such as the insistence that parents who want a child baptized take some significant part in congregational life. These elementary disciplines are entered with discovery and joy; they are not barriers arbitrarily erected in ritual life. They are signs of the church being intentional about its central business.

As to signs of change which apply largely to *adult Baptism*: There have always been adult converts and adult baptisms in the Episcopal Church, and they have often had a vitalizing impact on the congregation in which they took place. But as a rule they have been pastorally, catechetically, and liturgically exceptional. The thing for which the church's ritual and educational processes were tooled was infant Baptism, to be followed in time by adolescent Confirmation and admission to Holy Communion. (What was to happen after that was something for which the church could scarcely be said to be tooled at all.)

When persons came to faith and Baptism in adulthood, it was always a welcome event, but the ritual was full of anomalies. Often adults were baptized in an empty church, with only the family present. Such baptisms would be timed to fall a few days before the bishop's visit for Confirmation (inevitably suggesting that Baptism was a preliminary rite, while Confirmation was the principal moment of reception into the family of Christ). The Prayer Book liturgy for use with adults was (since 1662) an adapted form of the rite which had been drafted in the 16th century for infant Baptism. A short time after the baptismal promises had been intelligently made by an adult (occasionally within the same service), the newly baptized person was asked to "renew" them before the bishop—an act that seemed either to cast doubt on the seriousness with which the promises had been made not long before or to suggest that in the days (or moments) since Baptism there had been some lapse. The Church was structured for incorporating its own children into the baptized life, but it was ill equipped to hold the fact of adult conversion and ritual initiation before the collective life.

Changes in pastoral priorities have been going on within the Episcopal Church in these matters for some time. But now they have the liturgical material of the 1979 *Book of Common Prayer* with which to work. The rite for Holy Baptism in this book is not adapted from a 16th-century service for infant Baptism, but is designed along the lines of the initiatory ritual which the early church devised with adults primarily in mind. The rite works well for children, for adults, or for a mixture of the two at the font.

In practice there seem to be more adult baptisms in recent years than there were—or else they are simply being made more public. When an adult and a child are baptized together, each form says something important about the other. In effect, the adult can look at the child and think: "Despite all those classes, the hard work, the discipline, the tears and the exhilaration, my Baptism is as much a gift and a witness to grace as is that baby's Baptism." And the presence of the adult might be a reminder that something must happen to validate the infant's sacramental initiation. In effect, it can say: "Some time this rite in which this child is inarticulate and passive must come to mean as much to him or her as the rite now means to this deeply dedicated adult."

Although the baptismal liturgy is much the same for an infant and for an adult, there are special factors in the preparation of adults. The provision for them is partly in suitable liturgical forms and partly in habits of congregational life. Both have developed rapidly and nearly simultaneously in a number of churches. The Roman Catholic Church led a little in time in this matter, so its development may be discussed first.

Shortly after the Vatican Council II (1963–65) mandated new liturgical texts, a revised form for the Baptism of children was issued, *Rite of Baptism for Children* (1970). Then several years later a sizable volume was issued called *Rite for Christian Initiation of Adults* (1974) —the RCIA. The Roman community thus has two rites in different books and with somewhat different approaches to the sacrament. The larger and less familiar RCIA text has begun to have an extraordinary impact on the church. It is the judgment of one discriminating writer that "in the restored Roman initiation polity lie the germs of a vastly revitalized sacramental theology and pastoral practice."[18] The new adult rite of Baptism was spoken of in the supporting documents which presented it to the Roman Church as the "norm" for Christian Initiation.[19] That does not mean that abruptly there will be more adult baptisms than infant baptisms—that is not going to happen. Rather, it means that what Baptism signifies is more amply stated and enacted in the case of an adult than it can be in the case of a child. When one looks at the two forms, it is clear that the infant form is derived from the adult—not the other way around. The reality expressed in the adult form is the criterion for judging the adequacy of the infant form.

The RCIA text is structured with a full catechumenate leading to Baptism. This catechumenate assumes a serious process of education and formation prior to Baptism and first Communion at the Easter Vigil. One is, as in the Church's early centuries, to go through a period of discovery—moving from separation from the old to incorporation into the new. Through this process, the congregation is continuously aware of Christians-in-the-making in its midst.

Now, if this form of Baptism is the initiatory norm, the liturgical rite is raising an ecclesial question. It asks: What should be expected in normal membership in the Church? Why are there not more informed, responsible adult Christians than there are? And how can the ritual and catechetical processes of initiation raise the level of common expectation? With such concerns about the quality of life and faith in the Church, many Roman parishes have begun a regular catechumenate. It is a period of training and real participation for new Christians in the life of the Church, marked by moments of public ritual in the Sunday congregation, culminating in Baptism at the Easter Vigil.

Some of the persons who are most aware of the importance and the power of the RCIA are fearful that it will be treated as a "church program," and be made part of American salvation by gimmickry. Of course, steps must be taken to make parishes aware of something that will be largely new to them. But what the RCIA opens is not an attractive "extra," but a vision of the church doing its central task. One writer has put it:

> The RCIA is not a "program"—it is the way the church is, the way the church lives. The kind of local church that it assumes and requires—one engaged in the constant process ...of a lifelong and ever deepening spiral of gospel-conversion-baptism-eucharist-mission—is the key to everything that community is and does. [20]

The amount of experience with the RCIA is now quite large, and there are exciting parish stories to tell. [21] One clear finding from these first few years is that the awareness of adult converts and their progress toward Baptism has an awakening effect on the entire congregation.

The Episcopal Church has addressed these matters in a somewhat different body of service material. When the Prayer Book texts were proposed, it was clear that there would be one Baptism rite, not two. But undeniably there are features of preparation and ritual that are special to adults. These have been provided for in the "Catechumenate" in *The Book of Occasional Services* (1979), pp. 112–130.

Such a service has not had a place in the official books before, so it is given a substantial introduction, "Concerning the Catechumenate" (pp. 112–114). There is nothing to prescribe the length of time for the catechumenate. (Presumably it might run for weeks or for years.) The whole process is given the title "Preparation of Adults for Holy Baptism." The first public step, "Admission of Catechumens," would follow a period of inquiry and initial clarification of what is sought and what is offered. The spoken text of the "Admission" opens with the splendid question and answer: "What do you seek?" "Life in Christ" (p. 115). The sign of the cross is given.

During candidacy there is instruction, each session concluding with prayer and laying on of a hand by the instructor, whether the catechist be lay or cleric (pp. 117–120). Candidates take part in the life of worship and service in the faith community. The "Candidacy for Baptism" would begin with an enrollment at the start of Lent (pp. 120–124), leading to Baptism at the Easter Vigil. The whole is a deeply serious, pastorally supported process carrying one to the sacrament of membership in Christ and his people.

Perhaps it should be emphasized that the material in *The Book of Occasional Services* is a liturgy, not a course of study. What is taught and learned and done in the time of preparation will depend on the experience of the catechumens and the resourcefulness and sensitivity of the instructors. But the progress of the catechumens toward Baptism will be noted by liturgical waymarks shared by the Sunday congregation.

Hitherto either infant Baptism or believers' Baptism has been used and defended within a given church body rather exclusively. Whole denominations have, of course, been organized around a single idea of Baptism and an ecclesiology that follows from it. This issue has made it impossible for at least some churches which practice believers' Baptism to recognize the initiatory rite of other churches as true Baptism. Those other churches, somewhat in reaction, have developed a considerable investment in the polemics of infant Baptism. It has not been possible for the positive side of each initiatory pattern to be recognized and for the two systems (not as opposing ideologies, but as varying pastoral judgments, parental wishes, and levels of involvement in the church) to be permissible and responsible usages within a single ecclesiastical community. But something of the kind may be emerging now.

Perhaps the specific meaning and vocation of adult Baptism and of infant Baptism within the ecumenical church will be enhanced when both are real possibilities and both are common enough within the same community to complement one another and to stand up to the corrective of one another. Clearly it is quite a different thing to practice infant Baptism, on the one hand, in a community which practices almost exclusively infant Baptism and, on the other hand, to practice it in a community in which there is an ongoing adult catechumenate and a generous proportion of members who have entered the church as deeply convinced adults. In a sense a faith community of converted adults creates the best conditions for infant initiation.

Questions of baptismal practice are questions of the nature of the church. The fact that the church has good liturgical texts for adult as well as infant Baptism will not cause them to be used. Talking persuasively about adult baptisms does not in itself bring them about. Churches do not drift into adult conversions and adult baptisms. These are marks of a vital, evangelizing church. Prior to the use of liturgical texts for adult baptisms is the question of the commitment of the church to mission.

But adult converts will have children—children who do not begin outside of Christian commitments as their parents did. (And those children will have children. The Church is always beginning freshly, and it is always persisting continuously.) The children of converts should not be expected to replicate the spiritual experience of their twice-born parents. They do not begin where their parents began. Their sacramental introduction to Christ and the Church should represent the shape of their actual second-generation experience. If a church in which adult baptisms are to be common is required to be an evangelizing church, a church in which infants are baptized needs to be a sharing, nurturing community in which the sacramental starting point can be sustained by growth into informed, honest adult faith.

The Episcopal Church, along with many other churches, has liturgical materials to encourage, interpret, and support an unprecedented condition of varying styles of Christian Initiation being permissible, expected, responsible uses within a single ecclesiastical unity. The "one Baptism" is adapted to different stages of individual development and to different ways of coming to faith, but it retains its integrity in all of them.

Persistent Issues:
2. Confirmation

Throughout its history, Anglicanism (with other churches of the West) has lacked clarity about the meaning and function of Confirmation. Sharply different points of view have been expressed—although the differences which divided scholars have often been disregarded by genial popular piety. Since the late 19th century a substantial literature in the Church of England has debated the relation of Baptism to Confirmation. In much of Anglicanism questions of a pastoral sort have been raised as to whether Confirmation does what it is meant to do. Dissatisfaction with existing theory and practice was summarized a few years ago with splendid irritation:

> A number of ill-assorted matters are packaged together in the grab-bag we call Confirmation. There is the concept that Confirmation is the fulfillment of the commitment of Holy Baptism. There is the imagery of the reception of the seven-fold gifts of the Holy Spirit symbolized by the laying-on of hands. There is the practical use of the service of Confirmation as a discipline of admission to the Holy Communion. Finally, this is all made the occa-

sion of an episcopal visitation to the congregation and a church. These unlikely matters are intertwined in utter theological and practical confusion."[1]

Confirmation seems to involve at least three kinds of issues: (1) liturgical issues which result from the unstable mixture of meanings and functions that have been compounded in Western forms of Confirmation; (2) theological issues arising from the effort to define the meaning of a second stage of initiation as distinct from the meaning of a first stage; and (3) the practical problem of how to administer a second stage of Christian Initiation at a moment of life when it can have its intended meaning. The following sections of this essay will consider these issues in sequence.

A. The Inherent Instability of the Anglican Pattern

The historical sketch in Chapter II has indicated that Confirmation as it has been understood and practiced in Anglicanism (and in some other churches of the West) has brought together actions, functions, and interpreting doctrines from different sources. A new and at least partially unprecedented unity was created in the Prayer Book tradition.

Two principal clusters of meaning, coming from different sources, are distinguishable: (1) One line of ancestry of Confirmation traces to a postbaptismal rite which was observed in portions of the early church. It has been observed above that, although such rites took many forms, they were always within a unified initiatory event in the early centuries. But by the later Middle Ages in the West, the bishop's anointing had become part of a second stage of initiation. (2) Another line of ancestry came from the Reformation period. Confirmation was taken to be the moment when the promises made at infant Baptism were ratified by a Christian come of age. This function had no ritual continuity with the early church. Of course, the early Christians did teach candidates before Baptism, and persons being baptized confessed their faith. But the transfer of these features of initiation to Confirmation, as a second and later stage of the process, has commended itself in many of the churches of the modern West as a way of dealing with what had come to be perceived as the psychological incompleteness of infant Baptism.

It is possible to contrast these two observances and these two clusters of meanings quite sharply:

- *One rite is* sacramental, *a part of the Church's faithful custody of the redemptive life. The other is* catechetical, *speaking of an individual's responsibility and competence.*

- *One is* initiatory, *an action derived from the liturgy of becoming a Christian. The other is within Christian life*—an act of a baptized Christian *at a certain stage of maturation.*

- *One signifies the Holy Spirit and* God's action; *the other expresses the renewal for oneself of promises made earlier on one's behalf by others*—obviously a human action.

- *One would properly be considered* unrepeatable, *for it is a separated bit of the baptismal ritual. The other, the renewal of the promises of one's Baptism, is* something that it is desirable to do and in fact is done repeatedly.

- *One came from* the early church; *the other from* the late Middle Ages and the 16th century.[2]

Part of the chronic uncertainty about Confirmation in Anglicanism is traceable to this mixed ancestry. Some Anglicans see Confirmation in the context of one of its antecedent sources, while some interpret it through the other. In general, it can be said that persons who approach Confirmation by way of liturgical and patristic history think of it in sacramental terms, and they seek the restoration of early practice. Others who approach Confirmation with education and nurture in mind think that the catechetical side describes what Confirmation really is, and they would like to adapt ritual to support something they judge to have become a practical necessity.

In the historical sketch in Chapter II, this tension was observed in the first Prayer Book. In 1549 the rubrics, which drew on Reformed sources, explained Confirmation by its catechetical function—making no reference to the gift of the Spirit. But the liturgy for the act was the early and medieval bishop's blessing, which spoke of the Holy Spirit and made no reference to baptismal promises.

When, after 1662, the Prayer Book rite of Confirmation brought these two sorts of action together, it was possible for Anglican apologists to speak persuasively of their complementarity: God confirms, and we confirm. But the uneasy relation between the two was always detectable. The efforts of those who thought in one set of terms to do justice to the things that were important to those who thought in the other were often unconvincing. Although both used the term "confirmation" for the observance they described, in many ways they were talking about different things.[3]

It is desirable to look more closely at each of these ingredients of Anglican Confirmation:

(1) The first, the postbaptismal rite from the ancient church, began as an enacted explication of some of the meaning of entry into Christ and his people. Christian baptismal practice was doubtless influenced by customs in the ancient world in which washing with water and anointing with oil were parts of the often elaborate customs of bathing.[4] In the rich biblical imagery which surrounded the ritual of the early church, an anointing with chrism spoke of the Holy Spirit. It suggested royalty and priesthood. Some of the church Fathers explain this postbaptismal act as speaking of Christ, the Anointed One. Cyril of Jerusalem uses the image of anointing to link Christ and the newly baptized Christians: "Now you were made christs (*christoi*)."[5]

It is difficult to trace these postbaptismal rites from antiquity into the present. There is no clear evidence in the New Testament or the second century that a ritual anointing or laying on of hands was given at Baptism, although imagery of divine anointing is present.[6] By the third century, such acts had become part of the sequence of initiatory actions. Tertullian, writing *c.* 210 CE, referring to the already quite complex baptismal actions, said:

The flesh is washed that the soul may be made spotless:
the flesh is anointed that the soul may be consecrated:
the flesh is signed that the soul too may be protected:
the flesh is overshadowed by the imposition of the hand that the

soul may be illumined by the Spirit:
the flesh feeds on the Body and Blood of Christ so that the soul
as well may be replete with God. [7]

From the third century on, a postbaptismal anointing is part of the rites of initiation in all our extant sources except those from Syria.[8] But the form of such rites varies greatly—so much so that one cannot be certain what part of an ancient practice is to be taken as the equivalent of a later custom. As Charles Davis once put it:

> *From the point of view of ritual, Confirmation has not remained identical with itself. Christian Initiation soon included several postbaptismal rites. Which is to be taken as the essential rite of Confirmation? It is not an easy question to answer, and history shows that now one rite, now another, was regarded as the essential part.* [9]

But Anglican historical inquiry must focus on Rome, the source (by way of the Carolingian reforms) of the English ritual inheritance. If the early third-century account by Hippolytus can be taken to represent Roman ways, initiation there involved an anointing immediately before Baptism (apparently taken to be a final exorcism) and two immediately after it. The first of these later anointings took place when the baptized persons emerged from the water and were anointed with an "Oil of Thanksgiving" which the bishop had blessed earlier in the rite; and probably the whole body was anointed. The second anointing was given by the bishop when the initiates, now reclothed, came to the eucharistic room where the community was assembled. The bishop placed his hand on the head of each and offered a prayer referring to the Holy Spirit. (Some editors read the text as a prayer for the giving of the Spirit; others read it as acknowledging that the Spirit has been given in Baptism and asking for grace that the newly baptized person may live as a Christian).[10] The bishop then anointed the head of the baptized with consecrated oil, sealed each one on the forehead, and gave the kiss of peace.

Perhaps heirs of Western practices cannot help but ask: Were these bishop's actions constitutive of the rite, and was the prior anointing by a presbyter preparatory and transitional? Or was the bishop's anointing a public continuation and acceptance of the anointing which had already been made in a darkened, private setting by a presbyter?

Such questions are unanswerable today. If they were asked of the persons who shaped the early rites, they would probably be unintelligible. Hippolytus' rite is striking for its use of many ministers serving complementary functions. In Rome (and eventually throughout the West, as Roman ways came to dominate), the presbyter's postbaptismal anointing became reduced in importance. The anointing by the bishop was continued and came in time to be reckoned one of the numbered sacraments. It was subject to the separate development, the practical difficulties, and the imposed interpretations we have noted previously.

In its early history, the postbaptismal anointing was part of a coherent sequence of actions within a unified initiatory ritual. In that setting it had a meaning and function as part of the enacted *kerygma* of Christian Initiation. Apart from that setting, what might it mean? Can a portion of a unified initiatory ritual become detached and then be the center of a true development of enriched, latent meanings? Or is it inevitable that such a rite will only seem diminished or problematic when it exists apart from the setting in which it emerged and which gave it its significance? Can one sign be removed from a complex of signs of which it had been an integral part without its removal flawing the shape of the whole?

(2) The second ingredient in traditional Anglican Confirmation, the ratification of baptismal vows, came from Reformation sources. The Reformers were mistaken when they supposed that their kind of confirmation followed early precedent.[11] They might have been well advised to disregard historical argument and to defend their catechetical practice on pragmatic, pastoral grounds. The Reformation was passionately concerned for catechesis and personal faith in a "second generation" Christian community—a matter in which the New Testament and the early church (both of them characteristically "first generation") gave no direct help, and in which medieval practice was thought to have been gravely defective.

A sympathetic grasp of the Reformers' intentions requires a consideration of the theology of faith. It is at this point, rather than in ritual continuity, that their work has enduring importance. They sought to recover an essential note of the believing community, Christian life, and sacramental theology.

Faith, in the biblical sense, reaches toward utterance. Service of the "lips" without participation by the "heart" was condemned by the prophets.[12] This biblical judgment suggests a state of alienation in which the human unity of "heart" and "lips" is broken so that heart and lips often speak differently. Faith knits up that broken unity, so that one's words are as oneself. Then a restored believer addresses God out of that wholeness. Thus, belief which remains unexpressed and which does not order life around an articulate center, could hardly be called belief. Salvation, according to St. Paul, comes when one confesses vocally "Jesus is Lord" and believes inwardly that God has raised him from the dead.[13]

The early church retained much of this vital sense of faith. Initiation was a conscious, adult event, a sacrament of conversion. It was preceded by instruction and examination; it required explicit renunciation of evil and confession of the rule of faith; and it was followed by responsible moral discipline. The historian A.D. Nock put it this way: "Judaism and Christianity demanded renunciation and a new start. They demanded not merely acceptance of a rite, but the adhesion of the will to a theology, in a word faith, in a new life in a new people."[14] Lapse from such commitments might require public repentance. Inward experience was taken by the church Fathers to be a constituent of sacramental reality. In a famous sermon, Gregory of Nazianzus urged those who had postponed Baptism to "run to the Gift" while they were still master of their thoughts. Old age or the approach of death might make them unaware of what was signified. Only a body would be washed for burial. It was important to be baptized "while the grace can reach the depth of your soul."[15]

This conscious element had been eclipsed as infant Baptism became universal in both East and West. No equivalent devices had been introduced in the medieval church to demand or elicit personal commitment. The supportive admission into the Christian myth, community, and life which the social environment itself provided were regarded as sufficient.[16] Of course, many Christians in the Middle Ages had intense vocations as ascetics, mystics, theologians, missionaries, workers of charity, and the like; and many of these vocations were entered upon by way of strenuous discipline. But no call to articulateness and no training in a way of life belonged to membership and its ritual as such.

The Reformers rejected the idea that faith could be merely "implicit." A faith which did only what the Church did, without serious thought or decision, was scorned by John Calvin as "ignorance tempered by humility."[17] The Reformers rejected just as emphatically an intellectualistic account of faith. True faith was not consent to authoritative teaching about God. It was trust, or *fiducia*. Yet it could be described as a kind of knowledge—knowing God in his mercy, his gracious will. "Faith consists in the knowledge of God and Christ." Calvin was wise enough to see the mystery and dimness at the heart of religious knowledge. "Most things are now implicit for us," he said. Some "implicitness" belongs to the very nature of faith. Moreover, the implicit level might be a needed preparation for truer faith, but it was not a place to stop. Faith has and conveys meaning—albeit the meaning exceeds any discursive account that a believer might give of it. Vital faith always seeks greater understanding. It is only true to itself as it reaches toward explicitness.

This emphasis on explicit faith stood in some tension with infant Baptism—a rite defended by the Reformers on the basis of God's promise, but a rite in which the child who is baptized is incapable of personally confessing the faith. To achieve, in a society of persons who had been baptized in infancy, the level of adult competence which they sought, the Reformers gave to Confirmation a distinctive development. It was made an occasion when youths who had been baptized in infancy were to make for themselves the promises that inhere in Christian profession. This restatement of basic promises by a Christian was often compared to the covenant renewals in the Old Testament.

This idea of what Confirmation could be was present in a germinal way in the thinking of John Wycliffe, and stated more fully by the Bohemian Brethren, followers of Jan Huss.[18] But it was developed in the teaching and pastoral practice of the Reformation churches. The effectiveness of Confirmation as redefined, depended on postbaptismal teaching, and the Reformers wrote catechisms for such instruction.[19] Often these catechisms were in pairs—a larger, more detailed explanation for the teachers, and a shorter, simpler text for the children. (One should add that the Counter-Reformation was also an educational movement which produced schools and instructional literature in profusion.) At its best, in the churches of the Reformation, the rite of Confirmation and the teaching that led to it have marked a genuine period of religious development for children. Pastors take seriously their duty as educators; they carry out the rite itself solemnly; and the event is long remembered by the confirmands.

In the Church of England, the rubrics of the Confirmation service explained its pastoral function. A brief catechism was printed between the services of Baptism and of Confirmation. (This official catechism was less popular than some that were later issued privately.)[20] The canons required the clergy to catechize and assigned heavy penalties for failure to do so. Obviously the Reformed sense of explicit faith informed Anglican thinking about Confirmation. A form of initiation in which the initiate was passive was inappropriate to the nature of the Gospel, of faith, and of the Church's task. It was incomplete; something more was required.

Valuable though it was, this Reformation emphasis held some ambiguities. The search for explicit faith doubtless contributed to the verbal, intellectualist character of the protestant scholasticisms of the 17th and 18th centuries. (All traditions, however, developed scholastic styles at the same period—as well as pietistic reactions to scholastic aridity. It was in the cultural climate.) The effort to make an informed faith normative in a large and varied Christian community is likely to lead to schematization of complex issues, to adults putting words into children's mouths, and to compelling what ought to be a free, inward, personal response.

Even though it is not easy to handle this dimension of Christian experience wisely, it will not do to disregard it. In our self-conscious, critical modern world, a faith that is true to its own potential must grip persons deeply and press for authentic expression.

In our own time, the acceptance of explicit faith as a theological necessity is no longer a distinctively Protestant emphasis. Vigorous catechetical and biblical revivals have accompanied the liturgical awakening in the Roman Catholic Church. The ideal of conscious, instructed, articulate participation in the Church's life and worship has been declared to be the right of every baptized person.[21] There is widespread agreement that in our critical, pluralistic, self-conscious age, faith should have as much explicitness as possible. There is also dissatisfaction with the measures now being taken to attain that goal and little pride in past accomplishment.

These two sources of Confirmation—the bishop's postbaptismal blessing, signifying the Holy Spirit, and the confirmand's renewal of baptismal promises, signifying acceptance of adult responsibility— were brought together in Anglicanism. The conscious, informed response to Baptism was combined with the ancient rite of the bishop's laying on of hands. The now detached bishop's part of Christian Initiation was thus given greater pastoral significance than it had had in the late Middle Ages. By the same stroke, catechetical work was given a sacramental completion not possible for those churches with no bishops and no equivalent historic rite. In a typically Anglican move, the old and the new were combined in a way that seemed likely to benefit both.

The idea of such a combination was certainly defensible; and it has demonstrated some practical strengths. For the Church, the retention of infant Baptism has kept the Church from thinking that the relation to God is constituted solely in verbal and conscious ways, while the expectation that the promises of Baptism will be assumed for oneself has kept within the Church the ideal of a committed Church with committed members. For the individual born within the faith community, the two-stage rite has no doubt in many cases expressed the interdependence that persists between one's inheritance at birth and what one does about it later. This Anglican pattern has had a certain credibility. It has doubtless worked at some moments and for some persons. Much has been built up around it: theological statements, priestly and episcopal role definitions, personal expectations, and pastoral and parental duties.

Yet the combination may be rather fragile. Do the two elements of Anglican Confirmation—each with an integrity of its own: one as part of a once-for-all rite of initiation, the other as sign of a long process of growing up in the Christian life—benefit by being combined? Do these two observances have any inherent connection with one another, or has their association been imposed?[22]

In Anglican treatments of Confirmation, the tension between these two historic components could sometimes be observed within the covers of a single work. In the two-volume English symposium of sixty years ago, *Confirmation: or the Laying on of Hands*,[23] the historical and doctrinal material of Volume I, much of it still of considerable value, described largely the history of the ancient sacramental rite. In Volume II the practical essays, now very dated, dealt with education for intelligent religious commitment. The same observation could be made of the material in the American volume edited by Kendig B. Cully called *Confirmation: History, Doctrine and Practice,* 1962.[24] The historians and theologians dealt in the early chapters with one agenda; they spoke of the Holy Spirit, and they referred to such authoritative sources as the Book of Acts and Hippolytus. In the later chapters, the Christian educators dealt with another agenda; they spoke of stages of maturation, and they referred to studies in developmental psychology. More recent work in the Church of England demonstrates the same duality. Some authors are able to argue liturgical and theological matters from early and medieval sacramentary and ordo texts, with little recognition of what the Reformed inheritance has contributed to the teaching and ethos of the Church of England.[25] By contrast, the report, *Christian Initiation: Birth and Growth in the Christian Society,* 1971, treats Confirmation in the context of developmental and educational understandings.[26]

The tension has its practical side. Those who think of Confirmation primarily in sacramental terms usually have wanted it to be administered at an earlier age, so as bring it into closer relation to Baptism and to admit baptized persons to Holy Communion sooner. Those whose thinking about Confirmation was primarily along educational lines have called for it to be moved into later years, for only so could it be a truly adult rite. These two directions were difficult to reconcile. The issue of the right age for Confirmation has often been raised without awareness that different contexts of history and understanding lay behind the conflicting recommendations.

Two bodies of scholars have been working with developed literatures and assumptions about Confirmation. Each has looked at the history and function of Confirmation differently, and each has criticized the present administration of the rite by different criteria. Each has sought a different sort of remedy.

Two rites, each from a different context of meaning, were combined at a past moment by responsible persons. If in a changed situation the combination seems to have developed interior stresses, it can be responsibly altered, as long as its demonstrated values are recognized and kept.

B. Theological Confusion

In the early church a great complex of meaning came to focus in Christian Initiation. The whole reality of the Christian revelation—redemptive, trinitarian, Christocentric, ecclesial, eschatological, ethical—was signified in one relatively simple rite. It could not be otherwise. The meanings were not separable. In dynamic, biblical terms, there could be no forgiveness without the positive new relation to Christ and his people; there could be no relation to Christ without the Holy Spirit as the pledge of the age to come. Because the redemptive work is God in personal action, it is not divisible.

But we cannot apprehend or state this meaning all at once. Thus, it is understandable that as the rites of Christian Initiation came to be used for Gentile converts and grew more complex, they underwent a kind of stretching-out of actions and significances. This stretching-out seems to have moved in both directions from the central Christian washing. Prior to Baptism, in addition to the prebaptismal catechesis, there were, late in the preparatory period, exorcisms, signifying an emptying (as the fasting also did), an expulsion of all evil powers. Some writers speak of a sealing of the forehead, ears and nose, as though to prevent the return of the evil powers. In some places, the celebrant would breathe on the candidates, an action called the *ephphetha,* based on Jesus' healing miracle in Mark 7:31–37. Following the time of Constantine, there was a giving of salt (whose significance is variously explained and may, in fact, have been largely forgotten) and a signing with the cross at the enrollment in the catechumenate. After Baptism, an anointing (doubtless thought of as a completion of the washing) came, on the basis of biblical imagery, to be associated with the gift and seal of the Holy Spirit. In some places, following the water action, there were the sign of the Cross, the washing of feet, the giving of a white garment, and other ritual acts. The baptismal Eucharist, with which the series of initiatory actions concluded, expressed incorporation into the common life. Third-century writers speak of a special cup of milk and honey at the baptismal Eucharist; it carried the meaning of nourishment for the newborn, and, as the food of Canaan, it spoke of entry upon the promises of God.

Such a list of acted-out meanings, by no means complete, suggests the rich significance for which only a rich enactment was suitable. As long as these initiatory rites were observed in one continuous sequence, each action had its identity within the complex totality. Together they expressed the one fundamental Paschal Mystery—the redemptive reality in which sacramental life participates.

In the early third century, Tertullian, in *On Baptism,* the first treatise devoted to one of the sacraments, made a distinction. He said: "Not that the Holy Spirit is given to us in the water, but that in the water we are made clean by the action of an angel, and made ready for the Holy Spirit."[27] He says, in effect, that while the water cleanses from sin, it is an essentially negative agent, like John the Baptist preparing for the Christ. But the anointing, which follows the water step, imparts the Holy Spirit. It is the positive granting of divine life.

This unargued proposition did little damage at the time. The forgiveness and the new life were two sides of the same thing. The washing in water and the anointing with oil took place within moments of one another. But this comment by Tertullian is the earliest trace of a distinction from which has come a history of mischief. Although some of the early liturgies expressed such a distinction, it was never closely defined. Meanings were not attached exclusively to a single act or thing. Often the water spoke as clearly of the Spirit as did the chrism. The entire complex of actions could be spoken of as "baptism" (*baptisma*), or it could be spoken of as "the seal" (*sphragis*).[28]

In the West, by the process that was traced in outline in an earlier chapter, Christian Initiation became divided into two ritual moments: a washing and an anointing. It was inevitable that it would be asked what either might mean apart from the other. In the defining style of thought which prevailed, one of them came to be understood as carrying a largely negative meaning, a major exorcism, a remedy for inherited sin; while the other was understood positively as speaking of new divine life. The dismemberment of the unified rite led to the dismemberment of the unified meaning which it had enacted. Significances which had mingled came to be distinguished. The Western churches have been struggling with this inherited confusion.

Anglican discussion of the theological problem has come to focus on the role of the Holy Spirit in Baptism and in Confirmation. Anglican formularies have used many phrases expressing the agency of the Holy Spirit in Baptism: in the 1928 revision and before, "...regenerate of water and the Holy Ghost," "...baptized with water and the the Holy Ghost," "...Give thy Holy Spirit to this child," "...to sanctify him/her with the Holy Ghost," "...that all things belonging to the Spirit may live and grow in him/her." The 1979 Prayer Book (in addition to the affirmations made concerning the Spirit in the virtually "pentecostal" lessons that are appointed for this sacrament and in the creed which is confessed) the rite itself asks that the baptized be filled with God's "holy and life-giving Spirit." It affirms that by Baptism we are "...reborn by the Holy Spirit," and "by water and the Spirit" given forgiveness and raised to "the new life of grace." It prays that the baptized may be sustained in God's Holy Spirit (whose gifts are specified), and it thanks God that they are sealed by the Holy Spirit. The catechism speaks of "new life in the Spirit" as one aspect of the inward grace in Baptism. It would be difficult to say more. Baptism, according to the Prayer Book tradition, is a Spirit-filled event.

Yet the Holy Spirit is also taken to be active in Confirmation. In the older Prayer Books, Confirmation was clearly spoken of as "...strengthening with the Holy Spirit," and "...increasing in the Holy Spirit." The bishop, using one of the oldest prayers of the liturgical heritage, prayed at Confirmation for the gifts of the Spirit; and the Scripture lesson read at the service after 1928 spoke of "receiving" the Spirit. In the Prayer Book of 1979, the bishop asks that those who are confirmed be sent forth "in the power of the Spirit," to perform the service God sets before them. And this revision repeats from previous Prayer Books the themes of being "strengthened" and of "increasing in the Holy Spirit more and more."

Such a duplication of themes is certain to suggest questions: Why are there two sacramental occasions, commonly separated by several years, in which the relation with the Holy Spirit is specified? Do we meet the Spirit twice? If so, was there something insufficient about the first meeting? Or do we meet the Spirit in different ways at these two times? If so, how do the two times differ? Is one more important than the other?

Questions such as these have provoked an extensive literature in which two general positions have been formulated:

(1) The Anglican view that came to expression at the Reformation in the official formularies, and has been maintained by many persons since, is that Baptism is complete Christian Initiation. Entry into Christ and his Church and the gift of the Holy Spirit belong to water Baptism. Confirmation is desirable as an occasion for those who are baptized as infants to ratify for themselves the promises that others made for them; it may be thought of as conveying gifts of the Spirit appropriate to adult responsibilities; and it introduces one to the Lord's Table.[29]

In favor of this position is the claim in the liturgical and theological tradition that Baptism is complete. The water imagery in Baptism should not be associated exclusively (or even predominately) with washing or cleansing, understood negatively. It speaks of the sharing in divine life, of new birth and of the self-imparted Spirit. In the New Testament, it cannot be shown that the gift of the Spirit was regularly associated with a ritual action which followed after and completed Baptism. Moreover, in the New Testament, the laying-on of hands, rather than being primarily initiatory, is often a designation for ministry. Further, this view recognizes as a sign of Christian unity all trinitarian Baptism; there is no necessity, on doctrinal grounds, of finding some essential inadequacy in the Christian Initiation of persons baptized in groups which do not practice episcopal Confirmation. In an ecumenical era, the self-evidencing fruit of the Spirit in all Christian groups is part of the data for theology.

The principal difficulty with this view is that Confirmation is left somewhat problematic. It is defended largely on pastoral, practical grounds. If the public ratification of baptismal promises is pastorally desirable, why is it done only before the bishop? Why is it done only once? If this rite is defined in ways that complement infant Baptism, why is the renewal of baptismal promises required of persons who were baptized as adults and whose promises were made by themselves, responsibly and intelligently? If the Holy Spirit is fully given at Baptism, what is the specific additional role of the Spirit at Confirmation? If Baptism is really complete, a duplication of one of its major themes after the passage of a few years does not seem to say so.

(2) Another view, anticipated by Anglican writers from the 16th

through the 19th centuries, but stated most vigorously within the last hundred years, is that Baptism represents the washing from sin and incorporation into the Body of Christ, but the gift of the Holy Spirit is associated specifically with the episcopal rite of Confirmation.[30]

In favor of this view is the Lukan account (which has been regularly, but as has been noted, inappropriately applied to this sacramental situation) of the apostles' visit to bring the gift of the Holy Spirit to a Christian community which had received Baptism only. Some other New Testament passages (notably the way in which Jesus' Baptism is told) suggest that Baptism for washing, together with anointing for the Holy Spirit, form a sequence of distinguishable but inseparable steps. Parts of the liturgical tradition quite early used language that expressly made the gift of the Spirit the specific grace of Confirmation. And many Western theologians spoke quite clearly about Confirmation as the "completion" or the "perfecting" of Baptism.

But there are serious questions about this view. It tends to reduce water Baptism to a negative, almost pre-Christian rite. Any Baptism that lacks Confirmation (episcopal Confirmation) must be regarded as in some sense incomplete. The division which this doctrine introduces between Christ and the Holy Spirit is theologically intolerable; what God does, all of God does. That is the heart of trinitarian doctrine. Some expositors of this view have distinguished ways in which one may be related to the Spirit: "externally" at Baptism, but "internally" in Confirmation, for instance. But few people can attach distinct meanings to such metaphoric terms for a unitary personal activity.

These two general positions—with many ways of defending and stating each—have defined the Anglican dispute over Confirmation for several generations. The terms of the debate have not been productive. In the state of Anglican polemic that has prevailed, disputants seem to plead for the primacy of either Baptism or Confirmation at the expense of the other.

This static debate can divert attention from some of the more urgent questions concerning the Holy Spirit in Christian Initiation. It is possible to ask when, and by what act, and by what minister the Holy Spirit is given, as though it were perfectly clear what the giving of the Spirit means. What does the Church mean by a claim to minister the Spirit of God in its own initiatory rite? Is this idiom of the Spirit being "given" or not "given" compatible with the gracious, personal, sovereign character of God's relation with human beings? How does the gift of the Spirit relate to one's basic humanity? Is it some kind of ill-defined "extra" or "plus"? Does a person encounter the Creator Spirit for the first time only when the Spirit is sacramentally "given?"[31]

The terminology of "giving" and "receiving" the Holy Spirit is, in the New Testament, characteristic of the Book of Acts. The gift of the Spirit is depicted in Acts as a power with such unmistakable marks that one misguided person supposed it could be bought (8:9–24). The Spirit might come suddenly upon people, with or without tactual mediation. This is the biblical idiom that most specifically underlies the discussion of when and how the Spirit is sacramentally given. But the appeal to Acts must never make it sound as though the Spirit were somehow in the Church's control. In the Book of Acts, the Spirit is also depicted as sovereign over the Church—leading the Apostles, taking them by surprise, and frustrating their plans for purposes of its own. If there is a tendency for Anglican discussion of the Holy Spirit in Christian Initiation to make the idiom of this one New Testament source—or, indeed, only part of its idiom—normative, the tendency should not go unquestioned.

Other New Testament writers develop their conceptions of the Holy Spirit in ways that give no comparable place to divine power coming upon people in ecstatic signs or being given by official ministers or to its belonging to a second moment of initiation. St. Paul identifies the Holy Spirit by ethical characteristics. The Spirit is the one by whom "God's love has been poured into our hearts" (Romans 5:5). The fruit of the Spirit, according to Paul, is love, joy, peace, patience, kindness, goodness, faithfulness, gentleness, and self-control (Galatians 5:22). The "gifts of the Spirit" that Paul affirms and about which he cautions (1 Corinthians 12–14) are God's own self-imparting within the baptized community, and are not initiatory. The Spirit, for Paul, is not separable from being "in Christ." To be in Christ is to be in his Spirit-filled people (1 Corinthians 12:12–13). Paul loads the rite of Baptism with all the reality of the redemptive Mystery, and he speaks of no further ritual act by whch one is brought into the life in Christ. A writer comments: "Paul not only fails to mention the imposition of hands, but his theology definitely excludes it."[32] If Anglican theology of Christian Initiation were to take its governing ideas rigorously from St. Paul, some of the issues in the discussion of the sacraments of initiation would have to be recast.

The other great theologian of the New Testament, the author of the Johannine literature, similarly allows no separation between Christ and the Spirit. The Spirit is described as given by the risen Jesus in one of the resurrection incidents—the "Johannine Pentecost" of 20:22–23. The realities of Easter, Ascension, and Pentecost are, in the Johannine writings, essentially one reality. No reader using categories from this strand of New Testament literature could envision anyone being in relation to Christ, but somehow not being so in and through the Paraclete, Christ's alter ego in and to his people.

Persons searching for New Testament evidence of a second episode in early Christian Initiation have pointed to expressions in which salvation or baptismal references are followed by Spirit or imposition of hands references:

"...born of [1] Water and [2] the Spirit," (John 3:5).
"But you were [1] washed, you were [1a] consecrated, you were [1b] justified in the name of the Lord Jesus Christ and [2] in the Spirit of God," (1 Corinthians 6:11).
"...the [1] washing of regeneration [palingenesia] and [2] renewal [anakainosis] in the Holy Spirit," (Titus 3:5),
"...the elementary doctrine... of [1] ablutions (pl.), [2] the laying on of hands..." (Hebrews 6:2).

These wordings (some of them fairly obscure) are not in themselves evidence that a two-stage ritual existed in the first century, but they may indicate the sort of compound statement of the first-century faith that made the rapid development of a compound initiatory action natural.

When in time Confirmation became a separate event, the question was inevitable: "What does it mean, as distinct from Baptism?" But when this question is put to the New Testament and the early church—our principal guides in the economy of the divine life—they are of no help. They only know Confirmation (insofar as they know it at all) as one moment within the Baptismal complex. What meanings it has are part of the rich meanings of one initiatory rite.

One might ask: Can one bit of the early church's baptismal ritual properly break off and become something distinct in its own right? How will its separation affect the other parts of the initiatory complex? Insofar as those who have shaped the Western tradition have tried to explain what Confirmation means, they have used phrases or ideas such as: being enlisted for Christ in the conflict with the world, growing into maturity, joining the Church, the ordination of the laity....*But these are all baptismal meanings*. Baptism is the sacrament of birth and of maturity, of beginnings and endings; it is the sacrament of dedication to Christ's service for the sake of the world; it brings one into the common life of Christ's people; it gives the Holy Spirit. To ascribe some of these meanings in any distinctive way to Confirmation deprives Baptism of some of its richness. To affirm them as baptismal meanings and then to repeat them as Confirmation meanings gives two rites with the same signification.

It needs to be said clearly that *Confirmation has no independent meanings*. All the meanings that have been ascribed to it are drawn from Baptism, which says at the beginning all that can be said concerning Christ and ourselves as united in a single, divine-human life in a divine-human community. The Spirit is not divisible from the whole love, work, and presence of God, nor from the renewal of humanity. The Holy Spirit, in personal action, cannot be quantified, measured in separate moments, nor divided into distinct aspects.

But having said that Christ and the Spirit are inseparable and that the one initiatory act of Baptism is complete, more must be said. It is not a matter of indifference whether or not the liturgy of Baptism contains an express "Spirit-moment."

If the living Christ and the Holy Spirit are inseparable, they are not identical. In the New Testament witness, the revelation in Jesus sweeps on to the agency of the Spirit: Paul puts the two in sequence: "God sent forth his Son;...God has sent the Spirit of his Son into our hearts" (Galatians 4:4–6). In the Fourth Gospel, the departing Jesus pledges the Spirit to his followers: "I will pray the Father, and he will give you another Counselor,...even the Spirit of truth;...he dwells with you, and will be in you" (John 14:16*f.*). Although Jesus is leaving, he tells the disciples "you shall receive power when the Holy Spirit has come upon you; and you shall be my witnesses" (Acts 1:8). This New Testament idiom says that what the living Jesus is to the church he is through the

Spirit. The Holy Spirit is the immediate divine self-investment in human lives.

The Holy Spirit, as "God in action,"[33] represents the gift of fresh possibility within the human condition. The fundamental minister of the Spirit is the Spirit. "In ordinary affairs a gift may be distributed apart from the giver, but the Gift of the Spirit is his personal relationship with us, and the Gift cannot be detached from the Giver."[34]

The Spirit is self-imparted through the Church. Part of the Spirit's work is to bring into being a community of human response, a fellowship available for furthering God's purposes in the world. Within the Church, the divine life uses the word and the sacraments as foci of its activity—through them shaping the community, sustaining it, renewing it, and bringing individuals into living relation with it and its Lord. The Spirit works, in many subtle ways, to establish personal, reciprocal relationships. In those relationships, the Divine Spirit engages the depths of the personal life given first by divine creativity—"the Spirit bearing witness with our spirit" (Romans 8:16). The Spirit affirms and dignifies our humanity, drawing us in disciplined love to the intention of the Creator as shown in Christ.

One can think of the anointing in Baptism as explicative—something that brings to plain expression an otherwise unclear part of the compact meaning of Baptism. An English Jesuit liturgist has called it "simply an explicitation of a grace already conferred in Baptism."[35] Since the anointing or Spirit-moment is part of an action, not an explanation, perhaps it is not fully adequate to think of it as explicatory. But an antithesis of act or statement should not be pressed too far. There are things which are true but which become effectively true through being spoken. The acts and words of the Spirit-anointing do express something that is true, even if it is not expressed. What God does is done by the Spirit. But that being so, is it not better to name this fact than to let it remain mute in something as rich as the initiatory rite of the church?

It might be productive to think of the matter along the lines of the *epiclesis*—the prayer for the action of the Holy Spirit—in the eucharistic prayer. It is desirable that the liturgical recognition of the divine work contain both an *anamnesis*-cluster of meanings, in which historic redemptive acts are creatively recalled, and an *epiclesis*-cluster, in which the present life and power of God are named. Clearly the Spirit is active in the Holy Communion. But for many centuries in the medieval and the modern Roman Church and in many portions of the Anglican Communion, the eucharistic prayers were silent about the Holy Spirit. The absence of an *epiclesis* from these liturgies did not keep the Spirit from the sacramental action and the faithful people. But since the Spirit is constitutive of the sacramental reality, should not the liturgy say as much? The American Prayer Books (along with those of some other parts of Anglicanism) have said that it should, and they have included an express invocation of the Spirit in the Great Thanksgiving. As liturgical change has advanced, other churches have come to agree. The *epiclesis* at the consecration does not make the Spirit be present; its absence would not keep the Spirit away. But its presence in the text brings the wording of the church's prayers into accord with the Spirit-filled reality of which they speak.

The postbaptismal laying on of hands (or anointing) may be thought of as the *epiclesis* of Holy Baptism.[36] While economy in liturgy is desirable and no liturgy should try to say everything that could be said, it might be taken as a rule that it is better to say and enact the important things that are true in liturgical events than to leave them unstated and unrepresented, to be picked up by those who are good at gathering implied meanings. The association of an act involving water and washing and plunging in over one's head with an act involving hands (and oil and aroma) can fill out a range of significances that belong to Christian Initiation. It is an important part of the rich declaration that Baptism makes in behalf of a Christian at the very start of life in Christ and the Church.

Awareness of this fullness of meaning probably gave rise to the early postbaptismal actions. Awareness of it today is moderating old polarities. In the sacramental "convergence" of the present generation, a baptismal anointing appears in ecumenical rites and in the baptismal liturgies of churches which have hitherto not had such a ritual action. Its desirability is explained with a sense of discovery. A Presbyterian writer commended the postbaptismal actions of his church's new rite in the sort of positive terms that could hardly be bettered:

> *While the 16th century preoccupations with questions of sacramental validity drove Reformed sacramental celebrations in a minimalist direction, today sacramental validity is assumed. The*

CHAPTER V

modern quest is for theological depth of meaning in ritual activity, for grasping the mystery of the sacramental encounter with God. The multivalent imagery of the postbaptismal consignation-nointing is ideally suited to this need. It will bring a renewed emphasis to a whole cluster of scriptural images and ideas that help to explain the mystery of Baptism.[37]

Important as it is to include this explicit act and these words signifying the Holy Spirit, it would be misleading to think of them as constituting a specific, operative Spirit-bearing moment in the initiatory ritual. They are not a "formula"—a term and a way of thinking that has haunted Western sacramental thought and piety. The Spirit is not *absent* until and unless the epicletic action is performed. The words and the acted sign bring to expression a profound ingredient which has been operative, not only through the initiatory rite, but through the catechumenal period or the baptismal self-dedication of the parents and sponsors. The Spirit is not restricted. Where there is faith and prayer and true dying to sin and rising to newness of life, the Spirit is present in power. The sacramental sealing expresses a presence that permeates the entire ritual act and the personal history that has led up to it. As Aidan Kavanagh has put it, "The whole initiation procedure—before, after, and including the water event—is pneumatically charged. The Holy Spirit is not confined to one event, Confirmation."[38]

But the Spirit is not only present at and prior to Baptism. The Spirit is the actualization of the future—the guarantee of the final inheritance (Ephesians 1:14), the active power of the age to come (Hebrews 6:5). Baptism is not the first stage in a staged-out series of initiatory acts, as though one went beyond it to greater things. Rather, Baptism is total. It says at the start all that can be said about life and destiny. A Swedish theologian put it: "Nothing can be added to Baptism, and all that we receive after Baptism is the means by which the work of Baptism is continued."[39] What Baptism says can, of course, be forgotten and denied. And when it is forgotten and denied, it can, by the Spirit, be recalled and recovered. The reality of Baptism needs to be restated and repossessed in appropriate ways through a lifetime. It needs to be creatively remembered, and liturgy might be thought of as an ordered body of promptings for our memory.

Any theology of Christian Initiation which has led to the definition of two initiatory incursions of the Holy Spirit which can be put in sequence so that one is needed to complete the other, or so that one can be played off against one another has moved in a mistaken direction. The Holy Spirit, given in Christ, represents the presence now of that which is coming to be. A Christian's end is given from the start. Even though the Spirit works within us for a lifetime and more to accomplish God's intentions for us, the patient divine Counselor does nothing that is not pledged from the start. The liturgies and theologies of "the first sacrament" should say at the beginning all that can be said.

c. Pastoral Problems

There are at least two clusters of practical issues that gather around Confirmation: those that relate to the proper candidates for the rite, and those that relate to the proper minister. This section will look briefly at the status of these:

Who Shall Be Confirmed?

In the past practice of the Episcopal Church, two groups have been confirmed: (1) the Church's own children, who were baptized as infants, and who through Confirmation took for themselves the promises which had been made for them by others at their Baptism, and (2) persons who came into the Episcopal Church from communions which lacked episcopal Confirmation. The rite was their act of identification with a new church and its act of reception. Persons who came to the Episcopal Church from churches with the historic episcopal succession and a rite of Confirmation (or chrismation, in the case of the Eastern churches) were admitted by an act of reception, not Confirmation. Each of these sacramental and disciplinary functions carries a load of difficulties; each needs to be looked at separately.

(1) **Adolescent children who were baptized as infants:** Confirmation has served as a rite of coming of age within the Church. By it one passed from the relative dependence and limited rights of a child in the

Church to the competences and prerogatives of adulthood. For many years, pastors, bishops, parents, educators, and more recently young adults themselves, have reported that it has not worked as it ought.

A rite of entry on adult status is deeply rooted in culture and world religions. The parent religion of Christianity, Judaism, has long had a ceremony by which a boy (traditionally it has been restricted to males) becomes a "son of the Law." Such rites support and interpret an important transition, a moment at which a person ceases to be a child and assumes the rights and responsibilities of an adult. This time of passage is often associated with learning the lore of the group. Following this ceremony, persons can think of themselves as adults, because the community treats them as such.

To be significant and life-supporting, such a rite must correspond with the actual dynamics of growing up. It must express, shape, and interpret an experienced crisis.

The conditions of modern society are raising the question: *Is there a moment which can sustain believably the meaning of growing into adulthood in today's church and world?* Past designations of the "age of reason" were made without developmental studies and insights. Yet the time may have been chosen well, and the rite may have stood for a significant transition. But modern society presents the churches with a complex situation, for which past experience provides no adequate precedent. In an industrial and technological culture (and not all the world is yet industrial and technological), persons do not pass quickly from childhood to adulthood. We move through many stages in the process of growing up—stages having specific problems and specific characteristics. We perceive ourselves and our world differently as we grow; the priorities, logic, thought forms, and moral judgments of one stage are not those of the next. Developmental studies such as those of Erik Erikson, Jean Piaget, Lawrence Kohlberg, and Carol Gilligan have helped to identify the dynamics of the growing person.

It is not just that such investigators have analyzed the stages by which infants naturally grow into adults; rather, modern conditions are calling new life stages into being. The pioneer work on adolescence was done by G. Stanley Hall in 1904. He was probably documenting a change which had only recently come in human development. Once he had named and analyzed it, one could observe that some individuals in previous eras (because of factors in their life stories) had had a period of adolescence. But as a mass pattern of development, it seems to belong to the industrial West beginning some time late in the 19th century.

The forces which began the extension of the growing-up process have continued their shaping influence. One social analyst, Kenneth Keniston, identifies a recently emerged stage of life, still transitional, but having characteristics unlike adolescence. He terms it "youth," and locates it between late adolescence and adulthood.[40] He thinks of those within this stage as having been through an earlier crisis of adolescence, but they are still outside of and critical toward the adult world—a world they approach through "wary probes."

In general it can be observed that in the structures of modern society the passage from childhood begins earlier and earlier, while entry in to adulthood is later and later. Children take on sophistication and physical maturity and they begin separating themselves from their parents at measurably earlier ages. Yet the society is not prepared to consider persons as adults until their middle twenties, if then. Thus, growing to adulthood in the modern world carries one through a long, varied period of change, stress, quest, and often of reversal.

In addition to our awareness of the passage into adulthood, we have become aware that adulthood itself is not static. The stages and periods of life never stop. Adults of ages 35–45, of 55–65, and of 75–85, are facing markedly different circumstances and existential challenges to which they bring different configurations of inner resource. It would greatly oversimplify an account of human development if one were to think in terms of two stable categories: childhood and adulthood. If inherited ritual patterns are equipped just for those two stages and for one moment of passage, they are manifestly inadequate.

The question that past practices of Confirmation have asked is: What point within this developmental process can gather up and express its meaning for the individual's relation to God and membership in the Church?

Since a practical answer must be given, most congregations of the Episcopal Church have answered that it is about the age of twelve. However, the administration of Confirmation has extended in both directions from that age by five or six years.[41] Those who put Confirmation very early cannot intend that it signify adulthood; rather they

CHAPTER V

have meant for it to introduce a child to the practice of full sacramental life in the Church at an early age. Those who put Confirmation late can stress its adult, voluntary character, but (where participation in the Holy Communion depends on prior Confirmation) the later age has left baptized members of the Church unable to receive the Eucharist through important, stressful years of development—a practice difficult to defend. It is often argued that the age of twelve years, the point at or around which most confirming has been done, has combined the disadvantages of both extremes without taking much advantage of the strengths of either. It seems to locate the Church's only rite of passage just at the time at which children are becoming acutely aware of the clay feet of the older generation and are beginning to define themselves by questioning it. The conclusion seems inescapable that in the long, often turbulent transition to adulthood, so many stages are passed through, that any single moment for Confirmation is too early to capture some important possible meanings of the process, or too late to express others.

There has been widespread, persistent, ecumenical discussion among liturgiologists, Christian educators, theologians, and pastors about the best age for "a confession of faith."[42] But little consensus has emerged. Important authorities with weighty arguments have supported divergent solutions.

Perhaps it is not premature to propose that, at least for our moment in history, the wrong question has been asked. In the conditions of modern society, no single point can represent the meaning of growing into adulthood. Growth is a process—long and complex. Confirmation, insofar as it is part of Christian Initiation, is an unrepeatable event. Are these two things compatible? Can one observance—whether located early or located middle or late—sum up the meaning for faith and church membership of a difficult process that may last for more than fifteen years?

The wisest way to approach this question may be to observe that Christianity—in the New Testament, the early church, the Eastern churches, and the medieval West—has not had a puberty rite. In the modern world, most Western churches have tried to observe such a rite. (It takes the form of Confirmation in some churches, Baptism at an age of accountability in others.) When it has been functional, a rite of coming of age in the community of faith has probably been useful. One need not question the value of such a rite in one's own or in anyone else's past if value is claimed for it by persons for whom it seems to have worked. But neither must one feel that such a rite, whatever its use may have been in some times and places, is essential to Christian Initiation or Christian adulthood. It is not, by historical or theological criteria, a necessary thing either for the Church or for the individual Christian.[43] Of course, social or psychological needs might make such rites desirable; but the mandates for such rites as might be instituted for such reasons would belong to the economy of nurture within the redemption-bearing community, rather than to the economy of initiation into it.

Becoming a mature Christian is always a demand, a challenge, and an opportunity. It is both a human responsibility and a divine gift. But the process of entering on maturity is always within a specific situation, the situation of the church in its society. When that situation changes, the ritual and catechetical measures that may in the past have signified maturation may, rather abruptly, seem inappropriate. The same worthy ends that were served by one means in the past may have to be served by other means suited to an altered condition.

That is not to say that now that adolescence and youth have become more prolonged and difficult, the Church would be pastorally responsible to withdraw the involvement, interpretation, and help it has provided for these years in the past. The problem is that the help does not seem to help very much; the interpretation tends to obscure. Truly sensitive involvement of the Church needs to consider such basic questions as these: Can a long process of personal development be met effectively by a single rite at any point within the process? If it can, should any two persons find the same point to be suitable for themselves? Might not the dynamics of coming of age be better met by a flexible response—a rite corresponding with moments of need or of recognition, and open to being repeated as such moments recur?

The account that has generally been given of the pastoral intention of Confirmation has assumed birth, growth, and continued life within the practicing Christian community. It has talked as though the commitment to the life of a believer and a communicant that was expressed at Confirmation would continue—even though most persons realized that, for many confirmands, such future constancy was unlikely. Thus, some agreement to deceive and to be deceived has been present in the rite by which we have brought young people into their life as adult Christians. If a continuous life of faith could be taken for granted, the rituals of initiation as they have been practiced might well be adequate. But an untroubled relation with God and the faith community is more exceptional than usual in many portions of today's Church. Persons who begin life within the Christian community often detour out of that association, at least for a time. The drop-out commonly begins in teen-age years, and it may continue for ten or twenty years. Needless to say, some of those who break their relation with the faith and the Church never return. But many do. Thus, in our mobile, individualistic society, there is a pattern of discontinuous association with the Church. Moreover, among the adults who are committed to the Church and its faith, there are often times of lapse and disaffection, followed (often, but not always) by times of restoration.

The inherited pastoral understandings of Confirmation seem to have made the Church well equipped to ritualize what is not happening and ill equipped to identify and give expression to what is actually happening. By isolating the formal renewal of baptismal promises and making it a mark of puberty, we have made a life-stage rite of what might well be available for the varied occasions of Christian experience. So, to the questions above concerning the suitability of the Church's provision for persons coming of age, we add a further question: If the spoken ratification of baptismal vows is an important action of faith, why must that action be associated normally with childhood? We never stop in our encounter with developmental stages and their tasks—tasks rooted in divine judgment, care, and summons. We make lifelong response to the divine outreaching love declared in the Word and signified in Baptism. The privilege of bearing witness to that response ought not to end as though it were a childish thing to be put away.

(2) **Baptized adults from non-episcopal churches:** A search of the literature indicates that the widespread Anglican practice of "confirming" those who come to it from Protestant, non-episcopal churches and "receiving" those who come from the Roman or Eastern churches has never had the kind of scholarly explanation or defense that should be

required for a practice with such important ecumenical implications. It has been done; it suits some common reality-sense; but no adequate rationale for doing it has been put forward.

To at least some extent, the "Confirmation rubric" was used in explanation of the practice. It may have seemed clear and pertinent: "And there shall none be admitted to the Holy Communion, until such time as he be confirmed, or be ready and desirous to be confirmed," (*BCP* 1928, p. 299). The rubric may have been understood in ways something like this: "Christian persons who have been baptized in non-episcopal churches have not been, by our definition, confirmed. Roman Catholics and Orthodox Christians, by our definition, have been confirmed. Protestants coming to the Episcopal Church are in the same sacramental situation as we were when we were baptized, but unconfirmed and noncommunicating children. They must do what we did."

It was noted in an earlier chapter that this rubric traces to a canon from the late 13th century. It was Archbishop Peckham's prod to bishops and parents. It was not meant to make access to communion difficult, but to bring Confirmation into greater use by making communion depend on it. But it came to be applied to a very different set of conditions. All laws are written with reference to a situation. Anyone who seeks to apply a law in a changed situation needs to factor in what the law, whose meaning in its original setting can be known, might mean in different conditions. To apply its words literally in an altered situation may make it a different law. Yet, later generations, disregarding this hermeneutical rule, applied Peckham's regulation to the admission of non-Anglicans (Protestant non-Anglicans) to full communicant standing by way of Confirmation, even though religious pluralism was not part of the world for which it was written and therefore not part of the rule's intent. It was an internal discipline for medieval Christendom.

But more has been involved than a rubric. The practice implies a judgment as to the sacramental adequacy of other churches. The questions are complex and involve issues of ministry and intercommunion as much as issues of Christian Initiation. But some observations are pertinent here in inquiring "Who shall be confirmed?"

With respect to the communions whose initiatory rites seem fully acceptable, making a gesture of "reception" sufficient, the Roman Communion and the Anglican share the history of Western developments, and they have similar practice, similar understandings, and similar problems. Anglicans have accepted Roman sacramental initiation, but the recognition has not been returned, and until recently there has been no interconfessional forum in which the issues might be discussed. The relation to Eastern practice brings into a single discussion quite different customs, histories, and understandings. Since Anglicanism is willing to accept Eastern Baptism plus chrismation as full initiation, no Anglican problem arises about adequacy. But it is not at all clear that the Eastern churches equate their chrismation with what they regard as a strange Western development of a second sacrament of Confirmation. As one writer, speaking for his own tradition, put it: "Baptism and Chrismation constitute one single mystery. . . . The rite of Chrismation is not thus something which follows Baptism and can be separated from it. The Chrism is, so to speak, in with and under the baptismal waters and inseparable from it."[44] The acceptability of Eastern initiation is brought about to some extent by Anglicans imposing Western categories on Eastern rites.

With regard to those persons who are Christians in full standing in their former churches but who have been required to be confirmed when they come to the churches of the Anglican Communion, the issues are complicated, and not always cordial. Episcopalians can and do speak of Baptism as a great sign of unity and mutual recognition among Christian bodies. But insofar as persons baptized in Protestant churches (and often confirmed as well, by a serious catechetical observance) have not been clearly welcome as communicant members without Confirmation, the affirmations about unity in Baptism are to a marked extent subverted. Not Baptism, but something in addition to Baptism is made the constitutive thing in becoming a Christian of the Anglican obedience. If that additional thing were a formal welcome or admission, possibly by restating one's basic baptismal promises, possibly before a bishop, and accompanied by prayer, the action would be theologically understandable and ecumenically acceptable. Such an act would use the part of Confirmation that is an adult act of reaffirmation. But if the additional thing required for membership is understood as the gift of the Holy Spirit—the other part of Confirmation—it cannot help but reflect invidiously on one's past identity as a Christian and on the Christian tradition in which one stood. It implies a grave defect in one's prior life of faith and in one's former affiliation. It seems to say that hitherto the Holy Spirit has been lacking, because it was unavailable (except perhaps in some uncovenanted manner) in one's former church. Such a contention seems like the triumph of ideology over experience. Probably there are few Anglicans who would be entirely comfortable making it today. Indeed, many would be quite uncomfortable with it. Writing a few years ago, the late J.A.T. Robinson said:

> *When a person is admitted to Anglicanism from the Roman Communion there is a formal act of reception. Ought not such a service to be held in other cases as well—so as to let Confirmation in this instance stand out for what it is, part of the Catholic wholeness of Christian Initiation, and not something made necessary by our unhappy divisions? The disciplinary use of Confirmation, in relation to those outside Anglicanism, is a modern phenomenon and one much to be regretted. When Confirmation is allowed to become a sort of tariff wall in interdenominational trade discussions, I as an Anglican find myself shamed and embarrassed.*[45]

Such a comment is an expression of one person's deeply felt conviction. As such it is unassailable. But is it no more than that? Surely such a comment by an informed churchman implies serious questions: Is the Spirit of God the possession of the church—indeed, of the church, defined by a particular ministerial succession? Is it under the church's custody, limitation and control? Or is the church under the Spirit? Is the church so definitely under the Spirit that its task in history is to respond to initiatives of the Spirit—initiatives undertaken as judgment and renewal, and without asking the authorization of the official Church, and initiatives validated by unmistakable signs? At a late stage in history, with all of its embedded ambiguities, it will not do to lay the whole process under a neat doctrine.

This section has examined some of the difficulties with past understandings of "who shall be confirmed?" Earlier sections have perhaps made it clear that, because of the compound character of Confirmation, this question is really two questions: (1) "Who shall receive the seal of the Spirit?" and (2) "Who may renew the promises of Baptism?" There is no necessity that these two questions be given the same answer.

Some persons who might be suitable for one of the actions might not be for the other. Is it possible to separate these two acts so that a rite signifying the Spirit is expressly an episode within the baptismal action? Then is it possible to think of the renewing of one's baptismal promises in fresh ways? And can liturgy provide more adequately for both of these actions of faith than past texts and practices have? The discussion here has indicated that past Anglican practice has concealed many difficulties. This chapter has opened questions which must be dealt with in the liturgical provision and pastoral practice of the Episcopal Church. The extension of these lines of inquiry to the 1979 Prayer Book belongs to chapters VIII and IX.

Who Shall Minister Confirmation?

Chapter II has indicated that the development of the rites of Christian Initiation has been linked with the question of who should minister them. Note should be taken of the tension between the historic developments represented by the two adaptations outlined in that chapter and called there, "The Delegation of Ministries" and "The Division of the Rite." If the unity of the initiatory acts were to be maintained, they would ordinarily be performed by a presbyter. If the bishop were to be the regular minister of a postbaptismal anointing, the unity of the rites would shatter.

Confirmation (meaning specifically Confirmation by a bishop in the historic succession) has been an important mark of Anglican identity and ecumenical distinctiveness. It is not often recognized that this discipline belongs to a recent period. Historical study needs to be done on the matter, but it is clear that for a long time Confirmation did not occupy the place in Anglican thought and practice that it has come to fill within the past century and a half.[46] The rise of attention to Confirmation seems to have been part of the reassertion of Catholic identity that shaped Anglicanism so deeply beginning in the mid-19th century. Was it derived in some measure from the ecclesiology of William Palmer, whose learned and influential work *The Church of Christ* (2 vols., 1837) is usually credited with setting forth a "branch theory" of Catholicism? If so, the derivation was indirect. Palmer hardly mentions Confirmation. It is not an important topic in the Tracts. It seldom figures in the numerous Anglican works on episcopacy. Does it trace in the Episcopal Church to the establishment of episcopal order in which Bishop Hobart led so significantly? (Most adult Episcopalians had not been confirmed, but, with an energetic bishop present, they were coming to Confirmation in large numbers. Should they receive Confirmation and those who were coming to the Episcopal Church from outside not receive it?) There are impressive records of Hobart's practice, but although he wrote and preached on Confirmation a number of times, his words took the form of exhortation to confirmands to be loyal to their commitments. He seems to have left no extended account of his thought on Confirmation.

The unexplained but unquestioned acceptance given to confirmation practices suggests that episcopal Confirmation was considered a mark of the solidarity of Anglicanism with the Catholic West and at the same time a sign of its distinctiveness from Protestantism—a particularly important piece of corporate self-identity in the context of pluralistic, but Protestant-dominated, 19th century American religion.

If factors such as these were part of the rise of a distinctive Episcopalian practice, they are parts of ecclesiology that have undergone fundamental rethinking in Anglican theology and in interchurch dialogue since practices and understandings took their fairly durable form in the late 19th century. These issues cannot be raised in the old ways.[47]

Basic historical and theological work needs to be done on what is at stake when the Church asks freshly who should be the minister of Confirmation.[48] Does the inclusion of a Spirit moment in the initiatory liturgy require that such a moment be administered by a bishop? If it is contended that it does, what is the historical and theological basis of such a requirement?

But practical questions may be asked also. The retention of Confirmation as the bishop's prerogative has undoubtedly been felt by the church as a way of honoring the role of bishops; and it has been felt by bishops as a clear way of identifying a sacramental and pastoral role that is distinctly theirs. But has it worked that way? Now that the automobile has made even large dioceses more geographically compact than the smallest were at the turn of this century, have the demands of this sacramental ministry governed the priorities of bishops in a way they did not in previous epochs of the history of episcopacy? And has such a rearrangement of priorities come about without rigorous questioning? A Canadian writer on these topics has remarked on a crisis of *episcope*:

> Oversight of the local church cannot be defined in terms of the right to come and confirm. Indeed, given the practice of many Episcopal churches in which the bishop arrives shortly before the service and leaves shortly after it, it is difficult to see how bishops see this flying visit to a congregation as an occasion on which a pastoral relationship can be established with anyone, let alone with a large group of young people who are often not prepared to let themselves be known by this strange visitor they may never have seen before in their church and may never see again for years.[49]

Does the ministry of Confirmation as it has historically developed provide a fitting expression of the bishop's pastoral ministry? If it does, could it be modified for the better? If it does not, what alternative expression might be more adequate?

These are very large and basic questions—to some extent basic questions of authority and to some extent rather pragmatic questions. Until adequate inquiry is made into them, one matter may be noted. If episcopal Confirmation has been valued because, as the centuries-long tradition of the West, it evidenced and secured the catholicity of Anglicanism, this mark of identity has come to be more strictly observed in Anglicanism than it is within the other major church bodies which seek to keep the catholic substance within their ordered sacramental life.

It is obvious that any question about whether the post-baptismal Spirit-moment must be ministered specifically by a bishop is a peculiarly Western debate. For many centuries in the Eastern churches the usual minister of the entire baptismal act, including the chrismation, has been the local priest. To be sure, the priest anoints with chrism blessed by the bishop (or the Patriarch). Some writers on the Eastern churches speak of this blessed chrism as representing a token presence of the bishop in the Spirit-act of the baptismal complex. Others, however, make no point of the chrism being an extension of the bishop—a rationale that sounds suspiciously Western in character. Rather, as these writers see it, the bishop's ministry is to bless the oils, and the priest's ministry is to use the oils blessed by the bishop. In any case, the chrismation is done by a presbyter.

It has been customary to contrast this Eastern custom with the practice of Western churches, Roman and Anglican, in which Confirmation is administered by a bishop. Although tradition (since the early Middle Ages) has gone along such lines, there is no principle in such a tradition that places it above qualification and review. For many centuries in Roman theology and church law it has been possible for a bishop to grant permission to a presbyter to perform the anointing that has come to be called Confirmation. Such a faculty has seldom been sought, but it has been possible to secure it. While the bishop was the "ordinary" minister of the Confirmation rite (as the bishop had at one time been the ordinary minister also of the sacraments of Baptism and the Eucharist), presbyters could, by appointment, be made its "extraordinary" ministers.[50]

In our own time, an important qualification of past sacramental practice has taken place in the Roman Church. The Rite for the Christian Initiation of Adults (which has been spoken of in the previous chapter as opening new possibilities in thinking about Baptism) deals with the minister of Confirmation in somewhat unexpected ways. In the tension there must be between keeping the unity of the initiatory rites and preserving an integral role for the bishop, the RCIA (speaking of adult Baptism) comes down on the side of the unity of the rite. Baptism and confirmation are to be parts of one sequence: "According to the ancient practice maintained in the Roman liturgy, an adult is not to be baptized unless he receives confirmation immediately afterward," (Par. 34). The direction explains:

This connection signifies the unity of the paschal mystery, the close relationship between the mission of the Son and the pouring out of the Holy Spirit, and the joint celebration of the sacraments by which the Son and the Spirit come with the Father upon those who are baptized" (ibid).[51]

The bishop cannot be present each time there will be adults baptized; so the text says: "When the bishop is absent, the presbyter who baptizes an adult or a child of catechetical age should also confer Confirmation" (Par. 46).

Presbyters may also be associated with the minister of the Confirmation if the number of persons being confirmed requires it. Such presbyters should be those who hold diocesan office or who are pastors of the place where the Confirmation is held or who are pastors or catechists of the confirmands (Par. 46). Thus, in this germinal document, the Roman Church has said that when one must choose between keeping the actions of Christian Initiation together and keeping the bishop as the exclusive minister of Confirmation, the unity of the rites is the more important principle. The effect of this assignment of priorities is that whenever the adult rite is used, the initiatory actions will follow upon one another in their ancient and intelligible sequence.

This authoritative liturgical document has given its weight to restoring to a major church in the West the unity of the initiatory actions and adjusting the ministerial roles accordingly. Some liturgical scholars have gone further. As the previous chapter indicated, the RCIA is to be thought of as setting forth, in the Roman community, the norm of Christian Initiation. Liturgists are asking why, if this rite is the norm, the principles of all baptisms, whether of adults or of children, should not be brought into conformity with it. The Roman Catholic liturgist, Aidan Kavanagh, comments:

> The theological point made here [the unity of the paschal mystery] is of such seriousness that one feels compelled to ask why and how it can be construed as applying only to adults and not to infants and children.... Unless the theological point is dismissed as mere rhetoric, it seems inescapable that all who are deemed fit for baptism, no matter what their physical age, should also be confirmed within the same liturgical event.[52]

Anglicanism will, of course, go about the assignment of sacramental ministries and the reshaping of liturgical events in its own way and at its own pace. There is no need to do things in a certain way because someone else has begun to do them that way, and if what is being done elsewhere violates essential principle, there is every reason for Anglicanism to sustain custom whoever else may change. But in this matter, the Roman community and the Anglican look to the same early history and are parts of the same Western line of development. They are facing similar questions arising from broadly similar pastoral experience.

This rapid examination of an authoritative liturgical document from Rome suggests that new directions are being taken in that Communion. There is no need for Anglicanism to fear that if ministerial roles in Christian Initiation were to be rethought and to some extent reordered it would place in jeopardy the Church's catholic standing. Rigidity is not called for. The Eastern and the Roman churches are rather relaxed on the point. Anglicanism, confident in its catholicity, should do what seems best on its merits.

In 1985, at a meeting of liturgical scholars, an informal group of Anglicans met as "An International Anglican Consultation" to consider "Children at Communion." The issues of Christian Initiation are interconnected, and the Consultation, in listing some implications of its topic, spoke briefly about "the role of the bishop in a renewed pattern of initiation." Its comments include this suggestion concerning priorities:

> We would neither prescribe nor inhibit an episcopal role. We simply believe that the church must first get its initiation principles right, and then seek ways in which the ordained ministry, through presiding and participation, may be appropriately integrated in the rites. We do, however, favour an increased frequency in the occasions when the bishop will preside at baptismal eucharists. [53]

This chapter has dealt largely with (in a phrase of the 1985 Consultation) the church's "initiation principles." Here, as at the conclusion of the previous section of this chapter (which asked about the subjects of Confirmation), we may note that, in the light of earlier discussions, the term "confirmation" carries a compound history, and the question "Who shall minister Confirmation?" is really two questions: (1) "Who shall minister the post-baptismal seal of the Spirit?" and (2) "To whom shall baptized Christians make formal renewals of the promises of Baptism?" Again there is no inherent necessity that the two questions be given the same answer. Indeed, historically, it is unusual that the two questions came to be related. The ways in which the 1979 Prayer Book has dealt with these questions will be looked at in Chapters VIII and IX.

Persistent Issues:
3. First Communion

The classic sequence of Christian initiatory rites comes to its climax when the newly baptized persons receive Christ's Body and Blood in the Thanksgiving meal of the community of faith. This sequence, Baptism followed by Eucharist, was Christian practice from very early times.

Early History: It is difficult to say how early the two great sacraments were seen to be connected. St. Paul writes to other Christians of Baptism as a past action ("you were baptized") and of the Lord's Supper as a present action ("you eat this bread and drink this wine"). Each is integral to redemption in Christ. In 1 Corinthians 12:13 he speaks of Baptism as a participation in Christ's body, and in 1 Corinthians 10:16*f.* he attributes the same effect to the Eucharist. But he does not discuss the two together.

Similarly in the Fourth Gospel (taking the passages as actual sacramental references), both Baptism, "unless you are born again of water and the Spirit..." (3:5) and the Eucharist, "unless you eat the flesh of the Son of Man..." (6:53) are essential to eternal life. But a theological connection between these two rites is not traced, and how, if at all, they might have been related in first-century practice is not described.

Two late New Testament documents give substantial hints that the Christians may have set Baptism in conscious relation to the Eucharist quite early.

1 Peter is often taken to be a baptismal homily. Its themes suit the condition of new converts. Such references as it makes to baptismal actions are indirect. In 1 Peter 1:23*f.,* love for one's fellow Christians is commended on the basis that the converts have been born anew through the living and abiding word of God (1:23*f.*). This point is followed by imagery of putting away sin (2:1) and of taking pure spiritual milk—for growth (2:2) and for delight (2:3). The symbolic references thus pass from *new birth* and *putting away* something old to *taking nourishment,* and it is all spoken in support of mutual love in a new community. The imagery follows what could be simply a natural sequence: newborn children need to be clothed and fed. But does the sequence of word-pictures by this first-century homilist draw on a setting at a ritual event where persons who had been through a renunciation, the water of new birth, and a reclothing came to a table (perhaps offering milk and honey, as well as bread and wine) where they tasted the goodness of the Lord? Or was this passage just a homilist's rhetoric at the time 1 Peter was written (or preached)? And if it was, did such images encourage the rapid development of actual ritual? It is easier to ask questions than to be certain of answers.

A few years ago Massey H. Shepherd, Jr. put forward the thesis that the structure and elements of the Book of Revelation reflect the underlying pattern of the the the Paschal liturgy. By this analysis, in early sections of the Apocalypse, the letters to the churches (chapters 2–3) represent the scrutinies; washing and sealing represent actions of Baptism, while the "Marriage Supper of the Lamb" in the concluding episode of the book (21:1–22:5) corresponds with the Paschal Eucharist. In this reading, this early source evidences the early origin of a complex liturgical action which united the Paschal occasion, Baptism, and the Eucharist.[1]

The *Didache,* one of the earliest extant Christian documents (possibly as old as the later parts of the New Testament), contains directions concerning Baptism ("Now about Baptism,..." 7:1) and concerning the eucharist ("Now about the Thanksgiving,..." 9:1). Then something

CHAPTER VI

like a rubric or disciplinary rule links the two: "You must not let anyone eat or drink of your Eucharist except those baptized in the Lord's name" (9:5).

Baptism and Eucharist Clearly Linked: From at least the late first or early second century, the disciplinary, practical link between the two sacramental acts is secure. Baptism admits one to the Table of the Lord. The unbaptized do not come to the ritual meal. Holy things are for the holy. The two ritual acts are not only experienced in this order, they are observed in one compound event. At their Baptism, the newly reborn receive the sacrament for the first time. Each occasion of Communion thereafter would be a reminder of one's Baptism and one's initial welcome to the Holy Table. Most of our early liturgical sources do not describe either Baptism or the Eucharist alone; rather, they tell of the baptismal Eucharist, held at Easter, as though that were the plenary sacramental unit. When its order had been explained, other, derivative events (such as the Sunday Eucharist) would be clear. The sacramental acts that shaped the church and the consciousness of the individual Christian were intelligibly related, for they grew together from the Gospel as it formed the church. Once this link between the two great sacraments of the Gospel emerged, it proved to be coherent, expressive, and durable.[2]

Since this sacramental link between Baptism and Eucharist has been broken, and broken for centuries in the West, it has been known by many people, insofar as it has been known at all, only as the historically remote practice of the early church or as the practice of the somewhat exotic Eastern churches. The fact that, over a long period, in the West as in the East, newly baptized persons, including baptized infants, received Communion has dropped out of the awareness of the church.

A selection of the evidence may indicate the prevalence of this practice:

Cyprian, writing in North Africa in the third century, remarks it. Augustine, in a later century, says of infants: "Even for the life of infants was His [Christ's] flesh given, which He gave for the life of the world; and even they will not have life if they eat not the flesh of the Son of Man."[3]

In Spain, the eleventh Council of Toledo (675 CE) ruled that no fault belonged to infants who had received the host and threw it up. The point indicates not only that infants were communicated at the time, but that the church was less scrupulous about innocent human incapacities than it came to be later on.[4] A later Spanish document, the *Liber Ordinum* (known through an 11th-century manuscript, but referring to older customs), following the Baptism and the anointing, directs: "Then the priest sets a veil over the head of the baptized infants and communicates them."[5]

As to sources indicating generally Roman customs, the *Ordo Romanus XI*, a book of liturgical regulations which is taken to reflect practice as early as the sixth century, contains a direction: "After this [after Baptism and the postbaptismal signing] they go in to Mass and all the infants receive Communion."[6] This document commends care that the infants receive no "food or suckling" before the Communion. But such regulation was later relaxed. The *Gelasian Sacramentary*, a mid-eighth-century document, directs that after the infant is baptized and signed with chrism the Mass should be celebrated, and the infant communicates.[7]

When Baptism by a presbyter, followed at a later time by Confirmation by a bishop, became common, the infant might receive Communion at Baptism. The Gregorian Sacramentary says that after Baptism, "If the bishop is present it is fitting that he [the infant] at once be confirmed with chrism, and afterwards communicated. And if the bishop is absent let him be communicated by the presbyter."[8]

Such evidence is fairly common and quite consistent. Canon Fisher summarizes: "All churches in the West admitted infants to communion until the twelfth century."[9] Even after that time, the practice did not altogether die out.

Baptism and Communion Separated: But since this long-observed custom of communicating infants did, in fact, come to an end, it is important to establish, at least in a general way, when and why it ceased in the West.

Several factors appear to have figured:[10]

■ In the later part of the medieval period, among laity and religious, the act of receiving the bread and wine became infrequent. It was no longer a necessary or expected part of assisting at Mass. When non-communicating attendance became usual, there was little point in introducing infants at Baptism to something which adults did not in fact habitually do.

- From the ninth to the eleventh centuries, a series of controversies led to realistic, literal definitions of the presence of Christ in the Eucharist. An essay a few years ago remarked, "It is no coincidence that infant Communion disappeared in the same century that the dogma of transubstantiation was promulgated."[11] Such dogmatic affirmations led to a fear of accident to or desecration of the eucharistic elements. Moreover, for some time, when infants were communicated, it had been with the wine only. In about the 11th century, the cup began to be withheld from the laity, largely out of fear that it might be spilled. This change further removed Communion from infants.

- As Baptism came to be observed at a time closer to a child's birth and the link between it and Easter was broken, it became privatized and separated from a setting in a community Eucharist.

- St. Thomas linked receiving the Holy Communion to competencies clearly beyond the capacities of infants. In his *Commentary on the Sentences of Peter Lombard,* he drew on a saying of Augustine (himself, ironically, a strong advocate of infant Communion) that Christ is the food of the full-grown. Thomas argued that, since through the Eucharist the completion of spiritual life is given, the Eucharist is only for those of spiritual attainment. In his *Summa Theologica* he asks, "Whether those who have not the use of reason ought to receive the sacrament?" He replies that those who have had the use of reason but have lost it may be communicated because of their previous devotion. But those who have never had it (among whom he includes newborn children and the insane) should not be communicated, "because in no way has there been any preceding devotion."[12] He wants the act of receiving to be conditioned by the sort of discrimination that would "conceive some devotion for the sacrament." In a ground-breaking article, J.M.M. Dalby remarked:

There is then in St. Thomas an unexplained demand for strong faith, the use of reason, the ability to distinguish between the spiritual and the physical, and signs of discretion and devotion, and also a total unawareness of the novelty of this demand."[13]

Thus, by the late Middle Ages it was an established practice that infants be baptized, but not communicated. (Evidently when a bishop officiated, Baptism might be followed by Confirmation and Holy Communion.) Local councils gave their authority to this division, and theologians supplied it with a rationale—a rationale that was affirmed, to be sure, but hardly well argued.

In the years leading to the Reformation, there was some revival of interest in infant Communion among the followers of Jan Huss.[14] But for the most part, the churches of the Reformation sustained the inherited practice of bringing children to Baptism in infancy, but only admitting them to Communion much later. The requirement of intellectual competence for Communion was the principal justification for delay in admission to the Table. Calvin in particular argued from phrases of St. Paul that a capacity to discern the body and blood of the Lord, to examine one's own conscience, and to proclaim the Lord's death (1 Corinthians 11:26–32) all required reason. If the Lord's Supper was observed in remembrance of Christ and as a showing forth of his death, Calvin said, "What remembrance of this thing, I ask, shall we require of infants when they have never grasped it? What preaching of the cross of Christ, the force and benefit of which their minds have not yet comprehended?"[15] Just as the Passover (unlike circumcision) in the Old Testament, expected those who took part in it to be able to inquire into its meaning (Exodus 12:26), so the Lord's Supper is restricted to those who have some understanding of it.

The Anabaptists were quick to point out the discrepancy in the Reformers' treatment of the two sacraments. In effect they asked, "Do not the arguments you use for postponing admission to Communion serve equally for the postponement of Baptism? If what you say in behalf of infant Baptism is true, you should practice infant Communion as well. But you do not." This line of argument became a common part of the polemics against infant baptism.[16]

The Council of Trent ruled that infants, lacking the use of reason, would not receive Communion at their Baptism. They were incorporated into Christ by Baptism, and they would not lose the grace thus conferred.

The Prayer Book tradition entered in this period, and some factors that are special to it may be mentioned:

In the 1549 Prayer Book, the rite of Confirmation was not very long—only two pages or so in most printings. But it was part of a group whose overall shape indicates the priorities of the time. The service is titled, "Confirmacion, wherein is conteined a Catechisme for Children." In fact, the introductory rubrics explaining the pastoral intent of the rite are almost as long as the rite itself, and the "Catechisme" is about three times as long as the "Confirmacion" which follows. Clearly, the intent of the whole unit is to instruct. Rubrics require that curates shall catechize; fathers, mothers, masters, and dames shall cause the children to come to the church to be catechized; and severe penalties are set forth in the canons for clergy who fail to carry out this duty. The aim in these rites was to assure that the communion would be approached by those who had a pretty good idea of what they were about.

The whole sequence is brought to its close by the rubric: "And there shall none be admitted to the holye communion: until suche time as he be confirmed." This "confirmation rubric" was a regular part of the Prayer Books from 1549 and all later English and American editions through 1928.

The Separation Protested: The question of infant Communion hardly figured in the religious debates of the 16th century. As a wide spectrum of issues came to attention in the following century, only a few asked why Baptism and Holy Communion could be treated so differently.

Writing during the Commonwealth, Jeremy Taylor considered the argument of the Anabaptists that the groups that practiced infant Baptism were inconsistent in not also practicing infant Communion. Taylor knew infant Communion to have been early custom, and he regarded it as acceptable, but not required; for in having Baptism, infants have received Christ:

If infants can receive Christ in the Eucharist, to which they can no more dispose themselves by repentance than they can to Baptism by faith, then it were indeed very well if they were communicated, but yet not necessary; because if they can receive Christ in the Eucharist, they can receive Christ in Baptism. . . . Because infants cannot be obliged to the act or habit of faith, and yet can receive the sacrament of faith [Baptism], they receive Christ as they can, and as they can are entitled to life.[17]

In 1734 the learned nonjuror Thomas Deacon issued his *Devotions*. It is a quite complete Prayer Book containing a baptismal office for adults, whose rubrics ordered the Communion of the newly baptized. In 1747 he followed this liturgical text with two catechisms, published in a single volume as *A Full, True and Comprehensive View of Christianity.* The longer of these catechisms contains a section of fifty pages arguing in behalf of infant Communion. Deacon's argumentation draws on Old Testament analogy, on church tradition, and on pastoral considerations. He says, "What is in the institution said of the body and blood of Christ, does as much suit infants as any . . . adult."[18] Infants are part of the church; the Eucharist signifies the unity of the mystical body; therefore the exclusion of children from it obscures one of the purposes for which the sacrament was given. Deacon's liturgical work was not used by any church, and neither it nor the author's supporting argument had any direct influence, but it represents one 18th-century scholar's informed convictions on a subject that, after a long period of dormancy, has become current in our time.

In the 19th century, the Catholic Apostolic Church arose in England (and spread to a few places on the Continent and in the United States and Canada). This small group combined many unusual characteristics. Taking its rise from the preaching of Edward Irving, it was convinced that Christ would soon return and that the end of the age would be signaled by the restoration of characteristics that had marked the apostolic period. Although the group was charismatic and apocalyptic, it was also highly sacramental and aesthetic—with rich liturgical rhetoric, the use of incense, and dramatic architecture. It was the custom of this group to admit small children to Holy Communion at major church festivals soon after their Baptism. At the age of eleven children were received into regular Communion; and following a period of instruction, when a child turned eighteen years of age, there was a service of "sealing" which included anointing with chrism. This group has come to an end in this century, but it pioneered liturgical practices that have commended themselves widely in more recent years to other churches. Its practice of communicating children should be remembered.[19]

Although the churches in the modern West have given little attention to the matter, the instances cited here indicate that, in the centuries since the Reformation, exclusion of children from Holy Communion has been questioned, but only infrequently and by isolated parties.

Thematic, Theological Issues: This matter cannot be considered adequately from historical material alone. As a systematic, contemporary question it must be looked at on its merits and as an issue of our own time.

The Unity and Complementarity of Baptism and Eucharist: Part of the reason for treating the two great sacraments in a similar way is that there are between them many deep common levels of meaning. In a sense these two sacramental signs stood in the early period and they stand now for the same reality:

> *Both are sacraments of the Church and extensions of the atonement; both are concerned with incorporation into Christ, with death and resurrection; both are made powerful by the operation of the Holy Spirit; both stand under the sign of the cross; both are sacraments of inaugurated eschatology.*[20]

But if they represent and convey the same meanings, there are functional differences between them. The great difference is that Baptism is inaugural—an act done once at the start of life as a Christian, and never repeated—while the Eucharist is the climactic sign of incorporation into the divine life, and it is often repeated. Baptism signifies a basic cleansing and the entry into a new condition. It seals the relation in which a Christian stands with God. The Communion, to which Baptism leads, is the meal by which the baptismal bonding is sustained. This sacramental meal, signifying renewed absolution and sustenance in the redemptive life, is often repeated. One is a sign of birth—something that happens to each person once. The other speaks of the recurrent need to be fed. Kavanagh put it, "In Baptism the Eucharist begins, and in the Eucharist Baptism is sustained."[21]

Another difference might be noted. Baptism comes to focus on an individual. Each person baptized (if we except some mass baptisms in the recorded past which are not widely commended as models for today) is dealt with particularly, often by name. By contrast, the Eucharist is a communal act, done by persons acting together, and for the building up of the shared life. Neville Clark some years ago summarized a fine study of the sacraments by saying that Baptism incorporates an individual into a community which is continually remade by the Eucharist.[22]

There is, anciently and now, an impressive mutuality between these two great Gospel sacraments. It can be spoken of in terms of their imagery and in terms of their place in Christian life.

Washing and feeding have associations with our earliest experience. Newly born children need to be washed and to be fed. The priorities of a household in which there is a small child are rearranged around these events. Both washing and feeding are necessities, but infants cannot do either for themselves. Being washed and being fed are signs of gift, of dependence, of help that comes to one from others; hence they are signs also of community and human bonding. Through such connections with primal experience, the imagery of Baptism and of the Holy Communion stand in profound inner relation to one another.

The life in faith calls for them both. Faith brings one into a relationship with God in Christ which endures through every circumstance and every lapse from the new life, for it is rooted in God's character and promise. That is the reality for which Baptism, as an unrepeated act, stands. But, for our part, we are careless and neglectful; we need the meaning of that constant relationship to be gathered up and expressed freshly. We often act as though Christ were not Lord, as though God's name were not written upon us. We need a renewal of the awareness of God's favor. That is the reality for which the Eucharist stands. As an English theologian put it: "In Christian Baptism the whole course of the believer's life is summed up in one moment to be realized in all that follows, and this actualization is achieved primarily through the Eucharist."[23]

The Nature of the Church: The Church is a great time-embracing, space-embracing communion of persons who share in one life, as they share in Christ. The New Testament metaphors for this living unit of Christ and his people are in some instances physiological. Christ is "the Head, from whom the whole body, nourished and knit together through its joints and ligaments, grows with a growth that is from God" (Colossians 2:19; *cf.* Ephesians 4:16).

It is part of the faith of Anglicanism—as of most other large parts of the ecumenical Church—that children are included in this common life. In fact, at any one time children comprise a large portion of the members of this great living unit. The sign that one belongs to this *koinonia* is Baptism; and the Holy Communion is a sign for the body's members, not for those members who have somehow come to deserve it. A recent statement has said:

> *We wish to affirm on theological grounds that children of all ages are included among those for whom Christ died, that children of all ages are equally persons in the people of God, and that children of all ages have an active ministry in Christ among his people and in the world. We see no dogmatic or other credible basis for regarding some who are baptized as eligible to receive Communion while others are not. We believe this to run contrary to the inclusive character of the Gospel set out in Galatians 3:27–29.*[24]

The Accustomed Division: Persons who are familiar with the Western Christian tradition have had little opportunity to grasp this mutuality between Baptism and Communion. They usually have seen Baptism celebrated with no apparent connection with the Eucharist, and most Christians only began to receive Communion some years after they had been baptized. It called for an effort of the imagination to suppose that the two events had anything to do with one another.

This discontinuous initiatory pattern has been criticized for some time by persons who, through familiarity with history or with non-Western churches, had become aware of alternatives to it.

An initiatory pattern which has allowed a dozen years or so to elapse between Baptism and the beginning of its regular renewal through the Holy Communion is certain to cloud the unity of their meaning. The anomaly of baptized but noncommunicating Christians had become so familiar that it had gone unchallenged and unanalyzed.

But of course it is not an abstract issue of the complementarity of the Gospel sacraments and the desirability of bringing them together. It comes to a quite specific focus. There is no large group of baptized but noncommunicating Christians in the church (not penitents, with which the early church would have been familiar) *except for children.* We are accustomed to large numbers of noncommunicating baptized Christians in our midst—parish houses full of them Sunday after Sunday!

At some point one looks at the community with different questions. Why, if Baptism is initiation into Christ and his people, does it not lead at once to communicant status? The answers that would have been given in the past would have spoken, not of sacramental theology so much as of the peculiar place of children in the Church.

The Church has seemed to want to say that children both are and are not fully Christian. But this ambiguous affirmation has been made more by actions than by theological statement—a quite dangerous sort of nonargument to depend on when a challenge arises. Many people "know" that something old is right and that an alternative is wrong, but it is best not to ask how that certainty is reached.

The logic of the matter has seemed clear enough. A baptized person who is not yet admitted to Communion is a member of the Body of Christ and is not cut off from the the Holy Spirit or the redemptive life. Yet the question arises: If baptized children are Christians, why is their participation in the practice of Christian sacramental life only partial?

For generations the conviction had been widespread in the church that reception of Holy Communion belongs to a later stage of experience and is conditioned upon some understanding of the rite and the faith of which it speaks. It was difficult to say just how much understanding was thought to be necessary, or why tests should be imposed on children but not on adults. Similarly, it was seldom asked why the two Gospel sacraments were treated so differently. If understanding is a prerequisite for receiving the Communion, why should it not be required for Baptism? If infancy does not exclude a person from one of the sacraments, why should it exclude from the other? Any argument for infant Baptism is an argument for infant Communion. Any argument for waiting for an age of understanding for admission to Communion is an argument for "believers' Baptism."

But the issues over first Communion have been at least as practical as they have been theoretical. The educational processes of the Episcopal Church seem to have been ordered very largely for the task of preparing children for Confirmation and for communicant status. There have been and are important exceptions. But too often Christian education of children, despite devoted work by many people, has not been significant. A spurt of overambitious, content-centered teaching has led to Confirmation and first Communion.

This pattern tends to say that the educational work of the Church exists for the purpose of making communicants *in the Church*. Catechesis has been connected with a natural completion (confirmation by a bishop) and a new status (communicant). Such a thrust seems introverted and ecclesiastical at a time when the processes of the Church dare not turn in upon themselves. The aim of Christian education ought to be the making of servants of Christ (of whatever age) for his work *in the world*.[25] The redemption signified by Baptism is for the world. The administration of Christian Initiation ought not to appear to bring children to a new ecclesiastical status and then to have nothing more for them.

Yet something rather like that has established itself as a general pattern. The adolescent rite of Confirmation has seemed too much like an end, an achievement, a reward for going to all those classes. It closed one period of relation to the church, but it was not successful in opening and sustaining a new mode of relation. Following a time of attending the Eucharist and receiving Communion, the confirmands' involvement in church life in any form, instead of entering a more mature phase, declined rapidly. The "loss of confirmands" is often remarked in tones of alarm. Although there are exceptions in most parishes, the rite of Confirmation, as it has been known in the Episcopal Church, has statistically come to be what one eminent Roman Catholic, speaking of course of his own church, termed "the sacrament of exit from the Church."[26]

Although new liturgies, new understandings, and new pastoral practices are bringing about changes in all of these matters, their formative work has only begun. Many persons, it may be supposed, continue to think of the Church's sacramental occasions as separate from one another, for that is the way they have experienced them.

Changes Proposed and Put into Effect: For some time, reorderings of the initiatory actions have been proposed or carried out—many of them having the effect of bringing Communion into closer relation to Baptism.

Perhaps the first modern effort to realign the initiatory moments was in the Roman Catholic Church in Europe, where, in the 19th century, a practice was begun (later widely followed) which altered the sequence of the rites of initiation. Baptism was administered to infants by local pastors. Children made their first Communion, normally prepared for by first confession, at age six or seven. This first Communion traditionally became an important occasion for the parish, the families, and for each child. Confirmation came later—at an episcopal visitation when the children had reached the age of twelve or so.

Objections have been raised to this pattern. Why should the first occasion of doing something which is, by its nature, a repeated action be surrounded by heightened emotions and social excitement? It seems to build many false dynamics into the receiving of the Communion. The preparation for first Communion by first confession also seems to interpret the Holy Communion in a limiting way and to couple it with an awareness of guilt. Moreover, if the traditional sequence of actions—Baptism, Confirmation (understood as initiatory and sacramental Confirmation), Communion—is an element of the sacramental sign, the violation of this sequence in this modern practice makes the sacraments of initiation less coherent.[27] Yet something was being tried to bring the two great sacraments into closer relation to one another and to begin one's life as a communicating Christian at an earlier age.

Among the ways of adapting the initiatory actions, mention should be made of the custom which came into currency in the 1950s in the Episcopal Church of baptized children coming to the communion rail, usually with their families, to receive a blessing. In those years a great deal of emphasis was being put on Baptism as a sign of the acceptance and inclusion of children by God and the Church. They were members. Children were to know that they had been baptized, and they were to attend baptisms in church as observers—often taking places near the font, where they could see well. Many churches had a "Family Service" as a principal service of Sunday morning. Children attended with their parents. But what were the children to do when the parents and older sisters and brothers left their pews to go up to Communion? It was obviously an important action. Must the children be left behind? Would that not be an unmistakable sign of second-class membership? At that time (only a few years ago) hardly anyone proposed communicating baptized but unconfirmed children. But as a recognition of their inclusion they came to the communion rail, with the family, where they received a blessing, while others received the bread and wine. This step is easy to understand and explain. But it was surely less than fully satisfactory. On what basis were the children, who were in some respects cordially included, excluded from the central act? What did the parents and older children receive that the smaller children did not? Did this action speak of inclusion, or did it heighten the sense of discrimination? This act was clearly better than doing nothing. It continues as a practice in some congregations, and it deserves to be remembered as a first step —or at least a half-step.

At one stage of thinking through the rites of initiation, a proposal along rather original lines gained a following among some Roman Catholics, Lutherans, and Anglicans. In the late 1950s and early 1960s it was suggested that first Communion might be made quite early, while persons would only be confirmed at an age much older than hitherto (ages around twenty as a minimum were discussed) and only on their own initiative. Such a change would make Confirmation unambiguously adult in character. It was supposed that if this practice were widely adopted, only a portion of the baptized and communicating members would seek Confirmation; but if that step involved serious study and commitment, the confirmed members would bring vitality and vocational seriousness to the Church out of proportion to their numbers. Yet such administration of Confirmation would not, at the Lord's Table, create an elite within the Church, for all would have been admitted to Communion at an early age, without Confirmation. (Persons who put this idea forward emphasized the extent to which Confirmation had been adapted in the past; obviously it could be adapted further.) Perhaps this proposal seemed too obviously a sacrament devised by educators. In any case, it had largely stopped being discussed by the time liturgical revisions began in earnest.

At the Lambeth Conference of 1968, the Bishops of the Anglican Communion had this to report concerning Christian Initiation:

> *We commend the following alternatives as possible lines of experiment:*
> *[a] Admission to Holy Communion and Confirmation would be separated. When a baptized child is of appropriate age, he or she would be admitted to Holy Communion after an adequate course of instruction. Confirmation would be deferred to an age when a young man or woman shows adult responsibility and wishes to be commissioned and confirmed for his or her task of being a Christian in society.*
> *[b] Infant Baptism and Confirmation would be administered together, followed by admission to Holy Communion at an early age after appropriate instruction. In due course, the Bishop would commission the person for service when he or she is capable of making a responsible commitment.*[28]

These two directions which it was suggested that Anglican practice might take seem dissimilar, yet looked at closely, they may be two responsible ways of getting at much the same set of issues. Either of the recommendations of Lambeth would have the effect of associating Communion more closely with Baptism, although both have in mind some instruction after Baptism and prior to admission to Holy Communion.

To turn to the initiatives that were taken in the Episcopal Church, early in 1970 the Standing Liturgical Commission issued *Prayer Book Studies 18,* "Holy Baptism with the Laying-On-Of-Hands."[29] This document pioneered many features of the initiatory rites; clearly it was not a modest editing of the 1552–1928 texts, but a freshly conceived work. The baptismal action was meant to take place at a principal service of a Sunday or other feast; it was preceded by a full service of the Word; and it led to the Eucharist. The creed and promises, the brief prayers, the blessing of the water and of the oil, and the prayer for the Spirit all stood in this 1970 text substantially as they remain in the Prayer Book that was adopted later in the decade. The principal structural feature of this rite was "the reunion of Baptism, Confirmation and Communion into a single continuous service, as it was in the primitive Church," (p. 19). The introductory pages, which contained a good discussion of our experience of sacrament and symbol, said concerning Baptism and Communion:

> *Those who have been made members of the family of God have the right to be fed at the Lord's Table. Those who have been incorporated into Christ should be able to complete their eucharistic self-oblation in worship and love by receiving him. Those who are admitted by Baptism into the Communion of Saints should be allowed to partake of the Holy Communion (p. 18).*

A rubric said that "Those who have now been christened may receive Holy Communion" (p. 40).

The General Convention of 1970 authorized the initiatory rite of *Prayer Book Studies 18* for trial use, but with important qualifying provisions. The rite proposed that renewal of the baptismal covenant would principally take place in the Eucharist and at baptismal occasions. The action of the General Convention indicated the considerable attachment in the Episcopal Church to an act of individual "ratification" of the promises of Baptism—a feature which this rite was thought to have provided for inadequately.[30] But a part of what this rite sought was granted, for the terms of its adoption, which originated in the House of Bishops, said "That children [should] be admitted to Holy Communion before Confirmation, subject to the direction and guidance of the Ordinary." Louis Weil commented soon after the event that this action, "has restored in principle the ancient and long-standing practice of giving the Eucharist by virtue of Baptism and not by virtue of some ambiguous norm based on age or reason."[31]

The "Pocono Statement" issued in 1971 by the House of Bishops spoke mainly of Confirmation—specifically of the pastoral, catechetical side of Confirmation. But it also had implications for the matter at hand. It said:

It is the understanding of this house that in Holy Baptism a person is made fully and completely a Christian and a member of Christ's Body, the Church. God the Holy Spirit acts, so we believe, to bestow the gift of his grace in response to the affirmation of faith by his Church....

Confirmation should not be regarded as a procedure of admission to the Holy Communion; nor is it "joining the church."[32]

In December of 1972 the Theological and Prayer Book Committees of the House of Bishops held a joint meeting with the Standing Liturgical Commission to study the proposals that were emerging concerning Christian Initiation. A committee formulated a brief, carefully worded "Statement of Agreed Positions." Again, only the sections pertinent to the present topic are cited here:

A. Concerning Baptism

1. There is one, and only one, unrepeatable act of Christian Initiation, which makes a person a member of the Body of Christ.

2. The essential element of Christian Initiation is Baptism by water and the Spirit, in the Name of the Holy Trinity, in response to repentance and faith.

3. Christian Initiation is normatively administered in a liturgical rite that also includes the laying-on of hands, consignation [with or without chrism], prayer for the gift of the Holy Spirit, reception by the Christian community, joining the eucharistic fellowship, and commissioning for Christian mission. When the bishop is present, it is expected that he will preside at the rite.

B. Concerning a Postbaptismal Affirmation of Vows

...4. The rite embodying such affirmations [of the promises of Baptism] should in no sense be understood as being a "completion of Holy Baptism," nor as being a condition precedent to admission to the Holy Communion, nor as conveying a special status of church membership.[33]

CHAPTER VI

The principles put forward discursively in this statement moved generally along lines explicit or implied in the rites that were being drafted at the time.

The rite of *Prayer Book Studies 26,* which was issued in 1973, contained a rubric that said, "Baptized persons in good standing are eligible to receive Holy Communion" (p. 19). In the course of moving toward adoption, this rubric was deleted. Perhaps it seemed argumentative; or perhaps it was judged that the church was not ready for something so definite, but that the logic of the rites should win its way as it would.

However, as a consequence of this thinking, the "confirmation rubric" which had long stood as the final words of the Confirmation service was simply dropped. It was now clear that Baptism is the rite of admission to the Holy Communion. No other sacramental step is required and, if none is required, the gratuitous insertion of one flaws the clarity of sacramental order. Persons who are baptized are, by reason of the Christian standing that Baptism confers, eligible to receive Holy Communion. If they are competent to receive the first of the two great sacraments, they are competent to receive both.

In 1976 and 1979 the Prayer Book was adopted. Since that time, the Episcopal Church has had rites which bring Baptism and Holy Communion into close relation to one another. The Prayer Book achieves this effect, not by prescription, but indirectly through the structure of the rites and the relation among them and through what is not said. To identify factors which bring about this clear relation:

- Baptism normatively takes place in the liturgical setting of the Eucharist (p. 298), making it anomalous if the persons who have been central in one of two sacramental actions are excluded from full participation in the other.

- The Eucharist is obviously structured as a meal—a meal at which the baptized persons present who are in good standing will receive. Persons are baptized into a church in which attendance by persons not intending to receive the bread and the wine is uncommon.

- A rubric (p. 313) calls for the oblations of the bread and wine at the baptismal Eucharist to be presented by the newly baptized or their godparents. It would be strange if those who by rubric were named to offer were by custom forbidden to receive.

■ The Easter Vigil holds before each congregation the demonstration of the Redemptive Mystery which Baptism and Eucharist make together.

■ The "confirmation rubric" is quietly retired, and the Prayer Book suggests no other sacramental or catechetical hurdle that should intervene between Baptism and receiving Holy Communion.

These official rites ask for understanding and for pastoral implementation. But the rites only provide new structures within which pastoral understandings and practices can develop; the text and rubrics do not win their way by compulsion. Customs and judgments seem to be moving toward support of the authorized rites, but there is substantial lag. Moreover, not all churches in the Anglican Communion have moved in this direction at this time. So problems of the relation of Baptism and the Holy Communion continue to come up in the Episcopal Church and in the churches that are its near relatives. Persons in the congregations can be confused—and at times treated arbitrarily. A recent statement sought to provide some guidance in the matter. At a conference of liturgical scholars in July 1985, "An International Consultation" of the Anglicans in attendance met to consider these matters in an international, intercultural context. The findings of this group are summarized in the compressed statement "Children and Communion."[34] It is a brief, considered defense of early Communion and a valuable summing up (as of the date of its writing) of thinking which, as this account will have indicated, had been going on for some decades.

These pages have spoken principally of events in the Episcopal Church and in Anglican discussion, but similar trends could be traced in other churches as well. Inherited initiatory rites and understandings were similar in many Western churches; pastoral and theological issues appeared in the same ways ecumenically. A substantial literature has grown up on the subject of children and Communion.[35]

A witness to ecumenical thinking in this matter is the commentary section of the "Baptism, Eucharist and Ministry" statement which was issued (after years of broadly based discussion) by the Commission on Faith and Order of the World Council of Churches in 1982:

> *If Baptism, as incorporation into the body of Christ, points by its very nature to the eucharistic sharing of Christ's body and blood, the question arises as to how a further and separate rite can be interposed between Baptism and admission to Communion. Those churches which baptize children but refuse them a share in the Eucharist before such a rite may wish to ponder whether they have fully appreciated and accepted the consequences of Baptism.* [36]

Pastoral Rethinking: Is receiving Communion a privilege reserved for an elite within the baptized community, or is it one of the rights of the baptized?

Although the Episcopal Church has in place official rites which speak to this question, it has become clear that in this matter scholarly information and argument and even authorized liturgies do not in themselves persuade. Existing customs are embedded in deep emotions. Practices that have grown familiar belong to an order of reality; they are right—no need to ask how one knows; one knows. Children should be baptized. That is right and good. But they should not come to the Communion until... Well, until they know what they are doing!

The reactions to suggestions otherwise were often shock and outrage. But they were not uniformly so. Some parents saw at once that bringing their infant children to the Holy Communion was desirable. They did it as soon as it was proposed that it be done. Probably as time has gone by, many people who initially had reservations about the practice have been persuaded by seeing others do what at first scandalized them. But now they are not reacting to an abstract proposal, but to an action by persons they know and trust. In that human context, attitudinal change is possible. But at points where life touches the sacred, change is usually not easy.

As the foregoing sequence of documents has indicated, the Church, officially and collectively, moved to new positions slowly and sometimes painfully. Many persons who have been involved in this process can recall their own interior evolution in many of these matters.

Ritual behavior, important understandings, cherished personal investments, and deep feelings are all mingled. Continued coming to terms with a new pastoral and liturgical situation given by the Prayer Book text may not be rapid nor carried through at the same pace by everyone. The authors of "Children and Communion" said: "Change can involve some pain, and a time of transition is hard for those who liked things as they were, and also for those who want it all to happen everywhere immediately."[37]

Two quite specific, practical points come up when this change in practice is proposed:

■ If clergy and parents have not seen it done, they ask, "How can infants be communicated?" It is certainly true that feeding little children is not always simple. Infants who are too small to be given the bread can be communicated in the wine only. It is easy enough for the minister (sometimes a parent) to dip his or her finger in the chalice and then into the child's mouth. Toddlers can extend their hands. In many instances, parents help in giving the elements to their children; it needs to be quite human and unaffected.

■ Thinking of the old wish for some grasp of the meaning of the sacramental act on the part of the recipients, some parishes and dioceses have worked on some sort of special occasion of first Communion, prepared for by elementary instructions. The Eucharist is a meal interpreted by symbolically loaded words and standing in a special account of reality. It should not be distanced and forbidding, but it is surrounded with unusual solemnity, and it uses gestures that in some respects are not parts of everyday conduct. It is like parties and meals at home, but it is different from them too. Certainly some account of meaning appropriate to this stylized and unique meal needs to be supplied at intervals in the growing experience of a child, and parents can probably give it best. Any child begins with a tacit grasp of an action that is rooted in eating with a group of friends. A Lutheran theologian put it, "The one thing we do well at any age is to participate in fellowship by accepting nourishment."[38] Teaching or coaching helps can be given by capable people, and some good material for this sensitive educational task is in print. But it would seem to subvert the sacramental

CHAPTER VI

point if this desire for a context of stated meaning to surround the act of receiving Communion led to a formalized first Communion at a predetermined age with certain prerequisites. The sacramental link between Baptism and Eucharist should not be qualified by some further intervening step. A colleague has put it: "I myself think it is a principle not to baptize those one is not prepared to communicate."[39]

As, under new rubrics and new pastoral understandings, the Eucharist has begun to be reassociated with Baptism, and as, in appropriate ways, children have begun coming to Communion at a much earlier age than has been customary, some revision of the emphases of eucharistic spirituality is obviously involved.[40] Admission to Communion is no longer seen to belong to a second stage of initiation, presupposing some understanding of the act and corresponding to new opportunities and demands of teenage years. It belongs instead to childhood, corresponding perhaps to taking food with family and friends. Our earliest associations are with times of eating with others; and our most deeply buried memories are of being fed. The Holy Communion, like infant Baptism, stands as witness that God's love comes to one prior to one's ability to comprehend. The eucharistic life does not wait until a certain level of understanding has been attained; rather, understanding can grow within one's experience as a practicing communicant. A child might well grow up not remembering a time when she or he was not receiving, with the family, at the Lord's Table.[41]

A comment by a Church of England commission suggests that young children may find sacramental experience accessible in a way that older children will not: "To postpone the experience of sacramental worship until the child's best aptitude for it has deteriorated is...both theologically and pastorally indefensible."[42] The thrust of this remark is that instead of admitting children to the Lord's Table when they are ready, we have been keeping them away when they are most ready and admitting them when that readiness has diminished.

Pedagogically, Episcopalians using the 1979 Prayer Book are in a position to know in church the sort of thing they usually know very well outside of church in their more sophisticated awareness of psychology and learning: Our concrete experience does not happen because we have thought something through in advance. Rather, our thinking develops out of prior concrete experience. Our thinking develops richly out of rich concrete experience. We do not have some nonsymbolic grasp of reality which, by a process of symbolization, we turn into a symbol. Rather, we move toward thought, impelled by a primary contact with reality by means of symbols. For Christians in general, one may surmise, the Eucharist has been more powerful in itself than any of the ideas about it have been. It is, in a sense, its own authority and instructor. Explanations are answerable to it, not it to explanations. It can be trusted to impart its own significance. If the Eucharist is a meal of a disciplined, committed, apostolic, caring, supporting community —a community meal which speaks of Jesus sharing himself in the life of his people—its reality can impart itself to a child before he or she can think out its meaning or reduce it to words. When the child does begin to think, the ritual experience will have given her or him something to think about.

CHAPTER VII

The Freedom and Authority of Baptism

Baptism as a Rite of Passage: The repeated actions which shape and sustain the Christian community are elemental, human actions, which use the basic materials of the physical body, nature, and social ordering, in the service of an incarnational faith. Although they are understood as carrying out a specific Christological meaning, they use familiar ingredients and follow familiar communal patterns, and they are open to investigation by the human sciences. In recent years, liturgists have come to discuss Christian Initiation in terms of an anthropological category: rites of passage.[1]

In thinking of Baptism as a rite of passage, one needs to consider as one's unit for analysis the entire initiatory process (sometimes referred to as *baptisma*) that the early church devised for carrying the Christian faith and community into the Hellenistic world—the process (to compress an event that might well be described by a list of nouns twice this long) of conversion, catechesis, Baptism and related actions, Eucharist, and mystagogia. Clearly when this large unit is in mind, *baptisma* has many of the marks that are generally taken to describe the passage rites that are virtually universal in human cultures:[2]

■ The baptismal process is understood to bring one from one order of life to another.

■ It is described in images such as rebirth and cleansing—images that are virtually universal in such rites.

■ It is taken to be unrepeatable—another regular mark of rites of passage.

■ *Baptisma* moves by the classic stages by which rites of passage have been analysed: (1) *separation* from an old identity and an old order, (2) *transition,* when one is no longer in the old, but neither is one yet fully in the new, and (3) *incorporation* into the full life of the new community or status. Recalling the pattern of initiation in the early church it should be clear that the initial scrutinies and their judgment on a former way of life, the in-between period of the catechumenate, the final joining in the kiss of peace, the prayers of the faithful, the Communion, and the sharing of privileged insight following Baptism all exemplify this general pattern. Through such a rite of passage, one made a decided break with an old self-definition and old social solidarities and became a new person in a new order. Clearly the early church showed skill in shaping a powerful ritual of transition.

Baptism Adapted to Culture: In shaping this ritual, the early church was doing something so original that it would eventually break up the culture in which it was working. But what it did was not pure, in the sense of being culture-free. Nothing can be that. The rites of the early church, which worked in many ways against the culture, drew on materials of the culture for their expressive power. They were an adaptation to the culture, using the culture to subvert the culture. Only by thus adapting could they be intelligible and in some measure acceptable. One writer puts it:

> The baptismal rite (in the narrow sense) was linked with the bathing habits of the time, the anointing rites with the anointing customs in the thermae, in sport and medical practice, the signing or marking rites with the ways in which animals, soldiers and domes-

tic servants were branded or marked. The rites for catechumens were clarified by linking them with socially and culturally conditioned customs: kneeling and rising, turning round, stretching one's arms towards heaven, turning one's face eastward or westward, rejecting with a gesture of the hand, seeing the font, undressing and dressing, descending into and rising from the font. All this shows that the idea was to drive home and reinforce the way in which the liturgical ceremonies harmonized with the surrounding cultural habits. So the initiation ritual adopted during this period actions and gestures to which people were already accustomed through their ordinary behaviour. [3]

Baptism is a wet, earthy act, involving people in relation to one another, bodies acting and touching one another, hands, clothing, oil, light, and eating and drinking. It is often emotion filled. Baptism would not be more true to itself in some disembodied form. The rite of Baptism may in some sense be universal, but it is only carried out in contexts which are by necessity culture-specific.[4] Thus it will use the materials and take on the style of the culture in a very considerable measure.

Baptism (a) as the Birth-Rite of a Society: Often the church is quite at home in a culture, and its rite of Baptism becomes the birth-rite of a continuous, ethnic group. The church sees its vocation to be that of a redemptive, sanctifying, leavening presence throughout a society. Baptism hallows birth. But it is also a sign that it is not enough to be born; one must be reborn. Nature and culture do not satisfy the eternal destiny of each person. Baptism both witnesses to the transcendent in the midst of the everyday and provides a bond with the transcendent.

It seems almost inevitable that, when the Christian community is dominant in its social setting, its initiatory rites will come to focus on children. Surely most of the persons who now are and who ever have been Christians are and have been so because their parents were Christians. (Is 95 percent too high an estimate?) This is a fact not just of sociological, but of theological significance. It will fashion liturgy and pastoral practice. There is something essentially false about expecting children who grow up in a believing home to reproduce the twice-born life pattern of the convert who comes to Christian faith, and hence to Baptism, in mature years.

At times of relative social stability, in a community comprised mostly of Christians, it is difficult to suppose that Baptism should not do its quiet work of witnessing to the continuity of the generations in the age-old people of God. It is a mark of a faith held and handed on from generation to generation, reverently and little changed, like life itself. No one undertakes to redefine Baptism, for it is by Baptism that each person is defined.

This comfortable condition dare not be idealized or universalized. In how many times has it actually prevailed? And when it has, what deceptions has it concealed? The close association of Baptism with birth, with all of its value, carries the correlative risk of the society domesticating the church. Baptism becomes what the society lets it be, and no more. It is a fact of the natural and social order that one takes for granted—a terrible thing to happen to Baptism or to the Gospel for which it speaks! One comes to Kierkegaard's paradox that it is very difficult to become a Christian when everyone is a Christian.[5]

Baptism (b) Witnessing Against a Society: If Baptism is a rite of passage, it is a rite of passage with some differences. Anthropologists distinguish between, on the one hand, rites which belong to birth—to one's fundamental coming into being within a social solidarity and taking one's self-definition from it—and on the other hand, rites which belong to entering an elite. An instance of the latter would be taking monastic vows: (1) declaring one's intent and being accepted as a novice, (2) the time of the novitiate (a probationary period of testing a new life and of being tested), and (3) taking final vows and filling a place as a full member of the conventual community. Christian Baptism has at times been one of these things, and at times it has been the other. It has been a rite administered within a few days of birth, admitting one to a continuing social solidarity. At other times it has cut across social solidarities and selected persons for a distinct, adult vocation which isolated them from all they had known and held dear previously. At times it binds a society closely; at other times it is profoundly disruptive.

The rite of Baptism has this strange versatility because it serves a society of paradoxical character. The church, as its primary accounts of itself have it, is not an ethnic identity. It is a people "called out" to be distinct from the *ethnoi*. It owes its existence and vocation fundamentally to the purpose of God, who builds up and casts down, who is not captive of any people or nation, but judges and emancipates in all. The message of Jesus cuts across the limiting collectivities of nation, class, and religion to shape a new people which is to transcend the dividing lines of the old order (Galatians 5:28, in a baptismal passage). It unites persons on a new basis, a basis potentially universal. The Christian society is sometimes the creator and maintainer of important continuities and solidarities, but only after it has injected discontinuity by asserting its transcendence over old structures and sacralities. At times of cultural change, it may, out of its own spiritual resources, challenge the very continuities that it has itself established and maintained. In its disruptive, subverting role and in its constructing role (and in the ill-defined times when it is not quite one or the other), persons enter the church by Baptism. Thus Baptism sometimes takes the form of a community-controlled rite at infancy leading to long processes of socialization, and sometimes it is a highly intentional matter of adult decision. It is truly Christian Baptism, in service of the Gospel, in both of these social functions.

At times of rapid change, Christians may rediscover the revolutionary possibilities of their initiatory rite. In its familiarity and routinization, Baptism holds within its actions and symbols the potentiality that can power and interpret change. It may be heard by the baptized person —perhaps "remembered" long after it actually took place—as a divine summons to stand forth from the casually believing crowd. Baptism may be a sign (for the Christian and for the church) which reaches deep into life to shatter and rebuild. It may speak to and of the specifically, individually called Christian and be a source of summons to the collectively called church.

Who can say what Baptism is to be in our time? Is it clear that for everyone it must be one of these things or the other? Is it not often, for many Christians, many parishes, and many Christian populations, a little of both of them?

A Divided Initiatory Rite: But the question in the past has not been: Can Christian Baptism be the birth-rite of a society? Clearly it has been that. The question we inherit from Western European Christendom is more specific and more pedestrian: Can the parts of Christian Initiation be separated so that one of them marks birth, while others mark entry upon adulthood?

The preceding chapters have indicated the theological, liturgical and pastoral problems that have come of this progressive liturgy of initiation for a progressive entry into full Christian standing. The drift of this analysis has been to say that whenever the rites of Christian Initiation are used, they should be used as a unity. They are to mark becoming a Christian, not part of them to mark being partly Christian. They are intelligible as a complex unity. When a part is separated, it loses some of its significance (or takes on false significances), and the separation deprives the other parts of something they require for their sign value.[6]

A Unified Rite at Birth? If sacramental integrity requires that the rites of Christian Initiation should be a unity, and if as a practical thing they will almost inevitably be used in great measure for children, the result will be that the initiatory rites, as a single event (*baptisma*), carrying from Baptism through the Holy Communion, will be widely used for infant children of Christian parents. That is the direction taken in the foregoing chapters and the direction taken by the 1979 Prayer Book. All that was said earlier about the importance and in some respects the primacy of adult Baptism does not contradict the fact of church practice that the first-generation adult believer is always somewhat exceptional; the accustomed thing is for Baptism to deal with second-generation Christians whose parents were in Christ before them.

The administration of the baptismal rites in their entirety to infants is largely known as the Eastern pattern. It has proved a suitable pattern for large Christian populations of Eastern lands, and evidently also for their relocated congregations in the West. But is it suitable for others in the West? Could those groups which have had a staged-out initiatory practice in the past move to this single-stage Eastern pattern without loss? Is the two-stage form of initiation a trifling historical accident that the West could change readily, or does it represent by now a deep investment?

Such questions arose quite specifically when *Prayer Book Studies 18* was before the Episcopal Church. It proposed a unified sacramental initiation—Baptism, the postbaptismal signing, and admission to Communion—which was to be sustained by participation in the Eucharist and in the Baptism of others. The General Convention accepted this proposed rite in a qualified way, indicating the attachment of the Episcopal Church to a rite of individual "ratification." Was this action of the Convention a failure of imagination, or was it an intuition within the Church that needed to be taken seriously?

There are rites which do require some personal maturity on the part of the persons involved: marriage or ordination, for instance. Is Baptism a rite of this sort? Does it lack an essential ingredient in its infant form? Many Western theologians in the infant baptism traditions have felt required to say some sort of "yes" to the question. Ranges of human meaning—meaning constitutive of the baptismal sign itself— are missing when the subject is a child. If infant Baptism is to be practiced, it must, as these Western theologians see it, have some kind of complement to fill out this missing ingredient. The unwillingness of the modern Christian West to settle for Christian Initiation that provides full sacramental standing for infants, and builds in no expectation of more, should not be disregarded. At a time when Christian life seems likely to call for serious decision—not only at the "age of discretion" but repeatedly, over a lifetime—this characteristic intuition of the West is more than an attachment to an intellectualized form of faith. It represents some of the deepest cultural insights and commitments of the West.

The Dynamism of Western Culture: Ever since the Renaissance, and most intensely since the Romantic movement, the Western mind has been fascinated with individual persons and their development. The inner propulsions, the conflicts, frustrations, and satisfactions of personal growth have been recurrent themes of literature, psychology, and philosophy. Names such as Montaigne, Goethe, Kierkegaard, Dickens, Freud, Jung, and Joyce will perhaps suggest the dominance of such interests. The passage from innocence to experience, the ordering of self-awareness in spiritual autobiography, the generational conflict, coming to terms with authority and life's "givens," the personal quest, the sense that experience has marked seasons—in these are the materials of novel, drama, poetry, personality theory, and of modern self-definition. Most of us can recognize ourselves as *homo viator*.

Persons grow, as natural things grow. But consciousness, its pain and glory, means that persons can refuse to grow, or they can grow in distorted ways. In their persistent quest for themselves, they may mistake the mark. For human beings growth is not something that happens; it is a problem, a responsibility, a venture, and a fulfillment.

With such preoccupations as these having dominated the experience of the West for many generations, it is understandable that rites of the Christian community which take no account of process and of movement toward maturity seem to leave something out. The Church needs to be a place for children, as well as for adults, and initiatory liturgy and categories for its interpretation ought to say so. But the Church needs also to be a place in which children grow up. Should not liturgy be expected to say this too? If so, how? "Becoming a Christian" dare not settle for a childhood stage only. To do so risks settling for arrested development. If the problem of the Christian community in a post-Christian society is not "How can we make more children ritually complete Christians?" but "Why are there not more effective adult Christians?" how does one get from the desired beginning toward the desired end?

Rites in Support of Growth? Questions of personal movement or growth are raised in a curiously mixed setting. The culture is fascinated with development. Studies and interpretations abound, at rigorously academic and at popular levels. We understand ourselves when we understand where we have come from and where we might be going. Yet this same culture is standardized and unceremonial. The industrial West has little in the way of rituals that can help interpret us to ourselves as we grow from childhood to maturity. In a sense, young persons in modern American society are imitative and ritualistic, but the self-chosen rituals are not so much moments of passage into adulthood as they are insignia of conscious, somewhat abrasive collective self-definition against the adult world.

Persons who are aware of other cultures look at this unceremonial character of the West and think it impoverished. The common life lacks structures such as other cultures have had or still have—structures and processes that provide individual and shared meaning. In this comparative view, it seems that life would be richer if we had significant rites of passage. If the culture as a whole lacks them, perhaps the church, as a bearer of meaning, could at least supply them for its members.

Influenced by some thinking along this line, the work of liturgical revision in the Episcopal Church at an early stage gave some attention to passage rites. But it found, as others have, that there is something artificial about the enterprise. When a society has lost its agreed rituals, it has lost something important—something so important that the coherence of the society itself is in question. But can the society (or can a group of experts, acting for it) deliberately contrive rites which will at once be adopted and carry life-interpreting authority? The problem is important. In some way liturgists need to be involved in its exploration. But answers are bound to be elusive. The analysts who see the problem most acutely and are most sensitive to social dynamics may not be very good at filling the lack they detect. Their role can be a little like one person who directs another: "Be spontaneous!" Believable ritual grows out of common living and despairing and rejoicing and hoping and dying. When expressive ritual is lost, can it be intentionally restored or newly devised?

Persons who think about life's passages in today's Western industrial/technological society and the relation such times of passage may have to faith have a difficult assignment. Developmental studies ask how and at what points in life the sense of God emerges and how it grows. But persons are inwardly shaped by social configurations. Social factors which influence a Christian's passage—factors such as coming of age, family structure, child-rearing patterns, employment, the relationship between generations, and the stability of provincial religious and social traditions—vary so much throughout the United States (and even more if one thinks globally) that particular, diverse adaptations may be called for. Who can generalize safely from one's own experience today? Or even from extensive empirical surveys? New styles of life, thought, and community are coming into being. Individual histories and self-understandings vary greatly. In today's complex world, there may be several responsible ways of expressing with integrity the subtle and mysterious process of becoming a Christian. Flexibility, variety of custom, and openness to individual differences may be a realistic Christian response to a changing and varied situation. Christian rituals (like all other rituals) are traditioned actions. They need to show their own integrity and marks of identifiability, but they need also to respond to things that are taking place today which are in considerable measure unprecedented.

The Relationship of the Generations: When the Church asks Christian Initiation (or one part of it) to function as a mark of leaving childhood and entering adulthood, the Church and its past ritual and catechetical experience can bring little wisdom that equips it to deal with the relation between the generations in today's society.

As long as Christendom prevailed, rites of passage could be seen as moments at which young persons moved into patterns of life which, in most essentials, had been determined by, and were represented in the style of the older generation. Young persons would begin doing, in their turn, very much what their parents had done. The adults could look with satisfaction as this socialization process took each fresh step. But such assumptions hardly apply to the complex relationship between generations in today's society. A social critic has written: "Our chief certainty about the life situation of our descendants is that it will be drastically and unpredictably different from our own."[7] Young persons will live in a world for which the model of their parents will be of limited usefulness at best, and at worst it may be positively misleading.

Part of growing up in our time is that children rapidly come into a body of perceptions and ways which separate the young from the old, and often make them critical of the life patterns into which they seem to be expected to grow. Part of adult experience in our time is that, despite themselves, adults come to recognize that they learn significantly from the young. Roles are mingled. Neither is right or wrong against the other. Although the young may reject much of the older generation's ways and wisdom, they often do so on the basis of ideals acquired from that older generation. Adults often feel threatened by the young, yet ultimately many adults have been freed and changed by them. Each generation needs the other; each has difficulty understanding the other; each has been the teacher of the other.[8]

Probably all serious learning is mutual; we are able to teach others at the level at which we are meeting and dealing with our own existential questions; the effort to teach always confronts sensitive teachers with the need to repossess what they have. Teaching and learning are parts of a single process that takes place within and between both instructors and students.

Condescension must be ruled out of order. No part of Christian Initiation ought to appear to be a carefully controlled ritualization by which an older generation seeks to impose its structures upon a younger generation. The facts of the present time are that where Christian community is vital, both old and young, catechists and catechumens, pastors and parishioners, are assisting one another in greater awareness of God, redemption, community, and obedience. The process of "ratifying" in life the meaning of Baptism is not one in which the adults can appear to have dealt with the matter and to wait for youth to do what they have done. The only authority adults have for seeking a response to Baptism on the part of someone else is the authority of those who ask of others only what they ask freshly of themselves.

The Final Authority for Initiation: If life-cycle rituals are desirable and yet are generally missing from our society, their absence is a proper concern for pastors, educators and liturgists. There is a theological base for such ritual: Life is always in relation to God, but for persons of faith the relation draws to points of consciousness and articulateness when life is intense—times of decision, loss, discovery, threat, redirection, and pain. The *sturm und drang* of adolescence is predictably such a period, but not the last such period. Although some turning points may fall into similar patterns for many people, they are not really shared. For the persons involved, each is a unique, individual time when the forces of one's experience concentrate. These are obviously moments in which believers ask with special urgency about God and the divine purpose. One is no longer satisfied by old answers, deep questions lie open; persons are ready to grow, learn, and often to rededicate themselves to God. But if such moments contain opportunity, they also may bring one near to despair. Such experiences are not just things that happen. For a person of faith they are part of the relation to God. God, who may not always have been in one's mind, seems very near. For such times, the church might well seek words and actions whereby personal turning points might be set in the light of the Gospel of Jesus Christ and the Gospel be brought into engagement with life.

But if life-cycle ritual is desirable, is the need well served by dividing Christian Initiation so that one ritual act marks birth and another maturation?

The church is called into being by the Gospel, and its life is bounded and shaped by the sacraments—a foundational, unrepeated rite of entering and belonging, and a regularly repeated rite of sustenance and renewal. These two actions are constitutive of the church and necessary for the Christian as no others are. They are structural elements that one may draw on throughout one's lifetime—both at critical moments and in the orderly, habituated routines that give one something to turn to at critical moments.[9] But they are not themselves intrinsically life-cycle rites. As one writer put it:

> *If there are then to be rituals for the key-moments of the life-cycle they have a form and a meaning distinct from the traditional sacraments. They are rather rites to mark the occasions on which the question of personal passage symbolized in the sacraments is raised within the context of crisis moments belonging to the life-cycle as such.*[10]

The final authority for Baptism—the authority that gives it its universal relevance—is the prophetic Christian message. That message presents itself to us as a mysterious Word with whose otherness we must come to terms. That Word holds the redemption and the judgment of every institution and person which bears it.

For those born under Christian influence, God first meets us in here-and-now terms of birth, growth, parents, community, play, and work—in the love of those near us and in the discovery of an order into which to grow. If ultimately we must encounter God on God's terms, we are prepared by God's self-presentation to us on our terms. In every situation God stands in confrontation and grace, and we can reach toward an appointed future, or else draw back in unfaith.

But God cannot be adequately apprehended through the processes of personal and social life. A God who could be so discerned would be the God limited and defined by natural cycles or the traditions and customs of tribe or family. God, as made known in the prophetic witness, is the God of surprise rather than the predictable God of hallowed rule.

CHAPTER VII

The God who says "I Am" is not answerable to our expectations. The God of the prophets does not necessarily ratify prevailing concepts of home, nation, or personal development. God seems to show a reckless disregard for our schemes of what constitutes orderly religious growth and maturation. There is a subversive divine fondness for the creative nonconformist. We may first encounter God in Christ through our experience of parents, family, congregation, and social order. But the prophetic note of the biblical message implies that God may ask us to differ constructively with the supporting orders to which we stand in debt. We are creatures of time and space, and the awareness of God reaches us through the particular relationships and structures which inform and order our existence. Yet the God who reaches us can call attentive listeners to bring about change in the only social and religious structures they have ever known.

Baptism is a once-for-all introduction to the life in Christ. But it is a beginning which pledges and contains an ongoing relationship and a final ending. We do not go beyond it, but since it is foundational, we can remember it and claim it in new and critical moments. We are always in a sense contemporary with it.

Within the life of the baptized, and its many ordinary moments, there are moments of more than ordinary significance. The church may well provide for the recognition, in shared celebration or public words of commitment, of such things as growth, vocation, and crisis, whenever they come in Christian experience. Such occasions should not be observed as initiatory, but as episodes within the life of an initiate. J.B.M. Frederick warns against confusing rites of growth with rites of membership. "Such rites," he says, "marking the stages in all the varied conditions of life may have a role *so long as they have nothing to do with membership*."[11] The Church's rites do not center primarily on babyhood, parenthood, coming of age, or retirement and growing old. (Grant that they do, and sentimentality runs riot.) But for a believer, all of life's crises may in some creative way be brought into relation to the determinative death and resurrection which is God's own self-declaration. It is there that God's total gift and claim are extended and there that, through the sign of death and resurrection, the total human response is expressed. Thus as persons with ritual and pastoral skills give attention to supporting the critical times of life, they do not work to compensate for the inadequacies of the Church-and-Christian-making sacraments. The sacraments are not well *used* as psychological resources or supports. The sacraments do not need to be made relevant. As centuries of faith would attest, in ways too profound and subtle to be fully understood, they are relevant. The liturgical task, in connection with our troubled careers in faith, is reverently to uncover that relevance.

The rites of Christian Initiation in *The Book of Common Prayer*, 1979 have been asked by history to meet a demanding situation. They must say what the Church says concerning the sacramental starting place, rooted in the Gospel. Yet they must also have the pastoral openness to let them touch supportively, regulatively, and interpretively the varied experience of persons of faith in our time. The next two chapters consider these rites.

CHAPTER VIII

The Prayer Book Rite: Some Principles

Before turning to some general features of the new but old rites of the 1979 Prayer Book, two nontextual factors which influence liturgical life (both of them more than hinted at previously) may be remarked:

First, no church's practice of Christian Initiation is ever entirely a matter of words and rubrics in a book. No baptismal text ever stands alone. It is part of a rich but untidy corporate life and is always supported, and in some respects limited, by teachings and practices which particularize and fill out its meanings, perhaps in partially different ways. Such factors as theologies (in Anglicanism, some of them more adequate than others, but none of them official or definitive); popular understandings; preaching; catechetical handbooks; hymns; the design and location of the baptismal font; ceremonial; art; and role expectations of clergy, parents, and congregations all shape the process of becoming a Christian.[1] All them are part of the reception of a printed rite within the church. Any rite, as it is lived, is a combination of the text itself and the changing and varied things that are done to interpret and enact it.

New official liturgical texts can give important but limited direction. In a matter as significant for interpreting our experience to us as the rites of Baptism are, continuities must hold, even while new directions are being pioneered. But powerful forces, only partly understood, are at work. Liturgical changes can loosen uniform regulations which have come to seem arbitrary. They can open new possibilities where there has been widespread dissatisfaction with old practice; they can preserve, in the midst of change, the essential actions and meanings of the sacraments of initiation. That is a great deal, but it is not everything.

Second, both the Episcopal Church and the society in which it is set are pluralistic; hence the church-society relationship is varied. The church probably must expect, allow for, and learn to enjoy living with differences in baptismal understandings and practices. It is unlikely that any one pattern will be equally applicable everywhere—in the diversely situated provinces of the Anglican Communion, in the somewhat regional patchwork of the Episcopal Church, and perhaps even within a single congregation. In today's complex world, there may be several responsible ways of expressing with integrity the subtle and mysterious process of becoming a Christian.

People are mobile, and customs tend to be regional. Persons accustomed to one practice can quickly find themselves in an area where other practices prevail. It is necessary that the church engage in sustained discourse and that, through pastoral understandings or canons, churchwide norms be understood and observed, especially in matters in which liturgy interacts with sacramental prerogatives. Rights such as admission to Communion upon which one may have entered in one place must not be withdrawn when one moves to another parish or diocese, or to another province of Anglicanism. And of course, within the varieties of practice, there must be a core of recognizable identity, for the Baptism which appears in many guises is one; the rites that carry it out are fundamentally simple; and it is a mark of the Church's unity. But uniform customs and understandings are hardly likely.

The Shape of the Prayer Book Rites:

Several general observations may clarify features of the rites of *The Book of Common Prayer,* 1979—particularly features that would be new to persons familiar with former Prayer Books:

The location of the rite in the Prayer Book and in the liturgical system is an important indication of meaning. Since 1549 the Baptism service had stood first in the section of the Prayer Book often called the Pastoral Offices. These services, which were generally derived from the medieval *Manual,* with generous use of Reformed models, were printed in the Prayer Book in life-stage order, with Baptism standing first. This arrangement was continued in Prayer Books through the 1928 revision. (In that Prayer Book a new division began with its own internal title page, p. 271. Holy Baptism opened that division, pp. 273–282, followed by material for instruction and Confirmation, for marriage, childbirth, sickness, and burial of the dead.) This location in the Prayer Book has suggested that the infant form of Baptism is the expected thing, and the adult form exceptional. In this location Baptism was (except for its proximity to Confirmation) remote from any other rite with which one might seek to connect it theologically.

Insofar as form teaches, the relocation of the Baptism rite in the 1979 Book has something to say. It is now printed (on pp. 297–314) between the Great Vigil of Easter (pp. 284–93) and the Holy Eucharist (pp. 315–409). When on Easter Even they are used together, these three liturgical actions flow from one to the next. Neither the Vigil nor the Baptism rite is complete by itself. The *Vigil* develops its panorama of readings; the eucharistic room passes from darkness to light; the resurrection is announced; and then a rubric on p. 292 hands the liturgical flow on to the *Baptism* rite, beginning at the Presentation of the Candidates. (If there is no Baptism, the Vows of Baptism are renewed, pp. 292*ff.*) Then, after the Baptism(s) and the postbaptismal actions and the reception of the newly baptized (p. 308, and after such Confirmations, Receptions, and Reaffirmations as there may be when a bishop is present), the rubrics on pages 308 and 310 lead to the *Eucharist,* joining it at the Peace, the Prayers of the People, or the Offertory.

The two great sacraments of the Church and the Gospel are thus placed in intelligible relation to one another and to the heart of the Christian Year. These three, taken together (as they are on the printed page all of the time and as they are in action once a year) reassemble the great Paschal unit of Easter-Baptism-Eucharist—the unit which our earlier historical sketch noted as a theologically expressive and ritually powerful creation of the early church. In the layout of its text, the structure of the Prayer Book expresses the structure of the sacramental system. This Paschal center is the organic heart of both.

The location of Christian Initiation in ritual time is implied in the link with the Vigil, but it requires further comment. In the early church, baptisms took place, except in emergency circumstances, at Easter (and at Pentecost, the end of the days of Easter, if required). A Presbyterian liturgical scholar has put it: "Whereas the Supper has clearly been, perhaps since New Testament times, a *weekly* event, the evidence suggests just as clearly that Baptism has been an *annual* event."[2] In later centuries, the association of Baptism with this evangelically significant time broke down in both East and West. Rubrics of the Anglican Prayer Books have made no effort to specify times for baptisms. In practice, most baptisms have been governed, as to time, by when a child was born and godparents could be conveniently assembled.

In the 1979 Prayer Book the location of the rite in the book itself suggests, as noted above, the connection between Baptism and Easter. Not all baptisms will be at the Easter Vigil; but all, regardless of time, take their meaning from this great theological-liturgical-experiential center: the Paschal rites. All baptisms are occasions of union with the risen Christ, and all proclaim the Easter faith. This location of Baptism in ritual time speaks of Christian identity as bringing one into relation to a special time:

> *Baptism, as a rite of entry or initiation, has from the earliest days of the church meant stepping into a new kind of time, and that particular time is bounded by the Lord's resurrection on the one hand, and his return in glory on the other.*[3]

Not only is Baptism printed with the Easter Vigil, but a rubric on p. 312 commends the deliberate control of baptisms so that (as far as can be) they will coincide with appropriate moments in the yearly reenactment of redemptive history. The rubric cites: the Easter Vigil, which speaks of the death and resurrection of Christ against the background of Israel's exodus; the Day of Pentecost, which speaks of the Holy Spirit; All Saints Day (or the Sunday following it), which speaks of the Great Church; and the Baptism of Jesus (First Sunday after Epiphany), which speaks of Jesus' own Baptism by John. The visit of a bishop is also listed as an appropriate occasion for Baptism—of which more will be said in the next chapter. The Christian Year is a dramatic shaping of time into a sustained proclamation of the same Gospel that is enacted in Baptism. When the intentions of the Prayer Book, indicated by this rubric, are followed, the seasons and feasts of the Church Year interpret Christian Initiation, which in turn emphasizes the passing meanings in the Year.[4]

The structure of the Baptism rite itself helps with some past liturgical awkwardness. The Baptism rite as it had stood for centuries in the Prayer Book was rather inadequate when it was used alone. (Since many baptisms were essentially "private," the rite often did stand alone. Many people no doubt thought of it as so intended.) The Baptism service itself contained no creed and only thin scripture readings; it had little role for the congregation; and its language contained many expressions that were not echoed elsewhere in the Prayer Book. It was difficult to compensate for such inadequacies by combining Baptism with something else. It could not be "digested" easily by another liturgical event; it seemed to make a new start within a service already in progress. If one attempted to combine both Baptism and Confirmation with the Eucharist, the liturgical hesitations and repetitions were compounded. The Prayer Books made no provision of propers for a baptismal Eucharist; and the rubric (p. 273 in the 1928 revision), suggesting a setting in the Daily Office, assumed an English custom.[5]

The rite of Holy Baptism in the 1979 Prayer Book is clearly structured as a full congregational service. A rubric (p. 298) directs it to be used "within the Eucharist as the chief service of a Sunday or other feast day." There are participatory roles for the congregation: renewing the common Christian vows, pledging support for the newly baptized, and expressing the church's welcome. Sponsors, specifically, may be readers and offertory bearers (pp. 312f.). The Prayer Book text requires that Baptism be thought of, not just as an event for the individual who is baptized, nor for the family, but rather as an event for the congregation —the congregation representing the whole Church of God to which a new life is being joined.[6]

The liturgical unit is quite complete; the baptismal action is preceded by a full Service of the Word; and it leads into the Eucharist. The central initiatory actions reproduce the "shape" of Baptism, as the church had worked it out in quite early centuries.[7] The point is not that the late 20th-century church should do something simply because it was done that way in the third and fourth centuries. The early "shape" of Baptism, unlike the "shape" of the Eucharist, cannot claim to trace, in some measure, to Jesus and the Gospels. It represents a development made by the Church in its first generations. But it was a brilliant development—clear and economical. One follows it because one still wants to say something about life in Christ that the early church said well and that seems to be said less well when some innovative generation strikes off on its own.

The treatment of the postbaptismal actions is perhaps the most original feature of the rite of Holy Baptism in the 1979 revision. This Prayer Book separates two functions that have been combined in Confirmation as it has hitherto been known in Anglican liturgies and treats each of these separated functions in a distinctive way.

Earlier chapters of this book have traced the dual heritage in Confirmation and identified interior tensions that have come from its complex history. To review the matter for present purposes: One part of Confirmation, the postbaptismal blessing (which was represented in the 1928 Prayer Book by the prayer and action by the bishop printed on the lower half of page 297 in the Confirmation service) is a detached portion of the early church's baptismal liturgy. As such, it is inherently the rite of a moment, done once in a lifetime. The other part of Confirmation is the renewal of the promises of Baptism. (It was represented in the 1928 Prayer Book by the bishop's questions and the confirmands' answers on the lower half of p. 296, continuing to the top of p. 297.) This occasion of public "owning" of the pledges of Christian life was meant to speak for the faithful response to grace. But the learning and growing—and forgetting and starting again—which are a believer's response to the gift in Baptism, are a lifelong process. That response should have a ritual expression appropriate to itself.

The combination of these two significantly different functions in one rite (a rite separate from Baptism and often from the Eucharist) has detracted from each. We look for one expressive moment when a grow-

CHAPTER VIII

ing baptized person should ratify the promises of Baptism (one part of what has been known as Confirmation), and in our time there is no such moment. We seek, at the time of ratifying the baptismal promises, a divine gift which is definably distinct from Baptism (this gift being another part of what has been known as Confirmation), but we seek it in a rite which, in its origin, had no identity except within the completeness of the initiatory sacrament.

The rites of the 1979 Prayer Book make a different combination of these functions, and they let each part develop according to its own character. Baptism is followed immediately by the prayer for the gifts of the Spirit and a signing with the cross ("consignation"), at which Chrism may be used. This prayer and action are done by the bishop when a bishop is present (rubric, p. 298), otherwise they are done by the presbyter who ministers Baptism. In this location, the ancient postbaptismal ceremony is back where it came from and where it makes sense. It explicates and emphasizes baptismal meanings, but it does not take on a separate identity. (This relocation builds on the previous postbaptismal words and actions which, as earlier historical sections have indicated, had, in Cranmer's intentions, denoted presbyteral Confirmation.) The postbaptismal action signifying the Holy Spirit is an integral part of a unified sacramental rite which confers full Christian standing and should, in principle, reach its completion in the baptized person's first Communion and entry on full life in the Christian community.

That aspect of Confirmation which has not been initiatory, but rather catechetical, voluntary, and responsive, is now carried out within the baptismal Eucharist when the bishop is present and there are qualified candidates. (The same occasion and similar prayers also suit those who are received from other churches and those who are reaffirming the promises of Baptism.) This adult "ratification" is enacted in a liturgical context which contains the baptismal promises (at an actual Baptism or not) and ends with the Eucharist.

The vindication of this division of the functions of Confirmation must be found in the rites themselves as they are tested in the practice of the living Christian community, and as they are discussed critically over a period of years.[8] But a few further comments may clarify implications of this reshaping.

Baptism as the One Rite of Initiation:

The simple act of bringing the Spirit-moment (or the consignation, or the anointing) into immediate relation to the water-moment clarifies the completeness of Baptism. As the first rubric of the Baptism Order says: "Baptism is full initiation by water and the Holy Spirit into Christ's Body the Church. The bond which God establishes in Baptism is indissoluble" (p. 298).

This unified rite breaks the two-stage pattern whose logic required that Baptism be considered less than "full initiation." It also breaks the structuring that linked the parts of the baptismal act with moments in the life span. Baptism is not a birth rite. No part of Christian Initiation is by nature an adolescent rite. Nor is Christian Initiation necessarily an adult rite.[9] It is a rite of being joined to Christ and his people. As such it is appropriate, in its wholeness, when proper pastoral conditions are met. It is irresponsible at any life stage when such conditions are not present.

At whatever period of life a person is baptized, the Prayer Book rite is essentially the same, and in every case sacramentally complete. The one Baptism unites persons who come to faith by different routes. Various experience patterns can inform one another. The single, uniform, complete rite of Baptism is an objective sign that membership in Christ and his people is not bound to any one model of personal experience.

It has been noted earlier that the Prayer Book rites have, since the 16th century, placed important words and actions immediately after the baptismal act itself. In so doing, Anglican liturgies have deep tradition behind them. There is an emerging ecumenical recovery of such post-baptismal acts. At the same time that *Prayer Book Studies 26* was issued, the Consultation on Church Union (a long-running interconfessional discussion) put forward a baptismal liturgy for consideration by a group of churches, many of which had, by tradition, turned the New Testament into a liturgical book of discipline and had rejected the "auxiliary rites" that had grown up in connection with Baptism but which seemed to lack clear apostolic warrant. The Commission on Worship of COCU spoke of its proposal disarmingly, citing the authority of history and custom:

For most of the Christian world, during almost all of Christian history, when the candidate emerges from the water, there is some statement or prayer declaring the significance of what is happening, and this has usually been accompanied by one or more visible actions. Such actions generally relate back to what has just been done and forward to the practice of the Christian life in the future.[10]

The postbaptismal words and actions of previous Prayer Books are strengthened in the 1979 revision. Cranmer's indirect Confirmation references in the text are made more specific, and the actions are enriched.

The unified rite of Baptism-Consignation-Eucharist is set forth in the Prayer Book as the standard. Whenever the rite is administered (except in emergency conditions) and to whomever, all of it is administered. It is not liturgically fragmented nor theologically ambiguous. The significance of what has been done in the Baptism rite of the 1979 Prayer Book should not be underestimated. A Roman Catholic scholar, who has followed these developments with interest, has commented:

To a Roman Catholic viewing these revised rites it appears that the rite of initiation has been reunited after its millenium-long fragmentation; the sacraments of Baptism and Confirmation (in the Roman Catholic view) have been joined just as Baptism and Chrismation have always been joined in the Eastern Orthodox liturgies.[11]

In the interior structure of the rite, the prayer for the gift of the Spirit (p. 308) and the acts associated with it express something that is part of the meaning of Baptism, but something which seems to be less clear if it goes unexpressed. There should be no question. In Christian Baptism, all of God is linked with all of a person. All that is pledged for the future is signified at the start.

It is not just the redemptive meanings—forgiveness, new birth, Christ, Church, the Spirit, eternal life—that are declared in Baptism; it is also the commitments of Christian life. Baptism is—or ought to be understood as being—a commissioning for ministry; it is strength for spiritual struggle; it is the ordination of the laity; it is the sacrament of childhood and maturity. It pledges one to "resist evil" and to "strive for justice and peace among all people." It sets one within the people of God, the holy priesthood; it brings one into the eucharistic fellowship.[12] There is nothing in the way of initiatory ritual that must happen later to "complete" Baptism. Baptism is not incomplete.

Occasions of Renewal:

However complete Baptism may be sacramentally, it must always be considered the beginning of a process of participation, growth, and response. It is apparent in the case of infant Baptism that the demonstration of the meaning of the rite must come after it. The child is set within the new order and life. Momentous things are declared in her or his behalf by others. But any conscious difference it will make to the child will come later, if it comes at all. It may not be equally clear that many of the same factors apply in the case of adult Baptism. Adult converts, to be sure, bring articulate faith of their own at the time of Baptism. But faith is not a momentary experience. It is a deeply held orientation of all of life. The faith that underlies the baptismal event can at best be the start of the faith which must underlie the baptismal life from that point on. Momentous things are declared by the candidate at the time of Baptism, but the validation of those declarations will come later, if it comes at all. No Baptism, adult or infant, ought to be carried out without care for the antecedent conditions that make it a responsible act. But every Baptism is also an act of expectation and promise; it looks to what comes after it.

In the terms used by the New Testament and the early Church, anyone baptized was spoken of as newly born. The categories of infancy and age which were characteristically used of baptized persons were not terms of chronological age, but of salvation. The early sources would not have said that the newborn might be baptized; they would have said that all those who were baptized were newborn. Baptism spoke then and speaks now of life begun.[13]

The motivation of Christian life is often expressed as "become what you are." The Baptism rite should say as much as possible about "what you are." It is a summation, at the start, of that which can only be

CHAPTER VIII

fully apprehended at the end. But from the start, the "becoming" develops from the "is." To say much about "what you are" at the beginning, does not remove the urgency from the "becoming." Rather, it sets the process in perspective. From Baptism on, a Christian is always making response to the total, self-giving and claim of God which is declared in the Word and signified in Baptism. The demand for response is continuous and absolute. The actualization of response is limited and partial. At any moment, as much of a baptized Christian as one is capable of committing, responds as fully as one can, to as much of the love and will of God as one knows. Response to God moves in individual ways—gradual or impulsive, with crises, struggles, lapses, and restorations. The baptismal life which begins at the font never ends.

If Baptism is complete, its completeness needs to be remembered, drawn upon, renewed, or made creative in relation to subsequent life moments. An English scholar has put it: "As a rite, baptism is not repeated; but unless it is in its substance continually renewed it might as well not take place at all."[14] The Prayer Book provides expressions for this life of response. The sacramental system is concerned about the process of "becoming" as well as about the declaration of what "is." They are together signs of the "now" and the "not yet" of life in Christ.

Response to Baptism involves the whole texture of life: inward, unsharable depths; thought and imagination; one's conscious awareness of God and one's witness to faith; the relation with others—listening, giving and receiving, forgiving and being forgiven; work, play, citizenship; a passion for justice, and a thousand things. It may be fairly untroubled and fulfilling; and it may be full of doubt and struggle—a lover's quarrel with God. Ritual provides moments which gather up, express, inform, or reorient—routinely, or at occasions of personal urgency—the meaning of that constant response.[15]

The aspect of Confirmation that has spoken for one's conscious response to God's goodness—the renewing of the promises of one's Baptism—is intrinsically a repeatable act. The Prayer Book now allows it to develop in various modes of repetition: some routinized, and some quite unpredictable.

At least three *routinized* times of renewal may be observed in the Prayer Book text:

■ Every Eucharist is a renewal of Baptism. It is a repeated declaration of and sharing in the great redemptive reality which is enacted in an unrepeated way at Baptism. Such a connection between Baptism and the Eucharist—between being born and being fed—is largely left implicit in the liturgy. But the Prayer Book has at least two places in which a communicant can see the relation of the Eucharist to Baptism. In the first postcommunion prayer in Holy Eucharist II (p. 365), the congregation says to God:

> *You have graciously accepted us as living members*
> *of your Son our Savior Jesus Christ,*
> *and you have fed us with spiritual food*
> *in the Sacrament of his Body and Blood.*

By these words the act of spiritual feeding is connected with a prior act of acceptance and membership. (Fortunately, the language is indirect; the connection is as explicit as a worshiper thinks it is.) To cite another link, in the epiclesis of Eucharistic Prayer C (p. 371), the celebrant says, "...we who have been redeemed by him, and made a new people by water and the Spirit, now bring before you these gifts." This central prayer of the Eucharist recalls the prior reality of Baptism. But the bond between Baptism and Eucharist does not depend on explicit Prayer Book references. Both the sacraments are a participation in the same fundamental reality of the living Christ. For those who sense the relationship, Baptism, the sign of redemption once given, and Communion, the sign of redemption ever renewed, complement one another eloquently.

■ Another routinized time of renewal is when one takes part in the baptism of another. At each Baptism, one's own Baptismal promises are spoken freshly. In a deep identification, another's "yes" to God is said again for oneself. One's own past and future are made present. The active, vocal role of the congregation is bidden by the celebrant: "Let us join with *those* who *are* committing *themselves* to Christ and renew our own baptismal covenant." The already baptized community makes its own the promises of the one who is now being baptized and claims freshly the gift in which its life is constituted.

■ A third regular occasion of renewing the Baptismal Covenant is at the yearly Vigil of Easter. It was noted above that the Vigil is a powerful dramatization of the unity of the Gospel sacraments. As it rehearses the scripture-based saga of redemption, it passes to Baptism, and finally culminates in the first Eucharist of the Day of Resurrection. There may, of course, be baptisms at the Vigil, but even when there are not, "The Renewal of Baptismal Vows" is a part of the service (pp. 292–94).[16] A new people, free from Egypt, and sustained by bread from heaven, is bound in a new covenant of grace and obligation.

Perhaps the act of confession and absolution should be added among these routinized occasions, for although the liturgical system of the Episcopal Church provides for its private and individual use ("The Reconciliation of a Penitent," pp. 446–452), it is probably most often encountered as a part of certain structured, corporate liturgical events. Here, as in the Eucharist, the connection of the act with Baptism is largely implicit—although the form for confession on p. 450 refers back to Baptism, and the second of the baptismal promises, p. 304, refers ahead realistically to repentance. But the connection between the two is clear. Each time a Christian acknowledges his or her sin and is met by the unfailing forgiveness of God, this event in the life of a believer reenacts the repentance and faith, the renunciations and promises, and the dying and rising of Baptism. It is a fresh claiming of the grace of Baptism and a renewal of the baptismal condition.

The term "routinized" should not sound negative. It simply denotes occasions which belong to the ordered life of worship and which come before the members of a congregation with some regularity. These liturgical occasions can say much for us, if there is much within us needing to be said, and they can prompt within us things we did not know we were prepared to say. Liturgy can work from the inside out and from the outside in.

But in addition to these routinized and corporate liturgical events, some individualization of the renewal of Baptism seems desirable. Confirmation was thought to provide something of the sort—an occasion of dedication suited to a critical stage of one's life. But Confirmation tended to be regimented and rather pressured in many parishes. Moreover, it was one's only opportunity for a renewal of baptismal promises.

If that was an adult thing to do, one did it before one had much experience of adulthood. There might be better times for a solemn rededication of oneself. Perhaps some such times might come long after adolescent years. If the renewal of the promises of Baptism is a good thing for an adult Christian to do once, why might it not be done more than once? The response to grace is infinitely varied. Important events in one's conscious relation with and service of God happen throughout one's life span.

The late Urban T. Holmes, in his valuable small book, *Confirmation: The Celebration of Maturity in Christ,* drew a useful distinction between rites of *passage* and rites of *intensification*. The former bring one into a new status, and they are not repeated. The latter relate one to authoritative past moments; they are times of re-creation which may be repeated. Dean Holmes regarded Confirmation and all other modes of renewing the vows of Baptism as rites of intensification.[17]

The 1979 Prayer Book opens the renewal of baptismal vows as a rite of the sort Dean Holmes called intensification, an act usable in some *nonroutinized* circumstances where it expresses the deep stir of the Spirit in the unpredictable, unschedulable life in grace.

The Prayer Book identifies three such *nonroutinized* occasions. All are done at a visit of the bishop, and all are woven into the baptismal rite and use the common united affirmation of the promises of Christian faith and life.

■ The *first* of these nonroutinized occasions is *Confirmation*. The text is given in the Prayer Book within the Baptismal liturgy, pp. 303 and 309*f.,* where it fits smoothly when, at a Bishop's visit, there are baptisms as well as confirmations. The pertinent material is repeated in the Pastoral Offices, pp. 412–419, in a form suitable to a service where persons are confirmed, but no one is baptized. Both of these settings include, along with the liturgical material for Confirmation, the material for Reception and for Reaffirmation.

This rite provides words and actions by which persons who were "baptized at an early age" may make "a mature public affirmation of their faith and commitment to the responsibilities of their Baptism." This initiative of the confirmand is met by "the laying on of hands by the bishop."

It is a rite "expected" of such persons "when they are ready and have been duly prepared." This wording of the rubric leaves a great deal as to age and readiness up to the judgment of local pastors (who in many cases will be acting in the context of diocesan guidelines). The dropping of the "confirmation rubric" which had stood on page 299 of the 1928 Prayer Book, and which had been in all previous American and English books, was noted in an earlier chapter. With this deletion and with a history of decisions made prior to 1979 concerning early Communion, Confirmation is not a prerequisite for Communion. No sacramental privilege depends on this rite; it does not create an elite within the baptized community. The thrust of these directions should be to reduce, if not to eliminate altogether, the regimentation that has often marked the administration of Confirmation in a congregation. (All of the 5th graders every year!)

Yet the rite is to be "expected." This renewal in the gift and commitment to the responsibilites of Baptism ought to be something sought by a baptized and communicating Christian who would like to declare on her or his own something that had been received passively since childhood. Significant things happen in the religious experience of young people. The Church's ritual should be prepared to create conditions in which they can be recognized and named when they happen, and to welcome and celebrate them, but not to compel them nor to program them.

■ A *second* occasion of public renewal of the baptismal covenant by one who is brought to this act by individual biographical events is termed *reception*. (The text is on pages 310 and 412–418.)

It is to be used for persons who were baptized and who have come to mature faith in another Christian communion, but who wish now to carry out the commitments of their baptism in the responsibilities and satisfactions of the Episcopal Church.

This act recognizes the baptism already received in another part of Christ's Church: "We recognize you as a member of the one holy catholic and apostolic Church." A change in church affiliation marks discontinuity in one's experience. But if the change is from one baptizing Christian community to another, there should be, in the midst of the change, a recognition of the antecedent and continuing relation to God in the Church—the Church one, though divided.

The Episcopal Church has always gained a large portion of its members from other churches, but its official liturgy has had no provision for an act of reception. The formal act has often been carried out with dignity, cordiality, and pastoral understanding by the bishops; but now the Prayer Book itself not only provides a text, but it implies a theological account of meaning. One signifies an identification with the Episcopal Church, not by consenting to some peculiarity of doctrine or polity, but by renewing, before a bishop, the common Christian rule of faith. And one is received "into the fellowship of this Communion" by the bishop, the chief pastor of the diocese, the fundamental unit of an Episcopal Church.

There is need for pastoral judgment in this rite. Some persons who were previously baptized in another communion come to the Episcopal Church as part of their discovery of Christian faith. Their life in their former church was at no more than a nominal level. Other persons who come from other churches, however, are making the change as part of an intelligent, informed quest. In other words, they come to the Episcopal Church as persons who have not merely been baptized in another church, but who have grown into genuine Christian adulthood while related to that former communion. Such persons should be "received" as competent, practicing Christians. Those who were baptized, but little else, in their former churches are, in coming into the Episcopal Church, doing what the Prayer Book describes as Confirmation. Even though they may have been baptized many years before, they are for the first time making "a mature public affirmation of their faith and commitment to the responsibilities of their Baptism." They should be Confirmed.[18]

■ The *third* of the nonroutinized occasions for renewing the promises of Baptism is *reaffirmation*. (The text is on pages 310 and 412–419.)[19]

The provision for "reaffirmation" (new in the 1979 Prayer Book) is not tied to any one occasion of life, but is open to development as pastoral imagination sees its applicability to the lives of Christian persons. It is not initiatory, but it brings to expression critical moments of Christian life. This pastoral rite has little real history or model in parish life.

144   CHAPTER VIII

How it may be used is being roughed out now in the experience of individuals and of congregations. An earlier chapter of this book remarked the discontinuous nature of much Christian experience in today's society and the past inability of the church's pastoral rites to give ritual recognition to this struggle, interruption, and recovery. Rather frequently today baptized persons have some kind of religious awakening of such authority that they would like to be baptized again. "The first time meant nothing to me," they say. Of course, the Baptism should not be repeated. It is witness to God's involvement in one's life, whether the divine presence, discipline, and love are recognized or not. We are not baptized into anything as transitory as an experience. But when our awareness of Baptism and the faith of which it speaks has its moments of discovery—a thing that may happen more than once—our part of Baptism can be stated freshly in the reaffirmation of the solemn, inexhaustible promises of Baptism.

There is no requirement that this provision be used in any individual's life in the Church; and there is no reason why, if it is used once, it may not be used more than once. As a repeatable act, it suits occasions of return to Christian faith and practice after a time of lapse; it is available to celebrate moments of discovery in the spiritual life, or of dedication to new forms of the life of obedience, or of life-moments of personal significance.[20] There may be soul-searching and tears behind it. But by the time it comes to public expression in the liturgy, it should be celebrational. Usually the circumstances that lie behind an individual's wish to make this act of reaffirmation will be known in a congregation; but sometimes they may not be of the sort that can be fully shared. Bishops are understanding in what they say and what they leave unsaid, and a congregation of Christian people need only know that one of its members is making a self-declaration whose circumstances are only partly public knowledge; but the joy of that individual is entered into by all.

These functions—Confirmation, Reception, and Reaffirmation—use the promises actually made at a service of Baptism (or if there is no Baptism, they use the promises made by the baptized congregation, BCP, pp. 416–17). The persons having these special intentions are presented and identified early in the rite (pp. 303 or 415), and when they are presented, the Bishop asks them if they renew their renunciation of evil and their commitment to Jesus Christ. Thus it will be known that the baptismal covenant, when it is said by all is said by them with a more than ordinary weight of meaning. But apart from answering these two questions these persons have no special words to say. The common words of promise are regarded as seriously intended by all who say them. No one asks these specific persons, "But did you really mean them?"

This liturgical provision for personal response and affirmation may have flexibility suitable for our varied and changing experience. A renewal of baptismal promises, made before the Bishop, is not associated with any one designated moment of life; it can be used at any age; and it can be used more than once. No special status or privilege attaches to it. It imposes little and allows much.

Four pastoral and liturgical notes may be added to this account of principles of the Prayer Book rites:

(1) At an early stage of drafting the texts for the Prayer Book, it was proposed that the term "Confirmation" be dropped. It is neither ancient nor universal. Moreover, as this study has noted, it has come to be understood as designating two quite different things: (a) the post-baptismal laying on of hands, and (b) an occasion of adult owning of the promises of Baptism. Since in the rites that were being proposed these two components of traditional Confirmation were being divided and treated differently, it seemed that confusion would be avoided if neither were given the old name. New terms appropriate to the character of each of these two actions might be sought.

Further, it should be clear from the foregoing discussion that the persons who are presented to the Bishop for Confirmation, for Reception, and for Reaffirmation of Baptismal Promises are all doing essentially the same thing: at a critical moment in their Christian experience, they are renewing vows that belong to their fundamental standing as baptized persons within the life of Christ and the Church. It was not clear that the first time of doing something that is by its very character a repeatable action should have a distinctive name.[21]

But in the printed form of *Prayer Book Studies 26* the title "Confirmation" made an unobtrusive appearance, and it came into greater prominence as the rites moved toward adoption. Beginning with a text issued in 1975, the persons presented to the Bishop were distinguished by the three categories they have in the Prayer Book, one of them called "Confirmation."

These changes had more to do with the process of adopting the rite than with establishing a clear rationale for it. At no time were they subjected to serious churchwide discussion. One could argue that the retention of the term "Confirmation" and the attachment of it to the catechetical rite rather than to the postbaptismal rite (if it had to go to one rather than to the other) causes more confusion than clarification.[22] One could reply, of course, that unless there were a ratification rite, episcopally administered, and clearly called "Confirmation", the rites might have failed adoption.[23]

(2) In the past, the rite of Confirmation, generally speaking, stood as a dividing point between generations in the life of the church. Although probably no adult put it in such words, as a gesture it seemed to say to adolescents, "When you are confirmed, you will be mature, adult Christians, just like us." A statement of this sort is heavy-handed whenever it is said, but it is a particularly unfortunate signal to send to young persons who are at an age when disillusionment with the older generation begins in earnest. Confirmation seemed to be a ritual divide between those who had not yet arrived and those who had. In the present liturgical provision, the renewing of baptismal promises is not only something that the older generation expects of the younger; it is something that baptized Christians of any age may do. It recognizes the unfinished condition of all Christians. This provision may ease the abrasive relation that exists (in both church and society) between the generations. Since it is one form of the renewal of baptismal promises, Confirmation will ask the Church's young people to do—solemnly, before the bishop—what the Church's adults do or stand ready to do, as occasions in their lives suggest its appropriateness. This act of reaffirmation, by its repeatability, is not so much a mark of the separateness of the generations as of their unity and mutuality in the growing life of faith.[24]

(3) As rites with innovative features took shape, the drafters' thought processes (as well as comments from others) raised inevitable questions about liturgical authority, about bonds with other Anglican

churches, and about loyalty to long Prayer Book tradition. When change is proposed in a continuous tradition, the present touches the past; moments of origin call for fresh examination. The material in earlier chapters should have indicated some of the recent inquiry which seems to suggest a large measure of continuity between current revision and Prayer Book origins. Cranmer's two Prayer Books sought to emphasize the completeness of Baptism by bringing sacramental Confirmation (not, however, called by that name in those texts) into the total baptismal complex of signs. The historical evidence also indicates that Cranmer thought of the rite that carried the name Confirmation as an occasion for ratifying the promises of Baptism before the bishop and receiving the "increase" of a Spirit given in Baptism. In the light of history and theology, these general intentions seem as defensible now as they were in the 16th century. If these were the aims of the Prayer Book tradition, they would seem to be carried out more adequately and clearly in the Prayer Book of 1979 than they were in either of the Books that came from Cranmer's hands.[25]

(4) The third section of Chapter V raised two practical questions concerning Confirmation:

(1) *"Who shall be confirmed?* and
(2) *"Who shall minister Confirmation?"*

It was proposed there that, because of the dual character of Confirmation, each question was really two questions:

(1a) *"Who shall receive the postbaptismal seal of the Spirit?"* and
(1b) *"Who shall make formal ratification of the promises of Baptism?"*

(2a) *"Who shall be the minister of the postbaptismal prayer and consignation [and anointing]?"* and
(2b) *"Before whom shall persons make formal renewal of their baptismal promises?"*

Although these questions were raised in Chapter V, the character of the Prayer Book answers was only intimated. How are these questions answered in the initiatory rites of the 1979 Prayer Book?

(1a) **Who shall receive the postbaptismal seal of the Spirit?** The postbaptismal laying on of hands [and anointing], with prayer for the Holy Spirit, is given to persons as soon as possible after their Baptism. Ordinarily it is part of the baptismal rite and takes place only moments after one's Baptism. (In cases of Baptism under emergency circumstances or by a deacon, rubrics on pages 312 and 314 deal with subsequent supplying of this postbaptismal act, which is regarded as a priestly ministry.) The rite is administered because it is part of Baptism, not because one has qualified for it by age or achievement.

(1b) **Who shall make formal ratification of the promises of Baptism?** The restatement of the promises of Baptism is done frequently by Christian worshipers either by using the full promises, as at a Baptism service which one attends, or by using such liturgical prompters as the Eucharist or the Apostle's Creed or confession and absolution.

In a formal way, arising from one's individual circumstances, the promises of Baptism may be renewed:

■ by persons baptized at an early age who have taken no previous occasion to make a mature public affirmation of their faith,

■ by persons who were baptized in another church and who are identifying with the Episcopal Church, and

■ by baptized Christians who, for a variety of reasons, would like to restate publicly their pledges of faith and to claim freshly the gift in which those pledges stand.

None of these acts of renewal is initiatory. They are done by persons who have prior standing as baptized members of the Body of Christ.

(2a) **Who shall be the minister of the postbaptismal prayer and consignation [and anointing]?** The minister of these postbaptismal acts is a bishop or a priest. They are done in the baptismal liturgy by a bishop if one is present (rubric, p. 298), otherwise by the priest who is the minister of Baptism (rubrics, pp. 298, 304). (If chrism is used, it shall have been blessed by a bishop, p. 298.) In case of Baptism by a lay person or a deacon, this portion of the rite is omitted, to be supplied later at a service at which a bishop or a priest presides (p. 312).

(2b) **Before whom shall persons make formal renewal of their baptismal promises?** The formal renewals of the promises of Baptism, in their different forms, are made before the Bishop (pp. 303, 309f. and 412–419). The persons making these acts of reaffirmation are presented to and questioned by the bishop; then (following the Baptisms, if there are any) the bishop leads in a prayer for them, meets each one with an appropriate gesture, and prays for each by name.

The bishop as chief pastor is, in his person, the sign of the organic connectedness of the diocese, and the one through whom the life of the Church most obviously widens into the historical tradition and the present worldwide Christian community. The bishop confirms baptized persons who are making public confession of their faith, receives baptized persons from other communions, and responds in the name of the church to the reaffirmations made by adult Christians. The effect of this liturgical provision (plus the second rubric on p. 412 of the Prayer Book) is to bring all members of the Episcopal Church, in a manner appropriate to the situation of each, into pastoral contact with a bishop. The rites based in the individual, formal renewal of the covenant of Baptism bring the episcopal ordering of the Church very close to each of its members.

The historical, theological, liturgical, and pastoral rationale by which this set of answers might be understood has been set forth in preceding chapters. It remains to look in closer detail at the Prayer Book rite by which the principles set forth in this chapter are carried out.

CHAPTER IX

The Prayer Book Rite: A Commentary

The rites of the 1979 Prayer Book to be discussed here fall into two clusters: one is initiatory, words and actions by which persons are brought into the Christian community; the other marks events in the lives of individual baptized Christians.

(1) The rite of Holy Baptism (pp. 297–314) begins with a service of the Word, followed by the presentation of the candidates and questions to them. (The congregation joins in some of the answers.) After brief prayers and a thanksgiving over the water, the Baptism follows. Next is a prayer for the Spirit, the consignation [and anointing], and a welcome, after which the service joins the eucharistic order.

The parts of this service comprise a liturgical unity. If a bishop is present, the bishop presides, and certain parts of the rite are specifically the prerogative of the bishop. But more often than not, the rite in its entirety is led by a presbyter. (A rubric on p. 298 advises what parts of the liturgy are to be carried out by what ministers, clerical and lay.) Although this service is used in any parish several times a year, it would be used only once to baptize any Christian person. It contains the actions which give full sacramental standing within the people of Christ and access to the eucharistic life. It represents a gracious acceptance which God does not retract and whose sign is not repeated.

(2) The other cluster (pp. 309–10 or 413–19) comprises the actions done by and for those already baptized persons who are being Confirmed, or Received, or who are Reaffirming their baptismal promises. These actions are only done when the bishop is present. All of these are rites for adult, communicant Christians, but not for any age or stage within adulthood. They provide an opportunity to express, within the gathered community and before the bishop, some of the moments of restoration, recognition, and new beginning which mark the stir of life.

These two clusters of actions are so designed that they may conveniently be used together. When they are combined, the bishop presides over the entire sequence of actions, assisted by such other ministers as may be appointed. The promises that are renewed are those which are said in the order for Baptism with which the sequence of acts begins. The Eucharist follows, beginning at the Prayers of the People or the Offertory. For this combination of the two clusters, the rite as printed on pp. 299–311 (with due attention to the rubrics) is well suited.

The printed form of these rites must allow, however, for occasions on which there may be baptisms, but no reaffirmations of baptismal vows, either because a bishop is not present or because no persons are prepared for this special observance (in which case the material on pages 299–311, is usable, omitting the portions marked with a line in the left margin).

On other occasions there may be persons prepared for Confirmation, Reception or Reaffirmation, when the bishop is present, but when there is no one to be baptized. In that case, the vows, which are those of the baptismal order, are supplied in the service printed on pages 413–419.

The comments which follow speak in turn of the material belonging to these two clusters:[1]

A. Holy Baptism

Opening Versicles, Collect, Lessons, Sermon:

The rite opens with a doxology in dialogue form, which contains lines (from Ephesians 4:4–6) that set the baptismal tone. It proceeds to a service of scripture, psalmody, and preaching, which is structured like the service of the Word of the Communion order. (A rubric on p. 312 suggests that the *Gloria in excelsis* may follow the versicles. This canticle in this location provides a festal opening, and it duplicates another feature of the opening of the Eucharist.) On a Sunday or other feast, the collect and readings are those of the day. The tone of the opening of the liturgy would be that of the season or feast. On other occasions, the propers may come from the splendid group appointed for use "at Baptism," printed in the Lectionary, p. 928.

The opening of the rite with scripture and preaching signifies that Baptism is an enactment of the Word. Prior to the act of Christian Initiation stands the Gospel, its proclamation and its hearing. The readings and preaching at Baptism set this sacrament within the context of God's redemptive work and the faith and mission of the Church. Baptism is something the Church does for an individual, but as a thankful participation in something God has first done for the race.

A rubric allows for the sermon to come after the Peace. Ordinarily preaching immediately follows the scripture readings, but the presence of infants and small children may make this a bad place for a full sermon. Yet the location of the sermon after the Peace has disadvantages too. (Is anyone likely to be ready for serious listening immediately after the baptismal action and the Peace?) Perhaps a brief homily is advisable within the service of the Word—a homily that seeks to take account of the children. Or the children to be baptized may be brought into the church after the sermon and before the presentation.[2] If the Baptism falls on one of the major feasts, as the rubric on p. 312 commends, this calendar day may be the principal occasion in the year for preaching on one of the great themes of faith. The rubric invites the exercise of judgment.

Presentation of the Candidates:

The custom that persons coming to Baptism be presented by someone who sponsors them in their steps of entry traces to the early church. A trusted believer would vouch for the good intentions of an inquirer and otherwise assist in his or her later progress. Hippolytus speaks of candidates as "brought" to the church, and he says that "Those who bring them shall bear witness for them."[3] In subsequent centuries other meanings have been placed upon sponsorship.[4] In our mobile society, it is often difficult for sponsors to maintain close relationships with a godchild even though he or she is someone they truly care about; but the sponsors do not stand alone; they personalize the already baptized community and the responsibility it must take collectively for the initiates, before, during, and following their Baptism.

A bishop who is present at a Baptism presides. Candidates are presented to the bishop; and the questions are directed to the candidates, the sponsors, and the congregation by the bishop. In the absence of a bishop, candidates are presented to the priest.

The adults and the older children are presented, individually and by name, by their sponsors. The fact that they are mentioned in the printed text and dealt with in the action of the rite first is a reminder that Baptism was an adult rite before it became a rite for the children of the baptized. The place of adults has priority. The candidates who can answer for themselves indicate, by their response to the question directed specifically to them, that Christian Baptism is something they willingly seek.

Infants and younger children are then presented by their parents and godparents. Those who cannot make the baptismal commitments for themselves will be dependent on the communication of the love, order, and support of God to them through others. Their own growing life of trust, love, and obedience will begin by being imparted through older Christians. The fact that others speak for the child in this liturgy is not a ritual fiction; rather it expresses the reality that will prevail through many formative years.

The godparents, speaking for themselves, promise (in terms more significant than those in former Prayer Books) the Christian nurture of the one they present.

CHAPTER IX

Renunciations:

A part of an initiatory rite is a separation from a former loyalty or condition.

In early generations of the faith, the renunciation of "Satan, his works and his pomp" doubtless had specific reference to pagan religions which were regarded as manifestations of the great Deceiver. But in any cultural and religious situation, adherence to the one God implies rejection of all rivals.

But evil and the struggle against it are perceived differently in different ages. The three renunciations in this rite correspond generally to the traditional (but not early or medieval) threefold rejection of the devil, the world, and the flesh. All of these terms had become so trivialized in common American piety that it seemed to the drafters of the rite that it would be more misleading than clarifying to use them as they had stood in the past. Of course, old terms that speak of enduring realities can be explained, but a liturgy is no place in which to explain. Yet neither is it a place in which to continue the use of devalued terms.

The phrasing in the Prayer Book renunciations is meant to relate the heart of the persistent distortion of God's purpose to terms of modern experience. The first refers to a basic unmanageability in history. A discreative power is at work. "There was a war in heaven" (Revelation 12:7). At times, as persons living in this century know, monstrous evil prevails. But evil is not due to a few people who are particularly wicked. Even with good intentions, destructive things are done, and we all consent in that perversion of life. At times we are its partisans. In some early stages of revision, the term "Satan" was dropped; but on reconsideration, it was restored. No doubt some Christians think of a personal devil, and others do not. It is possible to take the Adversary lightly while conceiving him in personal ways; and it is possible to take the power of evil very seriously while thinking of it in impersonal terms. The traditional name is probably not offensive, regardless of the sophistication of one's theology, and it carries much religious and cultural weight. The second renunciation refers to the ordering of human affairs, on large and small scales, in ways that oppress and demean persons and misuse God's creation. We become skillful in supporting such systemic wrong by deeply held structures of justification; we are unreliable judges of ourselves. So the third renunciation turns from things outside us. It refers to that within us which mistakes our own good, finds evil attractive, and assigns final allegiance to something less than God. The complex experience of evil is represented in this threefold negation.

The rubrics of the Prayer Book are written so that these renunciations will be said by the adults who are being baptized and by the sponsors who speak for the children. They are not part of the promises of Baptism which are shortly to be said by all. But so much of the dialogical portion of the Baptism rite is now joined in by the congregation that in use these words are often said by everyone. The practice surely does no harm, even though that is not the intention of the text. It expresses the wish of the congregation for maximum vocal participation.

Occasionally sponsors are reluctant to say these renunciations in behalf of a child—feeling (although the words do not say so) that these terms carry the idea of inherited guilt, or that they sound like repentance for a sort of sin in which the young child has taken no part. But the renunciations, as much as the promises, look to the future. In a moral world, saying "yes" to God requires saying a correlative "no" to all that stands against God. The sponsors' words anticipate the realities of mature, committed life.

Profession of Faith and Commitment:

The congregation now takes a vocal, responsible part in the action:

It promises to support the persons who are being baptized. They cannot carry out the baptismal commitments alone. One grows in faith within a community of those from whom one receives and to whom one gives.

The baptized persons who are present also take occasion to renew their fundamental orientation to the great realities witnessed in this ancient rule. The celebrant bids the congregation, "Let us join with *those* who *are* committing *themselves* to Christ and renew our own baptismal covenant."

The term "covenant" has not been familiar in the liturgy or the theological discourse of Anglicanism. By contrast, it has carried a great deal of weight in some Presbyterian circles in which the church has been identified as a covenant people, pledged to covenant life. But the term is the property of no Christian group; it has a deep biblical background, and it can become significant in the function it occupies in the present Prayer Book.

A "covenant," in Old Testament terms, was a two-way agreement between God and Israel: "You will be my people, and I will be your God" (Exodus 29:45; Ezekiel 37:27; 2 Corinthians 6:16). But it was not entered upon by equals. The initiative lay with God—in what God had done toward Israel. The role of Israel was as a party called to make an adequate response:

> *Hear, O Israel. I am the Lord your God, who brought you out of the land of Egypt....*
> *You shall have no other Gods before me."*
> *(Exodus 20:2f.; Deuteronomy 5:1,6f.)*

What Jews owed to God, and to one another, and to the stranger within their gates was because of what God had first done.

This pattern is reproduced in "The Baptismal Covenant" of the service of Holy Baptism in the Prayer Book.

The first part of this formulary is the Apostles' Creed, spoken as a series of questions and answers. This symbol grew up (in regionally varied, oral form at first) in the earliest Christian generations as a distillation of the apostolic preaching. At first it was a part of the lore which the Christian community concealed from unbelievers. This was the faith to which new Christians committed themselves at the very moment of their Baptism and which would be explained to them from this symbol in the days following Baptism. This credal formulary has thus been associated with Baptism and with the commitments of a Christian from the time of its origin.

The Apostles' Creed celebrates the divine redemptive action in Jesus Christ, which the Church confesses, and in which confession the individual Christian stands. It is in three sections, giving it a broadly "triadic" form. The first paragraph speaks of the Father and of creation; the Creator and the Redeemer are one. The next and longest section is a summary of the apostolic preaching—the oldest stratum of the New Testament witness. This central section speaks of Christ in a series of short clauses emphasizing verbs: "conceived..., born..., suffered..., was crucified..., buried..., descended..., rose again..., ascended..., is seated..., will come again." God has taken action centrally in one life, under the conditions of human history—"in the days of Pontius Pilate." Yet that person, who was one of us, is the divine bearer of redemption. The third section of the creed was the least firm in the early texts; it is comprised of nouns: the Holy Spirit, the Holy Church, forgiveness, the resurrection, and eternal life.

In the Order for Holy Baptism in Prayer Books of the Episcopal Church prior to the 1979 revision, the Creed itself was not used. The candidates (answering for themselves, or their sponsors answering for them) were only asked: "Do you believe all the articles of the Christian faith as contained in the Apostles' Creed?" (If the baptism took place in the setting of the Office, the Creed would have been included in the combined liturgy.) The present rite uses the full text of the Creed.

Following the Creed, five promises are made, articulating the believing response to the redemptive initiative of God. They pledge the candidate to: (1) faithfulness in the Christian fellowship and its characteristic practices (using a list from Acts 2:42), to (2) the struggle against evil (including the realistic awareness of possible failure, and the good news that divine grace is always at hand for sin among the baptized), to (3) the duty and joy of mission, proclaiming the Good News "by word and example," to (4) a relation of loving service to other persons, seeing them as Christ, and to (5) the use of social structures in the pursuit of justice, peace, and mutual respect. These promises are stated simply, but they identify some of the deep commitments inherent in the baptismal life.

The Creed and the promises associated with it are followed by a short litany (pp. 305–306) for those entering on Christian faith and life. This litany and the collect with which it concludes hold important themes within a compact structure. Beginning with a request that the candidates may be delivered from sin, the prayer passes to a request that they may be open to God, that they may continue in the life of faith, love others, witness faithfully in the world, and come to the final peace and glory of God. The concluding collect turns "the mystery of faith" (BCP, p. 363) into prayer. This part of the liturgy merits the kind of attention it seldom gets, for it goes by quickly.[5]

A rubric (p. 312) suggests that these petitions be led by one of the sponsors. If the action of the rite has not begun at the font, the movement to the font now takes place—perhaps in a formal procession, during which the litany on p. 305 might be sung or said, or a suitable psalm, hymn, or anthem might be used. (The rubric suggests Psalm 42, whose opening image was used of Baptism by the early Christians, "As the deer longs for the water-brooks, so longs my soul for you, O God.")

Blessing of the Water:

Introducing the action by a call to give thanks, the bishop, or in his absence the priest, blesses the water of the font (pp. 306–307). This prayer of consecration is, on the model of Jewish blessings, expressed in thanksgiving. It asks what it does for ourselves on the basis of a grateful acknowledgment of what God has done for us.

It draws on the water imagery that threads the biblical saga. Texts for the comparable prayer in Prayer Books from 1549 through the 1928 edition made no use of the Old Testament imagery of water—a repository of material in which the typological mind of the early church found abundant baptismal references. In the spirit of the biblically saturated imagination of the early church, the present prayer finds symbols for the interpretation of its own rite in the story of the Spirit upon the waters at creation, in the account of passing through the water at the Exodus, and in the event of Jesus' baptism in the Jordan river by John the Baptist. Centrally, however, Christian Baptism is understood by the Pauline teaching (Romans 6:1–11) that it is death and resurrection with Christ. The prayer also alludes to the baptismal commission from the end of St. Matthew. This baptismal event and this water are set in a large context of creation and redemption.[6]

Following its precis of the biblical imagery, the prayer turns to the water in the font, and it speaks of the present action of the Holy Spirit to sanctify the water and sustain those who are baptized in it. A rubric bids the celebrant "touch the water" during this prayer.

[Blessing of the Chrism: Anointing has not been a specified part of the baptismal services of the Prayer Book since 1549 (when, as has been noted, the presbyter anointed the newly baptized, but the bishop did not anoint at Confirmation). However, whatever conviction there had been against anointing has moderated in recent decades. Chrism has become fairly widely used, and there seems to be little feeling that it should not be permitted, as long as its use is not required.[7] The 1979 Prayer Book allows for the blessing and use of chrism. A bishop who presides may bless the chrism (p. 307) for use at this service.[8] Chrism so blessed may be used by the priest when Baptism is administered at other times.

The prayer takes its imagery from Christ, the Anointed One. The very term "Christ" means "the Anointed," as does the derivative "Christians." In Luke 4:18, Jesus' ministry is spoken of as carried out by the promised anointing of the Spirit of the Lord, and Acts 10:38 speaks of Jesus as anointed with the Holy Spirit. Generally, anointing was used to designate publicly persons who were appointed by God as kings or priests. This prayer follows Acts 4:27 in specifying Jesus as anointed to be "servant," thus drawing attention to the evangelical paradox of the servant-king. This striking imagery of anointing, like the imagery of water in the previous prayer, links the Christian initiatory rite with Christ and his redemptive significance.]

The Baptism:

At this central action of the rite, the text (p. 307) follows the traditional rubrical directions to the minister concerning the manner of Baptism, and it uses the ancient trinitarian formula. The candidate is named, identifying each person's uniqueness. The solemn "triadic" wording expresses the link of each baptized person with the fullness of God's own life.[9] The congregation's "Amen" is a sign that it participates in this act of Christ through his Church.

The rubric speaks first of immersing the candidate in the water and alternatively of pouring water upon the candidate. This assignment of first place to immersion as the mode of Baptism is old in the rubrical tradition. Some Episcopal churches seem to be moving toward baptizing, at least on some occasions, by immersion; it does carry the imagery of dying and rising. (In the ancient world, however, burial was not necessarily descent into the earth; it might mean placing a body in a stone wall or scattering earth on a body). The number of churches practicing immersion is no doubt small. Other modes carry other imagery—imagery no less freighted with baptismal significance. (The rubric does not speak of "sprinkling.") From early centuries, practical considerations have allowed modes other than immersion to stand as fully acceptable.

Although most liturgists are practical and sensible, most of them commend the use of more water rather than less. The baptismal water is already a token of the death-dealing, vivifying, world-cleansing reality for which it stands. To use a minimum amount of water at Baptism carries out the action by a token of a token. A Lutheran comments, "It is irrelevant to ask how much water is necessary for Baptism to be efficacious. The point is, rather, how much water it takes for us to realize the radical nature of Baptism." She remarks that "to communicate central baptismal imagery, a font should contain enough water that one *could* bathe."[10]

[With respect to the actions that immediately follow Baptism, the rubrics introduce possibilities:

A rubric on p. 313 deals with space and movement. It suggests that, if the location of the font has taken the ministers, the sponsors, and the newly baptized persons away from "the front of the church," this is the point at which they might return. The prayer and actions which follow the baptism(s) would be in full sight of all. It is suggested that Psalm 23 or a hymn or anthem might be used at the time of this movement. The imagery from the 23rd Psalm of still waters, anointing the head with oil, and a table spread by God delighted the early church at baptismal occasions.

Following the Baptism(s), the rubrics (p. 308) allow a choice. Either: (1) After all have been baptized, and each adult has returned to a place with the others, and each child has been given to the parents or sponsors, the bishop or priest "at a place in full sight of the congregation," prays for the gifts of the Spirit and then goes to each person, giving the sign of the cross (using oil if desired). Or else: (2) While each adult is at the font or while the minister is holding each child, the minister gives the sign of the cross (and anoints) each one. Then, after all are baptized and signed, the minister prays for the gifts of the Spirit. The use of one order or the other—prayer for all, then individual action; or actions, followed by general prayer—is largely a matter of convenience.

Another rubric on p. 313 suggests that "after the Baptism" (conveniently indefinite as to precise sequence) "a candle (which may be lighted from the Paschal Candle) may be given to each of the newly baptized or to a godparent." This simple gesture introduces into the ritual action the image of light and enlightenment which was pervasive in the early church's baptismal hymnody and preaching.]

A prayer for the gifts of the Spirit (p. 308) has time-hallowed associations as an intercession for the newly baptized. In the Prayer Book tradition, through the 1928 revision, this prayer had been the bishop's prayer in the Confirmation service. Its origin can be traced at least to the rites described by Hippolytus and by Ambrose of Milan; its text appears in the Gelasian Sacramentary; in the early sources it is the bishop's prayer at the postbaptismal actions.[11]

The seven gifts of the Spirit, as they had passed through sacramentaries and Prayer Books, had become somewhat homogenized. The gifts sounded rather like one another. The gifts are based on a list in Isaiah 11:2 of characteristics needed by and granted to a wise and peace-loving king. The Hebrew text cites six gifts; the list of seven depends on the Greek version of the Old Testament and on the early Christian fondness for the number seven. The Christian use of this prophetic text to describe Jesus and Christian character is very old. It is a way of saying that by the Spirit, all baptized persons are admitted to spiritual royalty. The present prayer is a fresh paraphrase of the sources. It begins, in the manner of Jewish prayer, with a recital of what God has done. Then it asks for gifts and graces of the Spirit, in a list with greater precision and variety than hitherto.

The signing [and anointing] is an act of the bishop (whether the bishop has performed the baptisms personally or not); if the bishop is not present, it is done by the priest.[12] The minister's hand is placed on the recipient's head, and a cross is marked on the forehead (using chrism if desired). This signing with the cross, technically known as "consignation," represented a restoration by Archbishop Cranmer of an early and catholic, but non-Roman practice. It has been a continuous part of Anglican baptismal practice since the Prayer Book of 1552.

At the time of the signing, the celebrant says, "N., you are sealed...." "Sealing" is not a term with a history in the liturgical vocabulary of Anglicanism. But it is a useful designation for that portion of what has been known as confirmation which now is part of the baptismal rite. The "seal" suggests branding or stamping something so that it can be identified as belonging to its rightful owner. (There is graphic imagery of persons who are protected by being marked on the forehead in Ezekiel 9:3–8.) From very early times, Christians spoke of themselves as sealed by the Holy Spirit—as marked as God's possession until all who were God's own were claimed at the day of redemption. This figure is used, but hardly developed in the New Testament.[13] In later generations, it became a common expression for one of the meanings of the rites of Christian Initiation.

The bishop or priest continues: "N., you are sealed by the Holy Spirit in Baptism and marked as Christ's own forever." The words "in Baptism" (which entered the text at a late stage of the revision process) can be troublesome.[14] Although they are used at the signing (and anointing), they refer to a sealing by the Holy Spirit that takes place "in Baptism." If one thinks of "Baptism" as referring narrowly to the water action which has just taken place and of the "seal" as referring to the consignation (and anointing) which is now taking place, these words which associate the seal with the former action make one wonder why the later action is called for at all.[15]

But these words need not be taken in such specific senses. The term "Baptism" can (on ancient and authoritative precedent) refer broadly to the complex action which as a whole is an effective sign of the forgiveness of sin, union with Christ and the Church, the gift of the Spirit, and the pledge of eternal life. That is the sense which the words "in Baptism" should carry here. The Prayer Book is not interested in distinguishing a water moment and an anointing moment and assigning certain meanings to one rather than to the other. That could seem like the sacramental and liturgical legalism which has bedeviled Western discussion of Baptism and Confirmation for centuries. Rather, all is Baptism; all is seal. Meanings interpenetrate, for they speak of the unitary life of God which is joined to the unitary life of one of us in a complex, but coherent sacramental action.[16] To specify the gift of the Spirit as belonging to one point in the rite would impose restrictive definitions on the varied practice and the symbolic, nonlinear categories of the early centuries.

Yet the early church's postbaptismal sealing is an appropriate feature of Christian Initiation. It is part of the enacted *kerygma* of the sacrament. Anointing or signing with the cross are gestures of interpersonal physical contact which express some of the meanings of Christian membership and life.[17] But it is very desirable that all the postbaptismal actions, once again, be as close as possible to Baptism, so that it may be clear that they explicate parts of the rich, unified meaning of becoming a Christian.

Bidden by the Celebrant, the minister and the people welcome the new members into God's household (p. 308) and encourage them to continue in the service to which they are called.

If Confirmation, or Reception, or the Reaffirmation of Baptismal Vows is not to follow, a rubric on p. 308 directs that the Peace be exchanged. The liturgy then joins the eucharistic order, beginning at the Prayers of the People or the Offertory. These acts represent the point in the early church's rite which began the "mass of the faithful." For many months, the catechumens had been dismissed at the end of the service of the Word. But now, as newly baptized members, they took part in the characteristic actions of "the faithful" —the kiss of peace, the people's prayers and the people's offering, and receiving the Body and Blood of Christ. The peace, the intercessions, the offertory, and the meal are actions of the collective life into which a person is being incorporated.

A rubric on p. 313 says that the offerings of bread and wine at the baptismal Eucharist may be (Is it excessive to hear the rubric saying "It is certainly hoped that they will be?") presented by the newly baptized or by godparents. This simple direction links the baptismal action with the eucharistic action. Clearly, the act of offering is connected with the act of receiving. This rubric implies that baptized adults are expected to receive communion and that children sponsored by the godparents are part of the eucharistic community. When persons who were crucial in Christian Initiation (as persons who were baptized or as sponsors) are also prominent (as offertory bearers) in the eucharistic action, the connection of the the great sacraments is unmistakable.

If for any reason the rite of Holy Baptism is being observed apart from the eucharistic setting, the material on page 311 indicates ways of bringing the service to an adequate conclusion.

B. Confirmation: with Forms for Reception and for the Reaffirmation of Baptismal Vows:

Baptism declares what God has done, is doing, and will do for a person brought into the community which shares in divine life, order, and love. It is the basic sign of a relation with God that promises life abundant and everlasting.

Most persons, at Baptism, make the fullest response to God they are capable of making at the time. It is a sign of repentance and faith. Both godparents (who speak for a child) and adult converts (speaking for themselves) try to enter into what the Church means by Baptism, insofar as they grasp it.

But the baptismal life, which begins at once, is never simple. Children have a lifetime in which the relation with God, declared in their behalf in infancy, is a factor in the tumultuous business of growing into responsible adulthood, facing education, coming to terms with sexual maturity and (not always) marriage, seeking a vocation (and at times finding more than one), and assuming an authentic lifestance. The conscious relation with God may remain a creative, governing force in life —but there is no certainty that it will. Persons who are baptized as adults bring to their Baptism, along with much trust and idealism, many misunderstandings about what is involved in being a Christian. The life of faith on which they enter will have surprises and difficulties; it will require constant death and resurrection. Faith sometimes diminishes, at times to revive. Christian experience is usually somewhat inconstant—not necessarily through individual failure so much as through the sheer obstacles a sin-structured social order sets in the way of believing. But the awareness of God sometimes grows in sudden accesses of insight and clarity; a deeper relationship is entered, and new obligations and new disciplines are accepted.

The rites in this second cluster provide for and encourage the liturgical expression of some of the deep joy and serious rededication that mark the stir of the Spirit in every vital congregation. The rites provide a basic liturgical and theological structure which can help interpret ritually some of the significant moments in Christian experience.

These non-initiatory rites are only used when the bishop is present.[18] They may be used in connection with actual baptisms (in which case, the text on pages 303 and 309*f.* is followed), or they may be used when there is no Baptism (pages 412–19).

Versicles, Collect, Lessons, Sermon:

The structure of this opening portion of the rite (pp. 413–415) is the same as that on pages 299–301 and commented on above. When there are the various forms of renewal of vows, but no baptisms, special collects and appropriate readings (Lectionary, BCP, p. 929) are appointed and may be used (at the discretion of the bishop). The rubric on page 298 directs that the bishop is expected to be the preacher of the Word at this service.

The Presentation and Examination of the Candidates; the Baptismal Covenant:

Following the sermon, the candidates are presented to the bishop in the groups designated. The bishop asks them if they reaffirm their renunciation of evil and renew their commitment to Jesus Christ. (The renunciations, in the full form given on p. 302, are not restated by the persons presented.) The candidates reply that they do. As in the Baptism service, the bishop asks the congregation to promise its support to these persons in their life of faith, and he asks all to join in renewing the common baptismal covenant—the Creed and the five associated pledges.

The Prayers for the Candidates:

The bishop bids the people to pray for those who have renewed their commitment to Christ (p. 417). When the forms of renewal are used in combination with Baptism, the Prayers on pages 305–306 would, of course, be used. When the renewals are used without Baptism, these prayers might be used; the rubric referring to them is permissive—"may." A rubric also mentions a period of silence. Presumably prayers from elsewhere in the Prayer Book or prayers composed for the occasion might be used in this place.

[A word about space and movement:

Often a great deal goes on at this service, and in a limited space. When the forms of renewal are used together with Holy Baptism (pp. 299–310), it is important that each action and the group of persons connected with it be given unhurried time and adequate visibility. At the time of the baptism(s), the candidates and the sponsors, with the officiants, will occupy the center of attention. A rubric on p. 313 commends placing all of these persons at the time of the Baptism so "that the people may have a clear view of the action." (They should be near the font, but not completely surround it.) The persons being Confirmed or Received, or making Reaffirmations, with their sponsors, would at this point be unobtrusive. They will have been presented, and thus have been identified early in the service, p. 303, although they have no special role for a time.

But when the Baptisms are over and the newly baptized have been welcomed (p. 308), the part of the liturgical action in which these persons figure is concluded. Other actions and another group of people become central. A shift in location may take place. The persons who have been associated with the baptismal action retire from the central place, and the bishop and those on whom the following actions will focus take a front and center location in the room, the candidates standing clearly before the bishop—not necessarily near the font.]

The bishop's prayer for these persons (p. 309 or 418) begins with a compact but full thanksgiving for redemption. It speaks of God's work in Christ and the restored relation it brings about—"you have brought us to yourself." Coordinate with this thanksgiving, the prayer turns to the sealing of the Spirit whereby Christians are bound to God's service. Thus the divine work for us and the divine work in us—the good news and the ethical obligation—are linked. The petition asks that the covenant made with these persons at their Baptism be renewed in them. This request is made to God, by whose initiative the covenant was brought into being and by whose faithfulness it is made freshly. Such language traces to the Jewish Scriptures in which the covenant that identifies Israel is entered into solemnly; it is often violated, and it is often renewed.[19] Within the faithfulness of God and the givenness of redemption in Christ, old commitments are freshly restated. On this theological basis these persons renew their promises. The prior thanksgiving portion of the prayer had spoken of the baptized as "bound to your service." The petition picks up the theme of service—"the service you set before them." Life in Christ is life to some purpose. This God-given work is carried out in the power of the Spirit.

Following this prayer, the bishop turns (pp. 309*f.* or 418*f.*) to the persons in the three groups which had been presented (p. 303 or 415). Three categories are distinguished in the Prayer Book, and a slightly different prayer is provided for each. Although these persons are baptized adult Christians, all of whom are doing the same thing—renewing the promises of Baptism—they represent rather different sorts of Christian experience. The bishop will usually recognize the groups separately and speak to each in an appropriate way.

In Confirmation, the bishop is to lay hands on and to pray by name (a feature not in the parallel prayer in previous Prayer Books) for each person. There is a choice of prayers. The first is a tightly worded prayer, new in the 1979 Prayer Book, which speaks of God's service, an element that was no more than implied in the earlier prayer of Confirmation. The second is the Confirmation prayer common to all Prayer Books since 1552.

In Reception, the bishop's words are not a prayer, but they begin as an address (again by name) to the person being received. They recognize the person as a member of Christ's Church, there is a brief expression of reception "into the fellowship of this Communion," and a concluding sentence of blessing: "God, the Father, Son, and Holy Spirit, bless, preserve, and keep you." No manual gesture by the bishop is required or forbidden.

The circumstances in Reaffirmation may be quite diverse, so the words provided for the bishop cannot be very specific. They cite the beginning of God's work in this person, alluding to Philippians 1:6. They then speak of carrying forth that purpose in a life of service, and they look to the Spirit's future directing and upholding. Again, the bishop's words are spoken to the person, who is addressed by name; and no gesture is specified.

These actions of covenant renewal are summed up in a general prayer (p. 310 or 419) by the bishop. This prayer's use of the image of God's protecting hand is eloquent at the conclusion of a ritual in which hands have been important. The rite passes to the Peace, at which point it joins the Eucharist. The bishop is to be the principal celebrant.

The rubric (p. 309, repeated on p. 418) prescribes the laying on of hands (plural in this book—"The bishop lays hands upon each one") as the bishop's gesture at Confirmation. While no specific gesture is required or forbidden at Reception or Reaffirmation, to make no gesture at all seems inadequate. Even in social encounters, at times of welcoming or greeting or well-wishing or leave-taking, we usually mix words with actions. On occasion, when words are difficult, actions may be the more communicative. Many bishops, thinking of the laying on of hands as an appropriate gesture for Confirmation, Reception, and Reaffirmation, lay hands on the persons in all three of these groups.[20] Neither for those who were baptized in the Episcopal Church nor for those who were baptized in another church is this liturgical act meant to supplement or complete that earlier baptism as though otherwise it were defective. This non-initiatory rite provides a pastoral opportunity for the church, in the person of the bishop, to meet in appropriate ways persons who are at turning points in their journey in faith and in their relation to the church. The thing that is done (by the church, the bishop, and the individuals involved) draws on the basic sacrament of the union of God with persons of faith: Baptism.

These three episcopal actions will often be in a larger context. The Prayer Book sets forth the bishop's parish visitation as a rich liturgical event, the bishop presiding, in which the church is present to itself, celebrating the fullness of its life under God. This liturgy envisions Christian Initiation and the associated rites of renewal creating a sacramental and pastoral role for the bishop beyond that which has been customary in most parts of the Episcopal Church. Writing some years ago about "the reconstruction of the initiatory liturgy," Massey H. Shepherd commended changes that would "restore to the bishop his presidency and office in the *total* initiation of the Christian, and not just in that part we call Confirmation." He continued:

> *Indeed, I should go so far as to say that there is more meaning in the episcopal office, succeeding from the apostles, when it is viewed as a mission to preach and baptize than when it is restricted to a duty to visit and confirm.*[21]

Liturgy can be an important factor in exhibiting the meaning of episcopacy.

Note has been taken of the rubric (p. 312) which calls for Baptisms to be "as far as possible" on several specified major feasts of the church year "or when a bishop is present." The bishop especially represents, in and to the church, the familial unity of the diocese, the larger community of faith beyond the diocese, and the older church that traces to the apostolic witness. Bishops carry the sense of the church's past, and they lead it in its mission today. A visit of a bishop in itself creates a major occasion.

The matter might be put this way: One who is curious about what the Episcopal Church is can, of course, study and inquire. But to come to church on a Sunday or major festival when the bishop is present would provide a visible demonstration of the Episcopal Church in action. The church would be present to itself, standing before God, carrying out its most constitutive actions, and making its deepest declarations of faith.[22]

There would be a complex, but unified and orderly event at which the bishop presides (p. 298):

■ This ritual event will have been in long preparation. The adults who are to be baptized have come through the stages of the catechumenate. This act is one of the most intentional steps of their adult lives. They have prepared for this moment by self-scrutiny, rethinking, and fresh learning. There seems to be no end to the joy and the demand of this new faith. The parents and sponsors of children being baptized have similarly devoted time to serious consideration under God of their responsibilities. Young adults who have decided on their own that they should declare themselves as capable and intelligent persons of faith; persons who are finding, with joy and discovery, a new and chosen church home; adults who have come to a turning point in their religious experience—all have been getting ready with learning and prayer for this occasion. The self-dedication of these persons has been contagious. Anticipation has grown in the congregation for many weeks.

■ The bishop has come. The occasion is carried out with as much splendor as the resources of the congregation permit. The liturgical event itself opens with a service of praise and scripture, at which the bishop preaches the Word of God (p. 298). The Church is a people under the Word. It owes its being and continuance to acts of God whose primary witness is the Bible. In representing that biblical faith to the church, the bishop is teacher.

■ Persons, both adults and small children, are presented to the bishop for Baptism. The bishop asks the adults if they desire Baptism and the godparents if they will support the children. The renunciation of evil is made by the adult candidates and by the sponsors who speak for the children. Others are then presented for Confirmation, Reception and Reaffirmation. The bishop asks them questions appropriate to their status as baptized persons. The Church is a community which grows as new persons come to God through it in repentance and faith. It is a community engaged in conflict with evil and committed to discipline. Its members experience growth, struggle, modest success, failure and fresh starts. This vital human engagement with God, with the church, and with the world is presented before the bishop, who then asks the congregation to pledge its support for "these persons in their life in Christ."

■ As the entire congregation joins in the Baptismal Covenant, the deep confession of faith and the commitments of life that bind all Christians are spoken freshly. For some it signifies coming to a new faith, and for others these vows have often been repeated. All use old and general words, aware of present and particular significance.

■ The bishop gives thanks over the water [and, by ancient prerogative, consecrates the chrism]. The Baptisms (of adults and of children) take place next—the bishop usually delegating this task to the local priest. Following the Baptisms, the bishop prays for the Holy Spirit to sustain the newly baptized, and then signs [and anoints] each one by name. The congregation welcomes the newly baptized.

■ Then the newly baptized and their sponsors step aside, while the persons presented earlier for Confirmation, Reception, and Reaffirmation come before the bishop, who, after prayer, deals appropriately with:

> (1) *persons who had been baptized at an early age (in the Episcopal Church or in some other), but who now voluntarily take on their adult spiritual responsibilities,*
> (2) *persons who had been baptized and who had come to mature faith in some other church (and are therefore fully initiate Christians) and who now wish to carry out the responsibilities of their baptism in the Episcopal Church, and*
> (3) *baptized Christians who, for a variety of reasons, wish to celebrate an important moment in their life of faith by reaffirming the promises of their sacramental beginning point: Baptism.*

The visit of the bishop provides occasion for the quiet miracles of grace that take place in each congregation (but which often are well-kept secrets) to be celebrated.

■ The Peace of the Lord is exchanged—among people some of whom have been Christians for ten minutes and some of whom may have been Christians for eighty years. If this act in the liturgy has become somewhat perfunctory, on this occasion it is not.

■ Beginning with the Prayers of the People or the Offertory (at which the newly baptized or some of those who have acted as sponsors are presenters) the entire community proceeds to the Table of the Lord. The bishop, as the principal celebrant (p. 419), voices the Great Thanksgiving. In sharing in the living Christ, the congregation experiences concretely its oneness with him and with one another. The community of faith goes forth in peace to love and serve the Lord.

Notes

Chapter I: *Some Basic Theological Meanings*

1. Neville Clark, "Christian Initiation," in *Studia Liturgica*, 4 (1965), p. 161.

2. Keith Bridston, ed., *One Lord One Baptism* [Faith and Order Commission Report on the Meaning of Baptism], World Council of Churches, Minneapolis: Augsburg Publishing, 1960, p. 56.

3. The performative character of liturgy means that it characteristically uses the immediate, presentational language of metaphor rather than the secondary language of discursive explanation. Thus there can be a number of partially differing theological accounts which arise from and are renewed and corrected by one liturgy.

Chapter II: *A Sketch of Historical Development*

1. Flemington, W.F., *The New Testament Doctrine of Baptism*, London: S.P.C.K., 1957, p. 49, where the author has gathered passages which link Baptism with the Word and with belief or hearing.

2. The implied reference to Pentecost is included when the incident is referred to again in Acts 15:8, "And God who knows the heart bore witness to them [the gentiles], giving them the Holy Spirit *just as he did to us.*"

3. In Acts 19:1–7, a group at Ephesus had received the Baptism of John the Baptist, a rite which belonged to the old age, not to the age of the Spirit. When these persons were baptized in the name of Jesus, and Paul laid his hands on them, "the Holy Spirit came on them." Here again the pattern of actions seems dictated by a specific missionary situation and is not meant to represent a first-century ritual norm.

Reginald Fuller has commented that "These passages cannot be used as evidence for Confirmation as an apostolic rite. ... The separation of the laying on of hands in Acts 8 has nothing to do with the Western medieval separation of Confirmation from Baptism but is due rather to Luke's redactional interest in subordinating each successive new stage in Christian mission to the Jerusalem church and its apostolate." "Christian Initiation in the New Testament," in *Made, Not Born,* University of Notre Dame Press, 1976, p. 14. On this passage, see also O.C. Edwards, "The Exegesis of Acts 8:4–25 and Its Implications for Confirmation and Glossalalia" in *Anglican Theological Review,* Supplementary Series, No. 2, 1973, pp. 100–112. The author says, "There is no passage in scripture that was intended by its writer to prescribe Confirmation as a second stage of Christian Initiation after Baptism for the purpose of conveying the Holy Spirit" (p. 110).

Illuminating comments on the variety of baptismal patterns in Acts can be found in J.E.L. Oulton, "The Holy Spirit, Baptism and Laying on of Hands in Acts," in *The Expository Times,* LXVI (1955), pp. 236–240, and in C.S.C. Williams, *The Acts of the Apostles,* London: A. & C. Black, 1957, Appendix 3, "The Giving of the Spirit."

It is only in these places (Pentecost, Acts 2:4–13; the house of Cornelius, 10:46; and Ephesus, 19:6) that the Book of Acts mentions the manifestation of speaking in tongues, and only the first of these is spoken of as "Baptism with the Holy Spirit" (Acts 1:5). The author of Acts seems to represent these as inaugural and unrepeated events in the life of the church, rather than as ecstatic experiences for the individual.

4. 1 Cor. 1:16, Acts 16:15, 33; 18:8. See the remarks of J. Jeremias on "The *Oikos* Formula" in *Infant Baptism in the First Four Centuries,* Philadelphia: Westminster Press, 1962, pp. 19–24.

5. E.C. Whitaker's *Documents of the Baptismal Liturgy,* 2nd. ed., London: S.P.C.K., 1970, opens with an essay (pp. xiii–xxii) arguing generally that the anointing in the Syrian rites was exorcistic and preparatory. But others differ. See, among others, Gabrielle Winkler, "The Original Meaning of the Prebaptismal Anointing and Its Implications" in *Worship* 52 (1978), pp. 24–45 and Sebastian Brock, "Studies in the Early History of the Syrian Orthodox Baptismal Liturgy," in *Journal of Theological Studies* 23 (1972), pp. 16–64.

Texts of early rites are in Whitaker's *Documents.* L.L. Mitchell, *Baptismal Anointing,* London: S.P.C.K., 1966, surveys the postbaptismal practices in all parts of the early church.

6. There are four sets (double sets) of these baptismal addresses, all of them in good, but sometimes not very accessible English editions. A handy introduction to them as a group is Edward Yarnold, S. J., *The Awe-Inspiring Rites of Initiation:* Baptismal Homilies of the Fourth Century, Slough, Bucks.: St. Paul Publications, 1971. After a synopsis of the initiatory rites, this work gives texts from Cyril of Jerusalem, Ambrose of Milan, John Chrysostom, and Theodore of Mopsuestia.

7. E.C. Whitaker, *The Baptismal Liturgy,* London: The Faith Press, 1968, p. 38.

8. See Jeremias, *op. cit.,* pp. 87–91, and M.F. Wiles, "One Baptism for the Remission of Sins," in *The Church Quarterly Review,* CLXV (1964), pp. 59–66.

9. Augustine's mental processes can be observed in the early part of Book I of "On

the Merits and Forgiveness of Sins, and on the Baptism of Infants." See the chapters on Augustine in N.P. Williams, *The Ideas of the Fall and Original Sin,* London: Longman, 1929; and, as a statement of Augustine's doctrine as a proclamation of grace, see the article by E.R. Fairweather, "St. Augustine's Interpretation of Infant Baptism," in *Augustinus Magister,* pp. 897–903.

10. Whitaker, *Documents,* p. 121.

11. *ibid.,* p. 222f.

12. T.C. Akeley, *Christian Initiation in Spain c.300–1100,* London: Darton, Longman and Todd, 1967, p. 67f. See also Mitchell, *op. cit.,* pp. 131–143.

13. Mitchell, *op. cit.,* p. 125. See also the study of the early medieval Gallican documents, J.L. Levesque, "The Theology of the Postbaptismal Rites in the Seventh and Eighth Century Gallican Church," in *Ephemerides Liturgicae* 95 (1981), pp. 3–43.

14. Whitaker, *Documents,* ch. 10; and Mitchell, *op. cit.,* pp. 143–154. The best sources for investigating these developments from the early initiatory rites are Dr. Mitchell's book and J.D.C. Fisher, *Christian Initiation: Baptism in the Medieval West,* London: S.P.C.K., 1965. Canon Fisher devotes full chapters to Spain, Gaul, northern Italy, and the British Isles.

15. See Fisher, *op. cit.,* especially ch. VII, "The Shortening of the Interval between Birth and Baptism," pp. 109–119.

16. *Dialogue Against the Luciferians,* ch. 9, written in the East, but presumably reflecting Western custom.

17. Whitaker, *Documents,* p. 229f.

18. Letters IV.9 and 26.

19. Johnson, *English Canons* (1850 ed.), vol. 1, p. 415.

20. Fisher, *op. cit.,* pp. 120–140. See also the article by W. Lockton, "The Age for Confirmation" in *The Church Quarterly Review,* 100 (1925), pp. 27–64. Although the early portions of this article are somewhat out of date, it contains a great deal of fascinating historical information about the medieval period which is not readily located elsewhere.

How was an age such as seven determined? A recent investigation remarks:

> It is now clear that the "age of reason" or "age of discretion," typically identified in Roman Catholic sources as around the age of seven to ten years, is less a determinate stage of psychological maturity than a juridical-psychological convention. Thus under Anglo-Saxon law a child who reached the age of seven could no longer be sold into slavery, while under Roman Law a child of that age became liable for criminal acts. In general it was the age at about which children began to

mix with adults in medieval life and work.

Mark Searle, "Infant Baptism Reconsidered," in *Baptism and Confirmation* [Alternative Futures for Worship, vol. 2], Collegeville, MN: 1987, p. 51.

This book came to hand too late to be used in the preparation of this volume. It contains pertinent information and insight.

21. The factors cited here are only part of the complex story of the disintegration of the initiatory rites in the medieval West. The fullest account is Fisher's book already cited. Canon Fisher has given a summary in his chapter, "History and Theology," in M. Perry (ed.), *Crisis for Confirmation,* London: S.C.M., 1967. There are important insights in Nathan Mitchell, "Dissolution of the Rite of Christian Initiation," in *Made, Not Born,* pp. 50–82. A pioneer examination of these matters is J.G. Davies, "The Disintegration of the Christian Initiation Rite," in *Theology* 50 (1947), pp. 407–12.

22. Edward N. West, "The Rites of Initiation in the Early Church," in K. Cully (ed.), *Confirmation: History, Doctrine, and Practice,* New York: Seabury, 1962, p. 13.

23. *Summa Theologica,* III, q. 72, especially a.1 and 5–7, and q. 65, a.1. The crucial phrases by which St. Thomas explains the distinctive meaning of Confirmation came to him by way of (to abbreviate) Peter Lombard, Gratian, the Forged Decretals (where words are wrongly attributed to a Pope Melchiades), and perhaps ultimately Faustus of Rietz. There is a good brief discussion of Thomas in Nathan Mitchell, *op. cit.,* pp. 66–70.

24. Luther's best-known comments on this point are in "The Babylonian Captivity of the Church," specifically in the opening paragraph of the section "On Holy Baptism."

25. See the fine gathering of material in J.D.C. Fisher, *Christian Initiation: The Reformation Period.* London: S.P.C.K., 1970.

26. *ibid,* sections 33 and 51. A comment of Luther's is, "I allow that Confirmation be administered provided that it is known that God has said nothing about it, and knows nothing of it, and that what the bishops allege about it is false" (quoted here from Fisher, p. 172).

27. *ibid.,* p. 258.

28. Arthur C. Repp, *Confirmation in the Lutheran Tradition.* St. Louis: Concordia, 1964. Describes varieties of development in Lutheran thinking about Confirmation.

29. In the phrase "believers' church" there is some noble courage insofar as it affirms the church's spiritual independence from the state. There is also a measure of arrogance insofar as it implies that the folk-churches of Europe were without believers, while the sects, formed on the principle of self-selection, were the true churches.

On this strain of Protestant thought, good historical and constructive work can be found in H.F. Littell, *The Anabaptist View of the Church:* A Study in the Origins of

Sectarian Protestantism, Boston: Starr King Press, 1958; and George Williams, *The Radical Reformation,* Philadelphia: Westminster Press, 1962; and D.F. Durnbaugh, *The Believers' Church:* The History and Character of Radical Protestantism, New York: Macmillan, 1968.

Specifically on Baptism, see A. Gilmore (ed.), *Christian Baptism,* Philadelphia: Judson Press, 1959; G.R. Beasley-Murray, *Baptism in the New Testament,* London: Macmillan, 1963 (particularly the final chapter); and the same author's *Baptism Today and Tomorrow,* New York: St. Martin's Press, 1966.

The sectarian idea of the church pioneered the modern conviction that the church derives none of its authority from the state. Ironically, this sense that the church is not a creature of the state, but derives its prerogatives from God—an idea which took form in Radical Protestantism—was the starting point of the Catholic revival in the 19th-century Church of England. "Did the state make us? Can it unmake us?"

30. It is widely known that in 1533 (and thus well before the first Prayer Books) Princess Elizabeth was baptized by the Bishop of London when she was three days old and immediately anointed ("bishoped") by Cranmer. This incident indicates that, at least when a bishop was at hand, late medieval practice allowed for the union of Baptism and Confirmation.

31. See Lockton, *art. cit.,* pp. 54–64.

32. Marion J. Hatchett, "Thomas Cranmer and the Rites of Christian Initiation," unpublished dissertation, General Theological Seminary, 1967. This original, meticulous work brought together Cranmer's medieval and Reformation sources for his rites of initiation and sought to establish his theological and liturgical intentions. It has provided much necessary historical groundwork for the Prayer Book revisions of recent years.

33. John Taylor, "Christian Initiation in the Church of England Since the Reformation," in Basil Minchin (ed.), *Becoming a Christian.* London: Faith Press, 1954, p. 14.

34. See S.L. Ollard, "Confirmation in the Anglican Communion," in *Confirmation,* vol. 1. London: S.P.C.K., 1926, pp. 176–223.

35. See *ibid.,* p. 220. Bishop Wilberforce's confirmations "set a standard which was gradually followed in other dioceses until it became, as it now is, the normal use." For this period, see Peter Jagger's *Clouded Witness: Initiation in the Church of England in the Mid-Victorian Period, 1850–1875.* Allison Park, PA.: Pickwick Publications, 1982.

36. See Julien Gunn, "Bishop Hobart's Emphasis on Confirmation," in *Historical Magazine of the Protestant Episcopal Church* 24 (1955), pp. 293–310.

Chapter III: *The Situation Now: The Breakdown of 'Christendom'*

1. Karl Rahner, "The Present Situation of Christians: A Theological Interpretation of the Position of Christians in the Modern World," in *The Christian Commitment: Essays on Pastoral Theology.* New York: Sheed and Ward, 1963, p. 23.

2. Walter Ullmann in *The Individual and Society in the Middle Ages,* London: Methuen, 1967, pp. 7ff., has an analysis of the way in which the understanding of Baptism in the Middle Ages was adapted to imply citizenship. The rite which conferred personhood in the church also brought one into the public order and made one subject to its laws. The universal church was also the universal political order.

3. J.M.B. Frederick, "The Initiation Crisis in the Church of England," in *Studia Liturgica* 9:2 (1973), p. 150.

4. William H. Willimon, "A Liberating Word in Water," in *The Christian Century,* March 22, 1978, p. 305.

5. A splendid historical survey, with attention to liturgical and pastoral structures, is E. Glenn Hinson, *The Evangelization of the Roman Empire.* Macon, GA: Mercer University Press, 1981.

6. See Walter Buehlmann, *The Coming of the Third Church:* An Analysis of the Present and the Future of the Church. Maryknoll, NY: Orbis Books, 1977.

7. A brief book on this subject by an author who is informed in both histories is S.L. Greenslade, *Shepherding the Flock:* Problems of Pastoral Discipline in the Early Church and in the Younger Churches Today. London: S.C.M. Press, 1967.

8. Adapted from the author's booklet, "Adult Baptism: Getting Back to the Beginning." Cincinnati: Forward Movement, 1984, p.17.

Chapter IV: *Persistent Issues: Infant Baptism*

1. Figures of this kind are available in many places; they substantially agree. Perhaps the proportion of nominal baptized members is reducing in recent years, particularly in the cities of Britain. A summary a few years old is in Bryan Wilson, *Religion in Secular Society: A Sociological Comment,* Baltimore: Penguin Books, 1969, ch. 1.
One writer commented on the English situation that the lapsed baptized person or apostate "is not a freak on whom it would be artificial to focus attention. . . . He is statistically the standard case, by an overwhelming majority of at least 10 to 1." D. Kidner, "The Meaning and Efficacy of Baptism," in *Theology,* 68, 1965, p. 468.

2. An article sometimes cited as calling the matter to attention in terms that could not be disregarded is Alec Vidler's "Baptismal Disgrace" in *Theology,* July 1940. There were, however, discussions of indiscriminate Baptism in the late 1930s, and it

was at least briefly considered by the 1897 Lambeth Conference.

Anyone who seeks to keep abreast of the Church of England discussions of Christian Initiation is heavily dependent on the resources of the libraries to which one has access. There is too much of this ephemeral literature for any repository to have it all. For three decades, publications have followed one another rapidly; at times a reader is struck by the mind-numbing repetition; at other times by the shifts of emphasis. Two older surveys of the various statements and commission reports are F.J. Taylor, "Baptism in the Church of England To-day," in J.R.S. Taylor and F.J. Taylor, *Baptism in the Church,* London: Church Book Room Press, 1950, pp. 34–46; and F.C. Tindall, "Anglican Principles and Practice" in *Church Quarterly Review,* 52 (1951), pp. 53–76. J.M.B. Frederick, "The Initiation Crisis in the Church of England," an article already cited, is a discriminating recent study that pretty much picks up where the similar earlier summaries ended.

3. Karl Barth, *The Teaching of the Church Regarding Baptism,* trans. E.A. Payne, London: S.C.M., 1948. The most notable replies to Barth were Oscar Cullmann, *Baptism in the New Testament,* trans. J.K.S. Reid, London: S.C.M., 1950, and Pierre Marcel, *The Biblical Doctrine of Infant Baptism,* trans. P.E. Hughes, London: James Clarke, 1953. For a good review of the issues and the literature of this debate in Reformed and Lutheran circles, see Dale Moody, *Baptism: Foundation for Christian Unity,* Philadelphia: Westminster Press, 1967, chs. 2 and 3.

On the religious and political context, see Arthur Cochrane, *The Church's Confession under Hitler,* Philadelphia: Westminster Press, 1962.

4. For two recent statements, see Colin Buchanan, *A Case for Infant Baptism,* Grove Booklets on Ministry and Worship, No. 20, Bramcote, Notts.: Grove Books, 1973, and G.W. Bromiley, *Children of Promise:* The Case for Baptizing Infants, Grand Rapids: Eerdmans, 1979. Buchanan observes that, speaking for the English scene, a number of persuasive critiques of infant Baptism have come out in recent years and have received virtually no replies. A Prebyterian, Diane Karay, comments that so much has been said in recent years in behalf of adult Baptism that the case for infant Baptism must be restated—which she does very well in "Let the Children Lead the Way: A Case for Baptizing Children," in *Worship,* 61 (1987), pp. 336–349.

5. See George Saunders, "A Service of Dedication of a Child," in *Theology* 45, 1962, pp. 501–03, and the correspondence in subsequent issues for suggestions along this line. Similar proposals had been made before this article, and some continue to be made.

The discussion of infant Baptism has created an extensive literature. For a few items among many, see the appropriate passages in Basil S. Moss (ed.), *Crisis for Baptism,* London: S.C.M., 1965; Neville Cryer, *By What Rite? Infant Baptism in a Missionary Situation,* London: Mowbray, 1969; Richard X. Redmond, "Infant Baptism: History and Pastoral Problems," in *Theological Studies* 30, 1969, pp. 79–89; Robert Jenson, "On Infant Baptism," in *Dialog* 8, 1969, pp. 214–217. A radical proposal put forward by a Roman Catholic writing under a pen name, David G. Perrey, *Baptism at 21*, New York: Vantage Press, 1973, asks whether anyone is ready for the commitments of Baptism until about the age at which the society regards one as ready for the responsibilities of full citizenship. Perhaps the strongest contemporary theological argument against infant Baptism is Paul K. Jewett, *Infant Baptism and the Covenant of Grace*, Grand Rapids: Eerdmans, 1978, but it argues heavily from covenant ideas, which do not have comparable importance for all readers. There is a good exploration of the issues by an English Methodist, Neil Dixon, *Troubled Waters*, London: Epworth Press, 1979.

The survey of Reformed and Lutheran debate on infant Baptism between the mid-1930s and the mid-1960s by Dale Moody cited in note 3 is highly informative.

6. From a tough-minded Lutheran theologian:

> *Not every person is competent to make every contract....Parents or sponsors who have not communed for years and show no outward signs of any grasp of the Gospel...just are not able to make this contract about their infant....Those who, so far as the community of believers can judge, have evaded the risk of believing existence, do not have the simple human* right *to commit another person to that terrible risk.*

Robert Jenson, "Infant Baptism," p. 215.

7. There seems to be a tendency in Baptist churches in the United States for the age for Baptism to drift earlier and earlier—a tendency which some Baptists regard as subversive of the principles of the group. Occasionally some of this discussion is aired in the ecumenical press. For an example, G. Temp Sparkman, "Baptists and Baptism," in *The Christian Century*, April 13, 1977, pp. 349–50.

8. Galatians 2:20. The fundamental paradox of "I, and yet not I, but God-in-me" is part of the daring, yet reverent biblical faith, that comes to expression in the prophets, in Jesus, and in the early believers. Were the prophets' words their words, or God's words through them? Is prayer our words to God or the voice of God's Spirit in us? The answers to such questions touch the heart of the divine-human relation and have their applicability to baptismal theology.

9. It is surely wrong to emphasize the objectivity of Baptism so as to minimize the constitutive place of faith. But it is at least as mistaken to stress the subjective side so that Baptism becomes a human act of witness to one's faith, done for the benefit of others, and done only because the New Testament directs that it be done. But the worst error is to pose the issues so that they can be dealt with in these barren alternatives. Subjective and objective are categories that belong to certain modes of reflecting upon experience. They do not arise where life is most immediate and intense. Sacramental experience is simultaneously both deeply human and transparent to God.

10. A striking instance of such thinking is from a German Baptist, Johannes Schnei-

der, who in his *Baptism and Church in the New Testament,* trans. Ernest A. Payne, London: The Carey Kingsgate Press, 1957, says such things as: "The agent in the act [of Baptism] itself is God. . . . Baptism results in the forgiveness of sins. . . . A soteriological significance belongs to Baptism. . . . Baptism is a redemptive event" (pp. 28*f.*). Some English Baptists, such as Neville Clark, W.E.O. White, and (cautiously) G.R. Beasley-Murray, would be comfortable with such statements. For an American comment, see James W. McClendon, "Baptism as a Performative Sign," in *Interpretation* 23 (1966), pp. 403–416.

11. There have, since the 16th century, been ways of contending for believers' Baptism that made it impossible for persons of that persuasion to recognize infant Baptism as true Baptism. But the note above indicates that such polarization is moderating.

Some of these ecumenical matters were discussed ably in the *Louisville Consultation on Baptism,* a Consultation on Believers' Baptism held in 1979. The papers were published in *Review and Expositor* 77, No. 1 (1980), and are also available as Faith and Order Paper No. 97, from the World Council of Churches.

The remarkable ecumenical statement *Baptism, Eucharist and Ministry* [Faith and Order Paper, No. 111], Geneva: World Council of Churches, 1982, envisions mutual recognition among those who understand Baptism differently, and it proposes some ways of thinking that can comprehend the differing systems. See "Baptism," sections IV.A and C. A promising response to BEM is a recent symposium from a Conference on the Believers' Church, *Baptism and Church: A Believers' Church Vision,* Merle D. Strege (ed.), Grand Rapids: Sagamore Books, 1986.

12. The point was made concisely and tellingly a number of years ago by Donald Baillie in *The Theology of the Sacraments,* New York: Scribners, 1957. He asked simply "Are the children of Christians to be regarded as having a place within the church of Christ or are they outsiders? . . . Is there such a thing as a Christian child?" (p. 80*f.*). The question and Baillie's brief discussion of it appear to have stung some Baptist theologians, for there were a number of replies. Perhaps the strongest was G.R. Beasley-Murray, "A Baptist Interpretation of the Place of the Child in the Church," in *Foundations* 8 (1965), pp. 146–160. Other similar articles appeared, however, at about this time. One must read such accounts of Baptist thought about children in the church to decide whether they are adequate or whether they are trying to deal with a subject that rather took these theologians and their categories of thought by surprise and left them unprepared to report on much except the undeniable gratitude and affection that all Christian parents have for their children.

13. Frederick, *op. cit.,* p. 151. The fine recent presentation of a context of meaning for infant Baptism by Diane Karay, "Let the Children Lead the Way," was remarked in note 4.

14. The term "contractual," taken from political philosophy, would displease upholders of the baptistic tradition. For them, the church is not self-made by persons

agreeing to terms of association, but it is freshly brought into being by the summons of God. But this idea of the church came into Western history at about the same time that contractual theories of society were emerging and new states were being begun by popular consent. It carries an important, critical feature of ecclesiology. But what looks to a baptistic group like a new divine creation looks to a sociologist like a voluntary association.

15. Matters of this kind are discussed with honesty and ecumenical spirit by a Scottish Presbyterian and a Southern Baptist, see John Baillie, *Baptism and Conversion,* New York: Scribners, 1963; and Warren Carr, *Baptism: Conscience and Clue for the Church,* New York: Holt, Rinehart and Winston, 1964. Another Southern Baptist, Dale Moody, *op. cit.,* writes with a vast fund of information and much wisdom.

16. Jenson, *op. cit.,* p. 216.

17. A. Theodore Eastman, *The Baptizing Community,* New York: Seabury, 1982, pp. 31, 36.

18. Aidan Kavanagh, "Christian Initiation in Post-Conciliar Roman Catholicism: A Brief Report," in *Studia Liturgica* 12 (1977), p. 111.

19. Although the normative place of the RCIA is not stated in so many words in the document itself, it is clear from some of the supporting material. The point is presented in A. Kavanagh, "The Norm of Baptism: The New Rite of Christian Initiation of Adults," in *Worship,* 48 (1974), pp. 143–52. Fr. Kavanagh seeks to explain what is meant (and not meant) by a "norm." Some of this argumentation is repeated in the same author's *The Shape of Baptism,* New York: Pueblo Publishing, 1978, pp. 106–14.

A similar point was made in an exploratory way by a committee in the Church of England many years ago. A Commission on Indiscriminate Baptism reported to a conference sponsored by the Parish and People Movement: "The Baptism of those able to answer for themselves should be the norm. . . . We wish to see the Baptism of those able to answer for themselves made much more visible as the theological and pastoral standard of Christian initiation," in Basil Moss (ed.), *Crisis for Baptism,* p. 27. And in his summary article in 1951, F.C. Tindall reported: "More emphasis is now put on adult Baptism plus Confirmation as the *norm* of Christian Initiation, with the element of conscious response, in penitence and faith, as in New Testament and primitive days," in the article cited in note 2 above, p. 58.

20. Robert Hovda, "The Amen Corner," in *Worship* 61 (1987), p. 74f.

21. One of the earliest of the parish stories, and still one of the best, is Raymond B. Kemp, *A Journey in Faith: An Experience of the Catechumenate,* New York: Wm. H. Sadlier, 1979. More recent is Mary Pierre Ellenbracht, *The Easter Passage: The RCIA Experience,* Minneapolis: Winston Press, 1983.

Chapter V: *Persistent Issues: Confirmation*

1. Frederick J. Warnecke, "A Bishop Proposes," in *Confirmation Crisis,* p. 136. Bishop Warnecke might have added that the same overburdened rite also has admitted persons from non-episcopal church bodies. Another bishop, Frederick B. Wolf, cites a catalog of contradictions in Confirmation theology and practice in his essay, "Christian Initiation," in H. Barry Evans (ed.), *Prayer Book Renewal,* New York: Seabury Press, 1978, pp. 35–39.

2. At some point in the internal discussions of the Drafting Committee, I tried to clarify a distinction that had been emerging by listing the characteristics of these two strains of ancestry and meaning that had contributed to Confirmation as it had been known and practiced in the Prayer Book tradition. I called them "Confirmation A" and "Confirmation B." Reference continues to be made to this distinction, in these terms. See Reginald Fuller's chapter in K.B. Cully (ed.), *Confirmation Re-Examined,* p.17f.; Charles Price, "Rites of Initiation," *The Occasional Papers of the Standing Liturgical Commission,* Collection No. 1, New York: The Church Hymnal Corporation, 1987, pp. 28–29.

3. "The use of the same biblical and liturgical terms prohibited the underlying disagreements from becoming explosive," Frederick, *op. cit.,* p. 143.

4. See the material on "Pagan and Secular Use of Oil" in Mitchell, *op. cit.,* pp. 25–29, also a summary paragraph in A. Kavanagh, *The Shape of Baptism,* p. 28f.

5. *St. Cyril of Jerusalem, Lectures on Christian Sacraments* (F.L. Cross, trans.), London: S.P.C.K., 1952, p. 63. The Greek word *"christos"* means "anointed." For Jesus as God's anointed one, see Acts 10:38 and also Luke 4:18–21, citing Isaiah 61:1.

6. Notably in 1 John 2:27; also 2 Corinthians 1:21.

7. Tertullian, *De Resurrectione Carnis,* ch. 8, in Whitaker, *Documents,* p. 10. The ritual to which Tertullian refers evidently contained water Baptism, anointing, consignation, imposition of the hand, and the baptismal Eucharist.

8. The best survey of the variety in postbaptismal customs in the early church remains L.L. Mitchell's *Baptismal Anointing.* At the time it was done, this book gathered material that had not been put together in this way before. In the twenty years since it was issued, no subsequent work has replaced it, and no research has more than slightly modified Dr. Mitchell's findings.

On the Syrian rite, a scholar has summarized, "John Chrysostom found no postbaptismal rite of anointing in the tradition he inherited, and obviously did not feel that anything was missing." Georg Kretschmar, "Recent Research on Christian Initiation," in *Studia Liturgica* 12 (1977), p. 91.

9. Charles Davis, *Sacraments of Initiation: Baptism and Confirmation.* New York:

Sheed and Ward, 1964, p. 107.

10. The bishop's prayer is in *Apostolic Tradition,* 12.1. Hippolytus' work was lost, and it must now be put together from fragments embedded in other documents in several languages. Even though the textual problems for the document as a whole are complex, editors come to general agreement. The textual evidence and the issues are discussed in G.W.H. Lampe, *The Seal of the Spirit,* London: Longman, 1951, pp. 136–142. Dom Gregory Dix, in his edition of *Apostolic Tradition,* reads it as a prayer for the Spirit and for grace, while Burton Scott Easton, in his edition, reads it as a prayer for grace for faithfulness, the Spirit having been given in Baptism. Dom Bernard Botte in his succession of authoritative editions of *Apostolic Tradition* has changed his mind on this point—another indication that the textual evidence is closely divided.

11. Calvin made such a claim in *Institutes,* 1543 ed., 4.19.4. This claim that Reformed Confirmation practice followed early church precedent was often repeated over the next century and a half by apologists of the Continental Reformed churches and the Church of England. They were probably following Calvin, whose citations of the Church Fathers were usually reliable, but in this matter his reconstruction was entirely fanciful.

12. "This people...honor me with their lips, while their hearts are far from me," Isaiah 29:13, cited by Jesus in Mark 7:6f.

13. Romans 10:8–10. *Cf.* Paul's emphasis in 1 Corinthians 12–14 on the Body of Christ as built up through sharing intelligible words.

14. A.D. Nock, *Conversion: The Old and the New in Religion from Alexander the Great to Augustine of Hippo,* Oxford University Press, 1961 ed., p. 14.

15. Gregory of Nazianzus, Sermon 40, par.11.

16. A brief summary of the strengths and weaknesses of medieval catechesis is given in J.A. Jungmann, *Handing on the Faith,* New York: Herder and Herder, 1959, pp. 11–19.

17. *Institutes,* 3.2.2–5. See the wise comments on religious consciousness in O.C. Quick, *Catholic and Protestant Elements in Christianity,* London: Longman, 1924, especially ch. 3.

18. For the basic texts, see J.D.C. Fisher, *Christian Initiation. The Reformation Period,* sections 31–32.

19. Luther's "Short Catechism" and "Large Catechism" are among his finest works. For a gathering of Reformed catechisms, with a vigorous introduction by the editor, see T.F. Torrance, *The School of Faith: The Catechisms of the Reformed Church,* New York: Harper and Brothers, 1959.

20. The best known from the period was by Alexander Nowell, Dean of St. Paul's. It was published first in 1570, and republished for more than a century. There is a facsimile reprint of Nowell's Catechism with an introduction by Frank V. Occhiogrosso, *A Catechisme or First Instruction and Learning of Christian Religion (1570)*, Delmar, NJ: Scholar's Facsimiles and Reprints, 1975. On this and other English catechisms, see David Siegenthaler, "Religious Education for Citizenship: Primer and Catechism," in J. Booty (ed.), *The Godly Kingdom of Tudor England: Great Books of the English Reformation*, Wilton, CT: Morehouse-Barlow, 1981, ch. 4, pp. 219–49.

21. "The Constitution on the Sacred Liturgy," par. 14 & 34. In E. Koenker, *The Liturgical Renaissance in the Roman Catholic Church*, University of Chicago, 1954, the author speaks of concern for active participation in and comprehension of the liturgy as "the fundamental interest of the liturgical Apostolate wherever it is found." (p.45). See also J.A. Jungmann, "Christianity—Conscious or Unconscious?" in *Pastoral Liturgy*, New York: Herder and Herder, 1962, pp. 325–334.

An essay quotes Hans Kung in *Was Ist Firmung?*, 1976, as saying:

> *Confirmation signifies the point... when the child, having been baptized at the request of its believing parents publicly confirms its Baptism... and professes its faith before the community of the faithful. By means of a special ritual it is recognized and accepted as a full member of the community of the church and admitted to the celebration of the Eucharist. Confirmation and first Communion would take place at the same celebration.... [This] profession of faith [implies] an open affirmation and a responsible, publicly acknowledged decision of the young person to live his life according to the Gospel of Jesus Christ. Baptism, in the first instance only passively received by the child, now becomes fully effective through the active involvement of grace engendered by the young person's faith, profession and action.*

Quoted in Guenter Biemer, "Controversy on the Age of Confirmation as a Typical Example of Conflict between the Criteria of Theology and the Demands of Pastoral Practice," in D. Power and L. Maldonado (eds.), *Liturgy and Human Passage* [Concilium No. 112], New York: Seabury Press, 1979, p. 117. Martin Bucer would have wanted to say these things—and he could not have said them better.

22. More than forty-five years ago Cyril Richardson called attention to the disparate functions this one rite was asked to serve. See his article "What Is Confirmation?" in *The Anglican Theological Review* 23 (1941), pp. 223–230.

23. London: S.P.C.K., 1926. No editor was listed for this work. It is sometimes spoken of as having been planned by Canon Ollard.

24. New York: Seabury Press, 1962.

25. For instance, Cyril Pocknee, *Water and the Spirit*, London: Darton, Longman

and Todd, 1967.

26. Church of England Board of Education: 1971.

27. Tertullian, *On Baptism,* ch. 6 (E. Evans, trans.) London: S.P.C.K., 1964.

28. Patristic texts that make this point were gathered in an old, informative, but inconclusive article by John C. Sladden, "Baptism and the Gift of the Holy Spirit," in *The Church Quarterly Review* 146–47 (1948–49), pp. 220–245. See also G.W.H. Lampe. *op. cit.* for evidence that in the inexact but rich terminology of the early church, all was Baptism, and all was sealing.

A connection between water and the divine Spirit would have been suggested by such passages in the Jewish tradition as Isaiah 32:15; Ezekiel 36:25–26; Joel 2:28–29; Jubilees 1:23–25; lQS 4:19–21.

29. Representing this point of view, one should cite the apparent meaning of the Prayer Book texts and most of the 16th-century Anglican writers. When the subject comes up in the modern period, these writers take the same general line, although not with complete agreement among themselves:

A.T. Wirgman, *The Doctrine of Confirmation,* London: Longman, 1897.

Darwell Stone, *Holy Baptism,* London: Longman, 1899.

A.E.J. Rawlinson, *Christian Initiation,* London: S.P.C.K., 1947.

Archbishops' Theological Commission Report, "The Theology of Christian Initiation," London: S.P.C.K., 1948.

G.W.H. Lampe, *The Seal of the Spirit,* London: Longman, 1961.

E.C. Whitaker, *Sacramental Initiation Complete in Baptism* [Grove Liturgical Study No.1], Bramcote, Notts.: Grove Books, 1975.

30. Among those who thought of Confirmation along these lines in the earlier periods of Anglicanism, one might note Jeremy Taylor, *A Discourse of Confirmation,* 1664; and Thomas Deacon, *A True View of Christianity,* 1747. In the past century, this point of view has been represented by the following writers—again without complete agreement:

F.W. Puller, *What Is the Distinctive Grace of Confirmation?,* London: Rivingtons, 1890.

A.J. Mason, *The Relation of Confirmation to Baptism,* New York: Dutton, 1891.

G. Dix, *The Theology of Confirmation in Relation to Baptism,* London: A. & C. Black, 1946.

L.S. Thornton, *Confirmation: Its Place in the Baptismal Mystery,* London: A. & C. Black, 1954.

C.E. Pocknee, *Water and the Spirit,* London: Darton, Longman and Todd, 1967.

J.D.C. Fisher, *Confirmation Then and Now,* London: S.P.C.K., 1978.

One of the best guides to the literature and the arcane mode of argument in this dispute is chapter 4, "The Anglican Tradition: Baptism and Confirmation," in Dale Moody, *Baptism: Foundation for Christian Unity,* pp. 162–216.

31. A sacramental theologian has written:

> *In a very real sense, we cannot "give the gift of the Holy Spirit" in a liturgical service, in a sacramental celebration. Our sacraments must celebrate a deeper truth which exists in the community and in the life of the individual, if they are to have any truth at all, and consequently any power at all.*

Joseph M. Powers, S. J., "Confirmation: The Problem of Meaning," in *Worship* 46 (1972), p. 29.

32. E. Kenneth Lee, "The Holy Spirit in Relation to Baptism and Confirmation," in *The Modern Churchman* 12 (1970), p. 317. The great Roman Catholic exegete Rudolph Schnackenburg says: "One will seek in vain in the Pauline letters to discover a peculiar sacrament of the Spirit alongside baptism," *Baptism in the Thought of St. Paul,* New York: Herder and Herder, 1964, p. 91.

33. The title of a fine small book on the Holy Spirit by Bishop F.A. Cockin, *God in Action:* A Study in the Holy Spirit, Baltimore: Penguin Books, 1961.

34. E.K. Lee, *op. cit.,* p. 318. See the similar comments in J.G. Davies, *The Spirit, the Church and the Sacraments,* London: Faith Press, 1954, pp. 7ff.

35. Yarnold, *op. cit.,* p. 31.

36. The idea that *anamnesis* and *epiclesis* are applicable to the initiatory rites is not uncommon. The statement of it in Nathan Mitchell's chapter, "Dissolution of the Rite of Christian Initiation," in *Made, Not Born,* 1976, pages 73–75, seems especially full of suggestion. See also L.L. Mitchell, "The Place of Baptismal Anointing in Christian Initiation," in *Anglican Theological Review* 68 (1986), p. 207f.

37. Craig Douglas Erickson, "The Strong Name of the Trinity," in *Reformed Liturgy and Music,* 19:4 (1985), p. 210. Many modern liturgies have brought a prayer for the Spirit and an anointing or imposition of hands into their baptismal rites. The forms vary, and some churches make certain ritual features optional. The ecumenical "Lima" text includes this postbaptismal action (see Wainwright and Thurian, eds., *Baptism and Eucharist,* p. 96); the rites issued by COCU also include it. Recent liturgies of Lutherans, Methodists, Presbyterians, and of Anglican churches (perhaps others as well) contain this feature. For most of them, it is new, as it is for the Episcopal Church, but the logic of including it seemed to overcome the tradition of excluding it.

38. Aidan Kavanagh, *The Shape of Baptism,* New York: Pueblo Publishing, 1978, p. 174.

39. Gustaf Wingren, *Gospel and Church,* trans. Ross Mackenzie, Philadelphia: Fortress Press, 1964, p. 131.

40. Kenneth Keniston, "Youth as a Stage of Life," in *Youth and Dissent,* New York: Harcourt Brace Jovanovich, 1971, pp. 3–21. Keniston's essay influenced this section of the present study quite heavily. Perhaps the years have dated any work based on close interviews with young adults of the late '60s and early '70s. But if time modifies the conclusions of an observer such as Keniston, it only reinforces the point for which his work is drawn on here—the point that the stages of life are protracted in modern society, and they are in change.

41. Edric A. Weld, "The Church Report on Confirmation Instruction," in *Findings,* Oct. 1960, p. 10f.; an article based on a survey made for the Department of Christian Education of the Episcopal Church.

42. See the ecumenical symposium, "The Proper Age for a Declaration of Faith," in *Religious Education,* 58 (1963), pp. 411–442.

43. J.M.B. Frederick, *op. cit.,* remarks, "The adult's relationship to the Gospel is taken as so very different from that of the mere child as to require sacramental authentication which even scripture and the early church did not provide!" The central part of this article may be the most incisive critique of the dynamics of Confirmation ever mounted by a loyal Anglican.

44. P. Verghese, "Relation between Baptism, 'Confirmation' and the Eucharist in the Syrian Orthodox Church," in *Studia Liturgica* 4 (1965), p. 86f.

45. "Our Present Position in the Light of the Bible," in Basil Minchin (ed.), *Becoming a Christian,* p. 55.

46. Lacking more recent and more thorough research, we have the small but valuable work, J.W. Hunkin, *Episcopal Ordination and Confirmation in Relation to Intercommunion and Reunion,* Cambridge: W. Heffer & Son, 1929. The lengthy essay by Canon Ollard, cited in ch. 2 is also useful. But such works document the period prior to the mid-1800s better than they explain the changes of that period and since.

47. Dean Holmes spoke of "the brittle dogmatism of the nineteenth century, with its rather naive view of history" as a factor in punctiliousness about Confirmation. See *Confirmation: The Celebration of Maturity in Christ,* New York: Seabury Press, 1975, p. 48. The case for the rigid initiatory polity of Anglicanism was largely based on history, but it is history which has called that case into question.

48. A pioneer Episcopalian effort is Mercer L. Goodson, "What About Confirmation by Priest?," in *The St. Luke's Journal of Theology* 16 (1972), pp. 72–81.

49. David Holeton, "Confirmation in the 1980's," in Max Thurian (ed.), *Ecumenical Perspectives on Baptism, Eucharist and Ministry* [Faith and Order Paper No. 116],

Geneva: World Council of Churches, 1983, p. 82.

50. The best readily accessible study is Antonio Mostaza Rodriguez, "The Minister of Confirmation," in N. Edelby, T. Jimenez-Urresti, and P. Huizing, eds., *The Sacraments in Theology and Canon Law* [Concilium, vol. 38], New York: Paulist Press, 1968, pp. 28–36. This essay, based on the author's thesis, was written before the RCIA was issued, but it remains a basic, critical gathering of historical information. This researcher is persuaded that the restriction of Confirmation to the bishop is a matter of ecclesiastical regulation, not of theological requirement or of divine law, and is therefore open to change.

51. *RCIA*, U.S. Catholic Conference, Washington, D.C.: 1974.

52. Kavanagh, A., "Christian Initiation of Adults: The Rites," in *Made, Not Born*, p. 128; repeated in *The Shape of Baptism*, p. 138f.
For a second Roman opinion along similar lines, see James D. Shaughnessy:

> *The traditional sequence of baptism, post-baptismal anointing, and Eucharist is fairly well accepted and has priority of established position in the adult rite. But how long can we sustain the dichotomy of adult initiation going in one direction and the initiation of children in another? This schizophrenic approach to initiation cannot be productive.*

Initiation and Conversion, Liturgical Press, Collegeville, MN: 1985, p. 63.

53. *Nurturing Children in Communion*, Bramcote, Notts.: Grove Books, 1985, p. 46.

Chapter VI: *Persistent Issues: First Communion*

1. Massey H. Shepherd, Jr., *The Paschal Liturgy and the Apocalypse* [Ecumenical Studies in Worship, No. 6], Richmond, VA: John Knox Press, 1960.

2. Louis Bouyer, *Liturgical Piety*, Notre Dame, IN: University of Notre Dame Press, 1955, "According to the mind of the ancient Church, Baptism and Confirmation had no meaning except as milestones on the way to the Eucharist," p. 164.

3. Augustine, *On the Merits and Forgiveness of Sins and on the Baptism of Infants*, I.27.

4. J.D.C. Fisher, *Christian Initiation: Baptism in the Medieval West*, p. 95.

5. Whitaker, *Documents*, 1977, p. 122

6. *ibid.*, p. 204.

7. *ibid.*, p. 195.

8. L.L. Mitchell, *Baptismal Anointing*, p. 157.

9. Fisher, *op. cit.*, p. 107.

10. The best summary of this development is ch. 6, "The Separation of Communion from Initiation," in Fisher, *op. cit.*

11. J.M.M. Dalby, "The End of Infant Communion," in *Church Quarterly Review*, 167 (1966), p. 64.

12. On the *Commentary on the Sentences*, see Dalby, *op. cit.*, p. 61f.; the passage in *Summa Theologica* is in 3.q.80. art. 9.

13. Dalby, *op.cit.*, p. 63.

14. See David Holeton, *Infant Communion—Then and Now* [Grove Liturgical Study, No. 27], Bramcote, Notts.: Grove Books, 1981, pp. 9–15.

15. Calvin, *Institutes* 4.16.30.

16. Somewhat surprisingly this line of argument is vigorously restated in Paul K. Jewett, *op. cit.*, pp. 194–201. This author argues that "Believer's Communion," which is practiced by those who practice infant Baptism is inconsistent; it should correlate with believers' Baptism.

17. Jeremy Taylor, *A Discourse of the Liberty of Prophesying*, 1647, ch. 18, *ad.8.*, Heber/Eden edition, 1853, vol. 5, p. 576f.

18. Thomas Deacon, *A Full, True, and Comprehensive View of Christianity*, London: 2nd ed., 1748, pp. 343–393. The quotation is from p. 359. In this lengthy treatment of infant Communion Deacon writes as a teacher, not a controversialist. He has a thesis, and he sets it forth soberly and with some intellectual force. A number of years ago I acquired a period copy of this text. In following the literature of this subject I began to be concerned that Deacon's plea for infant Communion seemed to have dropped out of Anglican memory. But now, see David Holeton, "The Communion of Infants and Young Children," in Geiko Mueller-Fahrenholz, ed., ...*and do not hinder them*, Geneva: World Council of Churches, 1982, p. 67.

19. Kenneth Stevenson, "A Theological Reflection on the Experience of Inclusion/ Exclusion at the Eucharist," in *Anglican Theological Review* 68 (1986), p. 213.

20. Neville Clark, *An Approach to the Theology of the Sacraments* [Studies in Biblical Theology, No.17], Chicago: Alec R. Allenson, 1956, p. 83.

21. A. Kavanagh, *The Shape of Baptism*, p. 122.

22. Clark, *op.cit.*, p. 84.

23. J.G. Davies, *The Spirit, the Church and the Sacraments*, p. 124.

24. "Children and Communion," in *Nurturing Children in Communion,* p. 45.

25. For attempts to describe this kind of Christian education, see David R. Hunter, *Christian Education as Engagement,* New York: Seabury Press, 1963, and Letty M. Russell, *Christian Education in Mission,* Philadelphia: Westminster Press, 1967.

26. Piet Fransen, "The Oikonomia and the Age of Confirmation," in *Intelligent Theology,* vol. 2, Chicago: Franciscan Herald Press, 1969, p. 34.
   No one can be sure what practical flaws will develop in any pattern of initiatory acts which may replace past patterns, only that there will be flaws. But it is certain to improve things if the Holy Communion is not so specifically part of a package of actions one starts and stops in adolescence.

27. See some forceful remarks in Kavanagh, *The Shape of Baptism,* p. 69f.

28. *The Lambeth Conference* 1968, New York: Seabury Press, 1968, p. 99.

29. New York: The Church Pension Fund, 1970.

30. See the terms by which the initiatory rites were authorized in *Services for Trial Use,* New York: Church Hymnal Corporation, 1970, pp. v–vi and 21. On this 1970 rite, see D.B. Stevick, "Confirmation for Today: Reflections on the Rite Proposed for the Episcopal Church," in *Worship* 44 (1970), pp. 541–60. This article remains the only substantial comment on these rites which was made at the time of their publication.

31. The terms by which the rite of *Prayer Book Studies 18* was adopted for trial use are quoted (in addition to the reference above) in the Preface of *Prayer Book Studies 26,* 1973, and in the *Journal* of the 1970 General Convention. Louis Weil's judgment is in his *Christian Initiation: A Theological and Pastoral Commentary on the Proposed Rites,* first published in Nashotah Review 14 (1974), and later published (n.d.) as a booklet by Associated Parishes. The passage cited is in this booklet, p. 7.
   It is less clear from the words of authorization that the Convention was basing eligibility for Communion on Baptism than it is that it was not basing it on Confirmation. The directing hand of the ordinary suggests undesignated prerequisites. This action reads now like an effort to move, but not too far.

32. Text in *Anglican Theological Review* 54 (1972), p. 118f. This document was cited in this issue of *ATR* because it was the principal occasion for the insightful exploratory colloquium "Documentation and Reflection: Confirmation Today," pp. 106–118.
   It was at this occasion that the House of Bishops adopted a pastorally-wise, but little-publicized understanding that children who might be admitted to Communion in a diocese in which early Communion was the practice would be sustained as communicants if they moved to another jurisdiction in which the custom was different.

33. Also printed in *Prayer Book Studies 26,* pp. 3–5.

34. Published in the Grove booklet, *Nurturing Children in Communion,* pp. 42–49, and in *Anglican Theological Review* 68 (1986), pp. 185–197. *Nurturing Children in Communion* contains, in addition to the Boston Statement, some supporting papers.

35. With no hope of being complete:

Eugene Brand, "Baptism and Communion of Infants: A Lutheran View," in *Worship* 59 (1976), pp. 29–42.

Paul G. Bretscher, "First Things First: A Question of Infant Communion," in *Una Sancta,* 24 (1963), pp. 34–50.

Charles Crawford, "Infant Communion: Past Tradition and Present Practice," in *Theological Studies* 31 (1970), pp. 523–536.

J.M.M. Dalby, "The End of Infant Communion," in *Church Quarterly Review* 167 (1966), pp. 59–71.

David Holeton, *Infant Communion—Then and Now* [Grove Liturgical Study No. 27], Bramcote, Notts: Grove Books, 1981.

Urban T. Holmes, *Young Children and the Eucharist,* New York: Seabury Press, 1972.

Robert Jenson, "Communion: For Children?" in *Living Worship* 15:6 (June–July 1979).

Geiko Mueller-Fahrenholz, ed., *. . . and do not hinder them:* An Ecumenical Plea for the Admission of Children to the Eucharist [Faith and Order Paper No. 109], Geneva: World Council of Churches, 1982.

Nurturing Children at Communion [Grove Liturgical Study No. 44], Bramcote, Notts: Grove Books, 1985.

Lawton W. Posey, "Southern Presbyterians, Children and the Lord's Supper," in *The Christian Century,* April 29, 1981, pp. 480–483.

Frank C. Senn, "Confirmation and First Communion: A Reappraisal, in *Lutheran Quarterly* 23 (1971), pp. 178–191.

36. *Baptism, Eucharist and Ministry* [Faith and Order Paper No. 111], Geneva: World Council of Churches, 1982, "Commentary" to Paragraph 14, p. 5.

37. "Children and Communion," p. 43.

38. Robert W. Jenson, *Visible Words:* The Interpretation and Practice of Christian Sacraments, Philadelphia: Fortress Press, 1978, p. 164.

39. Lloyd G. Patterson, "Baptismal Renewal," in *The Living Church,* January 11, 1987, p. 9.

40. This is the thrust of Dean Holmes' small book, *Young Children and the Euchar-ist*, New York: Seabury Press, 1972.

41. See the fascinating personal account by the English liturgiologist Kenneth Steven-son, *op. cit.*, pp. 212–221. When he was a child, this author sometimes was taken to church with his family at the Catholic Apostolic Church, where he was welcome at the Holy Communion. At other times, the family attended the Episcopal Church of Scot-land. Stevenson says: "One thing I could not fail to notice: I never, *ever* went up to the altar-rail, because I was not allowed to receive Communion" (p. 215). The author re-flects on his mixed experience as a child.

42. *Christian Initiation: Birth and Growth in the Christian Society*, p. 44; a passage which came to attention through a quotation in J.B.M. Frederick, *op. cit.*, p. 155.

Chapter VII: *The Freedom and Authority of Baptism*

1. The articles in two volumes of the Concilium series look at liturgy and Christian Initiation in cultural context: D. Power and L. Maldonado, eds., *Liturgy and Human Passage* [Concilium, vol. 112], New York: Seabury Press, 1979. Especially valuable are Aidan Kavanagh, "Life-Cycle Events, Civil Ritual and the Christian," pp. 14–24; David Power, "The Odyssey of Man in Christ," pp. 100–111; and Guenter Biemer, "Controversy on the Age of Confirmation as a Typical Example of Conflict between the Criteria of Theology and the Demands of Pastoral Practice," pp. 115–25. Also: L. Maldonado and D. Powers, eds., *Structures of Initiation in Crisis* [Concilium, vol. 122], New York: Seabury Press, 1979. The article by Anthonius Scheer, "The Influ-ence of Culture on the Liturgy as shown in the History of the Christian Initiation Rite," pp. 14–25, is particularly fine. See also, Leonel L. Mitchell, "Christian Initia-tion, Rites of Passage, and Confirmation," in K.B. Cully, ed., *Confirmation Re-Examined*, Wilton, CT.: Morehouse-Barlow, 1982, pp. 81–92; and Roger Grainger, "The Sacraments as Passage Rites," in *Worship*, 58 (1984), pp. 214–222.

2. The anthropological classics are Arnold Van Gennep, *The Rites of Passage*, trans. M. Vizedom and G. Caffee, Chicago: University of Chicago Press, 1960 (originally published in French in 1909); and Mircea Eliade, *Rites and Symbols of Initiation: The Mysteries of Birth and Rebirth*, trans. W. Trask, New York: Harper & Row, 1965 (originally published as *Birth and Rebirth* in 1958).

3. Anthonius Scheer, "The Influence of Culture on the Liturgy," p. 18.

4. Aidan Kavanagh, "Life-Cycle Events, Civil Ritual and the Christian," p. 20, "While the source is trans-cultural, the recipient community is not: it hears the Word in place and time, with accent and idiom, and it keeps the covenant by *praxis* in the same manner."

5. Soren Kierkegaard, *Concluding Unscientific Postscript*, trans. D. Swenson and

W. Lowrie, Princeton: Princeton University Press, 1968. The pungent remarks on Baptism generally cluster on pp. 325–329 and 340f.

6. This point, which was labored in the three previous chapters was concisely summarized by Aidan Kavanagh:

> *There can be little doubt that conventionally relating Baptism and Confirmation to the life-cycle events of birth and maturity produces a host of difficulties in attaining an adequate grasp of what these two sacraments truly are. The analogies of Baptism with physical birth and of Confirmation with personal maturity or social majority have become practical univocities that require Baptism to be treated as the special sacrament of infancy and Confirmation correlatively as the special sacrament of adolescence. This assumption having become entrenched leads into an imperceptible transfer of one's own personal public confession of Christian faith from Baptism to Confirmation. It leaves Baptism as little more than a preliminary if major exorcism of sin, and inflates Confirmation into a de facto surrogate Baptism in the midst of adolescent socio-psychic individuation crises.*

"Life-Cycle Events, Civil Ritual and the Christian," p. 16.

7. Kenneth Keniston, "Social Change and Youth in America," in Erik Erikson, ed., *The Challenge of Youth,* Garden City: Doubleday, Anchor Books, 1963, p. 199.

8. Margaret Mead, *Culture and Commitment: A Study in the Generation Gap,* New York: Doubleday, 1970, especially ch. 1.

9. Kavanagh, in "Life-Cycle Events...," p. 22, quotes Alvin Toffler, "Repetitive behaviour, whatever else its functions, helps give meaning to non-repetitive events by providing the backdrop against which novelty is silhouetted," *Future Shock,* p. 394.

10. David Power, "The Odyssey of Man in Christ," p. 101f.

11. *op. cit.,* p. 157.

Chapter VIII: *The Prayer Book Rite: Some Principles*

1. Anyone inquirinq about the baptismal thought and spirituality of the Episcopal Church over the past generation would have to take account of the Prayer Book text, of course. But it is surely significant also that *The Hymnal 1940* had only two hymns in the section on Holy Baptism, and both of them were hymns about children. The six hymns elsewhere in the book that were designated as suitable for adult Baptism were hymns of self-dedication or of the inward Spirit. None were Easter in tone nor of a Christological or kerygmatic character.

It is some reflection of changed thinking that *The Hymnal 1982* has six hymns for Baptism and two for Confirmation, none of which is age specific.

2. Horace T. Allen, Jr., "The Time of Baptism," in *Reformed Liturgy and Music*, 19 (1985), p. 184.

3. *ibid.*

4. The ways in which Christian Initiation and the Church Year reinforce one another is one of the major emphases of A. Theodore Eastman, *The Baptizing Community.* It appears on pp. 39*ff.* but really is a running theme of the book.

5. This restructuring of the baptismal rite is the principal reason for there being no form of it in traditional rhetoric. The rite in the 1979 Prayer Book is not the former rite edited for new circumstances. In many respects, it is a new composition—made, however, with Prayer Book models and tradition always in mind. Having worked out the text in modern speech, it would have been artificial to cast it into older speech forms for a "rite 1."

6. The involvement of the congregation in Christian Initiation and the incorporation of Baptism into the life of a parish are the principal themes of Bishop Eastman's work cited in note 4.

7. The classic "shape" was described by L.L. Mitchell in "The 'Shape' of the Baptismal Liturgy," in *Anglican Theological Review* 68 (1965), pp. 202–211. Dr. Mitchell derives this "shape" largely from his examination of the rites of the early church. The recent Ecumenical Baptismal Liturgy—the "Lima" Document, 1983—follows this classic shape; see Thurian and Wainwright, eds., *Baptism and Eucharist,* Geneva: World Council of Churches, 1983, pp. 94–96.

8. Several liturgies of other churches have handled the postbaptismal actions along lines pioneered by *Prayer Book Studies 26* and the 1979 *BCP*:
The *Lutheran Book of Worship,* 1978, which was produced jointly by several American Lutheran groups, has (pp. 121–125) a service of "Holy Baptism," whose postbaptismal prayer contains both thanks for forgiveness and new life and petition for the gifts of the Spirit. Following the prayer, the newly baptized are signed with the cross, and oil may be used. A lighted candle may be given. A later section of the *Book of Worship* (pp. 198–201), contains an action called "Affirmation of Baptism," which is usable for "Confirmation," for "Reception into Membership," and for "Restoration to Membership." A good comment on a preliminary version of this rite is Frank Senn, "The Shape and Content of Christian Initiation: An Exposition of the New Lutheran Liturgy of Holy Baptism," in *Dialog* 14 (1975), pp. 97–107; and more recently, Eugene Brand, "New Rites of Initiation and Their Implications in the Lutheran Churches," in *Studia Liturgica* 12 (1977), pp. 151–165.
In 1980 the Methodist Church issued "We Gather Together" [Supplemental Worship Resources 10] in whose Baptism rite, immediately following the Baptism, the minister's hands are placed on the head of each person baptized, and the minister says: "The power of the Holy Spirit work within you, that being born through water and the

Spirit you may be a faithful witness of Jesus Christ" (p. 15f.). Provision is made (p. 16) for "Confirmation and Other Renewals of the Baptismal Covenant" at which a rubric suggests the sprinkling of water (optional); the minister calls upon all who are making this act to remember their own Baptism; as hands are placed on the head of each, the minister says the same words that were used following Baptism and were quoted above: "The power of the Holy Spirit work within you...."

In 1985 the Office for Worship of the Presbyterian Church U.S.A. and the Cumberland Presbyterian Church issued *Holy Baptism and Services for the Renewal of Baptism* [Supplemental Liturgical Resource 2]. In the baptismal rite of this text, immediately after the act of Baptism, there is a blessing and anointing (optional) of the baptized, pp. 31 and 39. The text also contains material for "The Renewal of Baptism," pp. 65–100. After a full explanatory section, the possible occasions of renewal are dealt with: those making public profession of faith, those who have been estranged from the church, a congregation making a corporate act of renewal, persons marking times of growth in faith, the sick and the dying, those engaged in pastoral counseling, and those being received as members by transfer. The pastoral intention of this provision is explained by Robert M. Shelton in an article, "Services for the Renewal of Baptism," in *Reformed Liturgy and Music*, 19 (1985), pp. 215–218; and on theological features of the Presbyterian rite, Craig Douglas Erickson, "The Strong Name of the Trinity," in *ibid.*, pp. 205–210.

The baptismal rite in the Anglican Church of Canada's new service book, *The Book of Alternative Services* (1985, pp. 146–165), follows the Episcopal Church's Prayer Book quite closely. (The Baptismal Covenant, however, is located between the Thanksgiving over the Water and the Baptism.) Immediately after the Baptism, there is a signing (chrism optional) with the words, "I sign you with the cross and mark you as Christ's own forever." The prayer for the Spirit follows the wording of the 1979 Prayer Book. A lighted candle may be given. On p. 161f. provision is made for three "modes of response to Baptism" when a bishop presides: Confirmation, Reception, and Reaffirmation.

A sympathetic comparative study of the Lutheran, Episcopalian, and Methodist baptismal rites, as of the time of writing, is Laurence Stookey, "Three New Initiation Rites," in *Worship* 51 (1977), pp. 33–49.

9. A few years ago I wrote, "It is psychologically self-defeating to try to associate one part of this initiatory unity with one stage of life, and other parts with other stages when no such staged-out meanings belong inherently to the rites themselves," in "Post-Reformation to the Present," in *Made, Not Born,* p. 116.

10. Commission on Worship of the Consultation on Church Union, *An Order for the Celebration of Holy Baptism, with Commentary,"* Cincinnati, OH: Forward Movement Publications, 1973, p. 20. The phrase "auxiliary rites" is from Louis Weil, *Christian Initiation,* p. 10f.

11. Gerard Austin, *The Rite of Confirmation: Anointing with the Spirit,* New York: Pueblo Publishing, 1985, p. 76.

12. An English Baptist says:

It is through Baptism that we are united with Christ, share his risen life, possess the Holy Spirit, are consecrated to God and made members of his church. How can the Christian thus share in his life and fellowship without being involved in the vocation of the Church? The Church is mission—the people of God elected for the service and salvation of mankind. There can be no incorporation into his people apart from the purpose for which God has called the people. We are baptised into the one body for service and witness.

Stephen F. Winward, in Basil Moss (ed.), *Crisis for Baptism*, p. 125

13. See the brilliant article by Clinton Morrison, "Baptism and Maturity," in *Interpretation*, 17, 1963, pp. 387–401.

14. C.K. Barrett, *From First Adam to Last*, New York: Scribners, 1962, p. 108.

15. A Roman Catholic document indicates thinking along similar lines. The *Newsletter* of the Bishops' Committee on the Liturgy of the National Conference of Catholic Bishops, vol. 14, April–May 1978, was generally on "Christian Commitment." It spoke of God's call through history and of Christian Initiation as "the entry of a Christian into the mystery of Christ and his Church."

After developing the theme of Baptism, the letter spoke of "Ways of Renewal," and identified them as: Eucharist, Sunday, Liturgical Year, penance, and "moments of personal decision." Some "nonliturgical events which call forth the renewal of baptismal faith" were mentioned. The document says: "In preparation for and sometimes in conjunction with these...events it is very appropriate to renew formally the promises of Baptism, those promises which accompanied our initiation into the mystery of Christ when we first said yes to his call." Some ways of carrying out such acts of renewal are described.

16. A rubric on *BCP* p. 312 commends the renewal of the baptismal vows on any of the days specified for Baptism when there are no candidates for Baptism. This interrogatory use of the Creed and the questions that follow would take the place of the Nicene Creed at the Eucharist.

One gets the impression that congregations are using this Prayer Book provision and restating the baptismal covenant at other times which seem to hold special significance for their common life.

17. *Confirmation: Celebration of Maturity in Christ*, New York: Seabury Press, 1975, pp. 57–65.

18. This point is made clearly in Charles Price, "Rites of Initiation" [Occasional Paper No.4] now collected in *The Occasional Papers of the Standing Liturgical Commission*, Collection No. 1. New York: The Church Hymnal Corporation, 1987, p. 32.

19. Neither this liturgical provision nor its intention is quite the same as "A Form of

Commitment to Christian Service" on pages 420–421 of the Prayer Book. That pastoral rite has in mind forms of service for Christ in the world. It uses the reaffirmation of baptismal promises, but it would also include a specific Act of Commitment. It need not be done before a bishop.

20. Urban T. Holmes, *op.cit.*, pp. 65–67.

> *There are critical times—in the sense of turning points—when we need to take a look once again at one's relationship to the Church and to ritualize that further step in the process of maturing within the context of the redeeming community. This may be only once in our life, but in our culture it is more likely to be three or four times over a period of forty or fifty years. There are the times when we move or when the rector or vicar moves. There are occasions when a divorce or a death in our immediate family calls our faith into question. The loss of a job, the discovery of or recovery from a serious illness, a sudden success, a return from a dangerous assignment, all might evoke in us a need to ritualize again our owning of our faith.... There is also the simple, slow erosion of our enthusiasm, which study and reaffirmation can seek to reverse" (p. 65).*

21. Dean Holmes again, *ibid.*, pp. 65–7.

22. The terminological morass can be illustrated. The consuming question from many groups considering the initiatory rites is, "Is a person who is baptized under the 1979 Prayer Book also confirmed?" The answer is: "It all depends. If you refer to the postbaptismal prayer and action, which has clearly been part—the oldest part—of what has been understood as Confirmation, your answer is 'yes.' But that is not the way in which the Prayer Book (nor the canons, nor the parish reports) uses the term 'confirmed.' What *you* mean by 'Confirmation' is now an act that immediately follows Baptism, but is not referred to by your term. If, however, you mean the ratification of baptismal promises, which is another part (less old, but quite important) of what the church has spoken of as 'Confirmation,' the answer is 'no.' For that ratifying action does not take place in the baptismal rite. There the promises are made, not renewed. But the baptismal promises made at Baptism are often renewed thereafter. The first occasion when, at a bishop's visit, one who had been baptized as an infant publicly renews the promises of Baptism is the action which the Prayer Book calls 'Confirmation.' Please ask easier questions."

23. The tension between what is required in drafting rites (especially rites whose use will be mandatory throughout a large denomination) and what is required in getting them adopted is remarked by several commentators on contemporary liturgical revision. L.L. Mitchell has some wise and temperate observations in "Christian Initiation, Rites of Passage, and Confirmation," in K.B. Cully, ed., *Confirmation Re-Examined*, 1982, p. 91f.

24. These sentences are taken from Daniel B. Stevick, "The Liturgics of Confirmation," in K.B. Cully, ed., *op.cit.*, p. 79. Copyright © 1982 Kendig Brubaker Cully.

25. This paragraph follows closely a passage in *ibid.*, p. 78. On the subject see also, Marion J. Hatchett, "The Rite of 'Confirmation' in *The Book of Common Prayer* and in *Authorized Services 1973*," in *Anglican Theological Review* 56 (1974), pp. 292–310.

Chapter IX: *The Prayer Book Rite: A Commentary*

1. There are other commentaries, all with valuable interpretive ideas, and each with special characteristics. When the initiatory rites of *Prayer Book Studies 26* were still at the Trial Use stage, Louis Weil wrote *Christian Initiation: A Theological and Pastoral Commentary on the Proposed Rites* (published first in 1974 as an article and later as a booklet). It combines wise interpretive insights with comments on detail and practice. In Marion Hatchett's *Commentary on the American Prayer Book* (1980), pages 251–288 give informative comments, largely historical, on the Prayer Book rites, their background, structure, and sources. Bishop Eastman devotes ch. 5, pp. 55–89, of *The Baptizing Community* (1982) to a running commentary on the Baptism rite with remarks on the words of the text, on fitting ceremonial actions, and on symbols which appeal to the imagination. Ch. 5, pp. 88–127, of Leonel Mitchell's *Praying Shapes Believing* (1985) is organized in the sequence of the rites of initiation, including the stages of the Catechumenate; the author's comments explain themes and content.

2. The first of these suggestions is favored by Bishop Eastman; the second by Louis Weil.

3. *Apostolic Tradition*, 16.2.

4. For the history of sponsorship, the finest work remains D.S. Bailey, *Sponsors at Baptism and Confirmation*, London: S.P.C.K., 1952.

5. The litany on p. 305f. of the Prayer Book is the primary intercessory material provided in the rite for Holy Baptism. It is focused quite specifically on the persons being baptized. If more intercession is desirable (as it well might be at a "chief service of a Sunday or other feast"), the order for Holy Baptism may join the Eucharist at the Prayers of the People (rubric, p. 310). It would be important to shape the intercession prayer so that those things are mentioned that really need to be prayed for but so that it does not overload a liturgical event which will have many strong elements in it.

6. The place of the consecration of the font is more problematic than might be realized. The earliest references to Baptism say nothing about prayer over the water. When it is mentioned first, by Hippolytus, it is rather incidental. As the ministers and candidates come to the water, prayer is made over it (*Apostolic Tradition*, 21). The prayer seems introductory, and not at the heart of the action. Later, the consecration prayer becomes quite full, but it is used several times a year rather than at each baptismal occasion. Does it come to have the place and form it does because of a parallel with the Eucharist? When Baptism and the Eucharist were understood to be members of a classification, "sacraments," they must have important features in common. In the Eu-

charist, the church repeats the action of Jesus, who, as a Jew presiding at a meal, took bread and "blessed" and broke it. The Eucharist requires an act of blessing. But there is no parallel necessity in the baptismal action. Among some Lutherans, it has been almost a point of honor to emphasize that the water of Baptism is common water— ordinary water made effective by the Word. The prayer of consecration, as they see it, must be carefully drafted lest it give a misplaced emphasis. Clearly, the church has accepted many Baptisms in which the water—like that in which Philip baptized the Ethiopian eunuch—was the water at hand. Of course, to say that when circumstances require, the consecration of the font is dispensable is not to say that when it can be done it should not be done.

7. A great deal of historical information on this subject has been gathered in L.L. Mitchell, *Baptismal Anointing*, Appendix I, "Anglican Use of Baptismal Oil," pp. 177–187.
Concerning the optional character of the anointing, Charles Price says, "Although the use of oil may be regarded by some as enriching the initiatory rite, its use cannot be regarded as indispensable, nor may a Baptism performed by a presbyter without it be regarded as incomplete," *Rites of Initiation* [Occasional Paper No.4], SLC, New York, p. 7. See the similar remarks in Louis Weil's *Christian Initiation*, p. 10f.

8. *The Book of Occasional Services*, 1979, contains, in the section of Episcopal Services, a rite for "Consecration of Chrism apart from Baptism" (p. 209f.) which may be used when it is desired, at a bishop's visit, to consecrate chrism but there is no Baptism. The *BOS* also contains "A Proper for the Consecration of Chrism" for use at a separate diocesan service (p. 211).

9. It will hardly do to pass without noting that objections are being raised to the baptismal formula because of its use of masculine names or metaphors: Father and Son. The terms seem to be evidence of the general male domination of the symbol-system. The words at Baptism are such a significant mark of church unity and tradition that it is difficult to propose change without inviting a charge of sectarianism. But they are so conspicuous in establishing Christian identity that objections, when they are felt, are likely to be felt acutely. The issues are complex and somewhat incidental to the subject here, which is to comment on the authorized text. Perhaps it is enough to remark that the "triadic" terms in the New Testament and in the earliest liturgical sources on which the Prayer Book (and the sacramental tradition) draws were in origin functional, existential, confessional, or doxological terms, gathering up the meaning of redemption. They were not credal or "trinitarian," although the developed trinitarian discussion took some of its rise from them. Believers' complex awareness that they had been brought into relation to God through Christ and given the Spirit, the firstfruits of the new age, came to immediate expression. Any substitute wording which might be proposed needs to be tested by whether or not it conveys this reality. These issues are discussed in a brief Appendix, "Concerning the Use of the Trinitarian

Formula," in Laurence Stookey, *Baptism: Christ's Act in the Church*, Nashville: Abingdon Press 1982, pp. 198–200.

10. S. Anita Stauffer, "Space for Baptism," in *Reformed Liturgy and Music*, 19 (1985), p. 176. Fr. Kavanagh, speaking more drastically, says, "Baptism into Christ demands enough water to die in," in *The Shape of Baptism*, p. 179.

11. Hippolytus, *Apostolic Tradition*, 22.1; Ambrose, *De Sacramentis*, 3.8; for the Gelasian Sacramentary, see Whitaker, *Documents*, p. 188

12. When the rite is used by a deacon (who is authorized by the bishop to preside), the postbaptismal prayer and actions (*BCP* p. 308) are omitted (rubric, p. 312). They are regarded as priestly acts, and "These omitted portions of the rite may be administered on some subsequent occasion of public Baptism at which a bishop or priest presides."

13. See 2 Corinthians 1:21*f.*; Ephesians 1:13; 4:30; and Revelation 7:3*f.*; 9:4 and 14:1 (the passages in Revelation are based on Ezekiel). Valuable material on this image can be found in G.W.H. Lampe, *The Seal of the Spirit*, London: Longman, 1951, and J. Danielou, *The Bible and the Liturgy*, University of Notre Dame Press: 1956, ch. 3, "The Sphragis." See the summary in L.L. Mitchell, "The Place of Baptismal Anointing in Christian Initiation," p. 205. The signing in Jewish custom was with the letter Taw. The Christians adopted the gesture and the shape, giving it their own meaning.

14. In *Prayer Book Studies 26* the text reads: "*Name*, child of God, inheritor of the Kingdom of heaven, you have been sealed by the Holy Spirit and marked as Christ's own for ever." This wording had in its favor some ambiguity. It could be taken as saying "You are sealed by the Baptism which has just been done," or it could be read as "You are now being sealed," or it could mean "You are recipient of an action with compound meaning. One important action, with water, has just taken place; another, with the sign of the cross (and anointing), takes place now. Together with other parts of the rite, they speak of the complex relation between you and the triune God. Do not be anxious about what parts are essential—as though the others were unimportant. Do not try to assign univocal significance to this sign and to that. 'You are sealed.' Do not ask specifically when or by what." The indefinite quality of this construction would be with respect to two actions closely linked in meaning and separated by only a brief time. The wording adopted for the 1976 Proposed Book threw the meaning explicitly to the first of these three constructions. None of the churches which has followed the Episcopal Church in other features of the baptismal rite has adopted this Prayer Book wording.

15. Gerard Austin, writing from a point of view for which the separate identity of two sacramental actions is taken for granted, says: "For the Roman Catholic theologian the phrase, 'in Baptism,' in the sealing formula ('N., you are sealed by the Holy Spirit in Baptism and marked as Christ's own for ever. Amen') might cause difficulty by implying that this act of sealing is not a distinct sacramental rite, separate from the water-

bath itself," *op. cit.* p. 76. The Prayer Book wording, as L.L. Mitchell remarks, "makes it clear that what is being done is intimately related to Baptism and is in fact a part of the baptismal rite," *Praying Shapes Believing*, p. 114. The Prayer Book's wording, however, by its strained explicitness almost reads as though it were arguing the point.

16. Eight sentences here are taken from "The Liturgics of Confirmation," in *Confirmation Re-examined*, p. 75.

From his examination of the fourth-century baptismal lectures, Hugh M. Riley observes:

> When Cyril says that the neophyte received the Holy Spirit in the anointing after baptism, he is thinking 'inclusively' and not 'exclusively,' for in the Eastern fathers, the communication of the Holy Spirit is seen in the totality of Christian Initiation. Hence, their thinking does not admit of too much application of a more linear Western mode of thought.

> Christian Initiation, Catholic University Press, Washington, D.C.: 1974, p. 399, quoted in Austin, *op. cit.*, p. 25.

17. A hand is not an isolated thing. It comes attached to a human being. It is an expression of a person, an extension of one person toward another, a touching, a bonding. It is capable of a range of meaning—from gentleness to hostility or cruelty. It speaks of persons in relation. For a superb thought piece on hands in liturgy, see Godfrey Diekmann, "The Laying On of Hands: The Basic Sacramental Rite," in *Proceedings of the Catholic Theological Society of America* 29 (1974), pp. 339–351.

18. It should be clear (but is it?) that any adult who is baptized at a service at which a bishop performs the postbaptismal signing (and anointing) has no need for a subsequent episcopal act. The vows made at Baptism were a "mature public affirmation" of faith and commitment. The bishop's action at Baptism surely satisfies the requirement of the second rubric on p. 412. *See* Canon I.17.1(d).

Adults who are baptized in the Episcopal Church, all parts of the rite being done by a presbyter, are expected, according to the rubric mentioned above, "to make a public affirmation of their faith...in the presence of a bishop, and to receive the laying on of hands." Since the vows at Baptism are a fully adult commitment, and the Prayer Book baptismal rite is sacramentally complete, the theological or liturgical reason for this rubrical requirement is not clear. (The bishop's act is not called "Confirmation" in the rubric.) Perhaps one may think along these lines: The person baptized and given the postbaptismal sign (and anointing) by a priest has not yet done something that Episcopalians do, *viz.* has not received the laying-on of hands from a bishop—expressing recognition and blessing. At a bishop's visitation, such a person may reaffirm the promises of Baptism and receive the laying-on of hands. (The bishop may use this gesture for those who are making an act of reaffirmation.)

19. For the establishment of the covenant, see Exodus 19–24, especially 24:3–11. Among many instances of covenant renewal, see 2 Kings 23 (Josiah); Nehemiah 8–10

(Ezra). The setting of covenant renewal is often strongly liturgical, "They beheld God, and ate and drank."

20. Louis Weil has remarked:

> The laying-on-of-hands was used [in the early church] to anoint the baptized; to designate the gifts of the Eucharist; to ordain to various offices; to absolve the penitent; to restore the sick; and to reconcile the lapsed. Surely, it is the liturgical content which clarifies the purpose of the gesture as the mind of the Church specifies the intention.

"Confirmation: Some Notes on Its Meaning," in *Anglican Theological Review* 59 (1977), p. 221.

21. Massey H. Shepherd, Jr., *Liturgy and Education,* New York: Seabury Press, 1965, p. 106. This passage is quoted in *Prayer Book Studies 18,* p. 26. Much of what this prophetic author sought is now available through the new rites.

Aidan Kavanagh makes a similar observation on the place of the bishop in the new adult rites of initiation in the Roman Catholic Communion:

> Far from constituting a restriction on episcopal ministry, it enhances this ministry by emphasizing the real sacramental importance of the bishop as the one who normally should preside throughout the whole process of Christian Initiation. Formerly this ministry was exercised almost wholly in confirmation.

"Christian Initiation of Adults: The Rites," p. 129.

22. In some fine remarks on "The Bishop at the Center," Louis Weil says, "The purpose is not that the bishop should swallow up all the other legitimate roles within the liturgical action, for . . . the norms of the rite make clear that a wide diversity of participation is presumed," *Christian Initiation,* p. 5. The presence of the bishop in the role of chief liturgical officer of the diocese makes possible a demonstration of complementary ministries.

Bibliography

BOOKS

Akeley, T.C. *Christian Initiation in Spain c.300–1100*. London: Darton, Longman and Todd, 1967.

Aland, K. *Did the Early Church Baptize Infants?* Philadelphia: Westminster Press, 1963.

Arndt, E.J.F. *The Font and the Table*. Richmond, VA: John Knox Press, 1967.

Austin, Gerard. *The Rite of Confirmation: Anointing with the Spirit*. New York: Pueblo Publishing Co., 1985.

Bailey, D.S. *Sponsors at Baptism and Confirmation*. London: S.P.C.K., 1952.

Baillie, J. *Baptism and Conversion*. New York: Scribners, 1963.

Baptism and Confirmation. Prayer Book Studies 1, Standing Liturgical Commission. New York: Church Pension Fund, 1950.

Baptism and Confirmation. Report of the Church of England Liturgical Commission. London: S.P.C.K., 1959.

Baptism and Confirmation Today. Report of the Joint Committees on Baptism, Confirmation and the Holy Communion of the Convocations of Canterbury and York. London: S.P.C.K., 1955.

Baptism, Eucharist and Ministry. Faith and Order Paper No. 111. Geneva: World Council of Churches, 1982.

Barth, K. *The Teaching of the Church Regarding Baptism*. London: S.C.M. Press, 1948.

Beasley-Murray, G.R. *Baptism in the New Testament*. London: Macmillan, 1963.

——. *Baptism Today and Tomorrow*. New York: St. Martin's Press, 1966.

Bohen, M. *The Mystery of Confirmation*. New York: Herder and Herder, 1963.

The Book of Occasional Services. New York: Church Hymnal Corporation, 1979.

Bouyer, L. *Christian Initiation.* London: Burns and Oates, 1960.

Brockett, Lorna. *The Theology of Baptism.* Theology Today Series, No. 25. Notre Dame, IN: Fides, 1971.

Bromiley, G.W. *Baptism and the Anglican Reformers.* London: Lutterworth Press, 1953.

————. *Children of Promise:* The Case for Baptizing Infants. Grand Rapids, MI: Eerdmans, 1979.

Buchanan, C. *A Case for Infant Baptism.* Grove Booklet on Ministry and Worship, No. 20. Bramcote, Notts.: Grove Books, 1973.

Carr, W. *Baptism: Conscience and Clue for the Church.* New York: Holt, Rinehart and Winston, 1964.

Christian Initiation: Birth and Growth in the Christian Society. London: Church of England Board of Education, 1971.

Commission on Education of the Lutheran World Federation, *Confirmation: A Study Document.* Minneapolis: Augsburg Publishing House, 1964.

Confirmation: or the Laying On of Hands (Vol. 1: Historical and Doctrinal). London: S.P.C.K., 1926.

Confirmation Crisis. New York: Seabury Press, 1968.

Consultation on Church Unity, Commission on Worship, *An Order for the Celebration of Holy Baptism.* Cincinnati, OH: Forward Movement Publications: 1973.

Crehan, J. *Early Christian Baptism and the Creed.* Westminster, MD: Newman Press, 1950.

Cully, K.B., ed. *Confirmation: History, Doctrine and Practice.* New York: Seabury Press, 1962.

————. *Confirmation Re-Examined.* Wilton, CT: Morehouse-Barlow, 1982.

Cullmann, O. *Baptism in the New Testament.* London: S.C.M. Press, 1950.

Davies, J.G. *The Architectural Setting of Baptism.* London: Barrie and Rockliffe, 1962.

Davis, C. *Sacraments of Initiation: Baptism and Confirmation.* New York: Sheed and Ward, 1964.

Dix, G. *Confirmation, or Laying On of Hands?* London: S.C.M. Press, 1950.

——. *The Theology of Confirmation in Relation to Baptism*. Westminster, MD: Dacre Press, 1946.

Dujarier, M. *A History of the Catechumenate: The First Six Centuries*. New York: Sadlier, 1979.

——. *The Rites of Christian Initiation: Historical and Pastoral Reflections*. New York: Sadlier, 1979.

Eastman, A.T. *The Baptizing Community: Christian Initiation and the Local Congregation*. New York: Seabury Press, 1982

Eliade, M. *Rites and Symbols of Initiation*. New York: Harper Torchbooks, 1965 (published by Harper in 1958 under the title *Birth and Rebirth*).

Every, G. *The Baptismal Sacrifice*. London: S.C.M. Press, 1959.

Fisher, J.D.C. *Christian Initiation: Baptism in the Medieval West*. London: S.P.C.K., 1965.

——. *Christian Initiation: The Reformation Period*. London: S.P.C.K., 1970.

——. *Confirmation Then and Now*. London: S.P.C.K., 1978.

Flemington, W.F. *The New Testament Doctrine of Baptism*. London: S.P.C.K., 1948.

Ganoczy, A. *Becoming Christian:* A Theology of Baptism as the Sacrament of Human History. New York: Paulist Press, 1976.

Gilmore, A. *Baptism and Christian Unity*. Philadelphia: Judson Press, 1966.

——, ed. *Christian Baptism:* A Fresh Attempt to Understand the Rite in Terms of Scripture, History and Theology. Philadelphia: Judson Press, 1959.

George, A. et al.. *Baptism in the New Testament,* Baltimore: Helicon, 1964.

Greenslade, S.L. *Shepherding the Flock:* Problems of Pastoral Discipline in the Early Church and in the Younger Churches Today. London: S.C.M. Press, 1967.

Hamman, A., ed. *Baptism:* Ancient Liturgies and Patristic Texts. Staten Island, NY: Alba House, 1967.

——. *The Paschal Mystery:* Ancient Liturgies and Patristic Texts. Staten Island, NY: Alba House, 1969.

Hatchett, M.J. *Commentary on the American Prayer Book*. New York: Seabury Press, 1981.

——. "Thomas Cranmer and the Rites of Christian Initiation." Unpublished dissertation, General Theological Seminary, 1967.

Hinson, E. Glenn. *The Evangelization of the Roman Empire:* Identity and Adaptability. Macon, GA: Mercer University Press, 1981.

Holeton, D.R. *Infant Communion—Then and Now.* Grove Liturgical Study No. 27. Bramcote, Notts.: Grove Books, 1981.

Holmes, U.T. *Confirmation: The Celebration of Maturity in Christ.* New York: Seabury Press, 1975.

———. *Young Children and the Eucharist.* New York: Seabury Press, 1972.

Holy Baptism with the Laying-On-of-Hands. Prayer Book Studies 18, Standing Liturgical Commission. New York: Church Hymnal Corporation, 1970.

Hunkin, J.W. *Episcopal Ordination and Confirmation in Relation to Inter-Communion and Reunion:* A Collection of Anglican Precedents and Opinions. Cambridge, England: W. Heffer & Sons, 1929.

Jagger, P. *Christian Initiation: 1552–1969.* London: S.P.C.K., 1970.

———. *Clouded Witness:* Initiation in the Church of England in the Mid-Victorian Period, 1850–1875. Allison Park, PA: Pickwick Publications, 1982.

Jeremias, J. *Infant Baptism in the First Four Centuries.* Philadelphia: Westminster Press, 1962.

———. *The Origins of Infant Baptism.* London: S.C.M. Press, 1963.

Jewett, P. *Infant Baptism and the Covenant of Grace.* Grand Rapids, MI: Eerdmans, 1978.

Johnson, L.J., ed. *Initiation and Conversion.* Collegeville, MN: The Liturgical Press, 1985.

Kavanagh, A. *The Shape of Baptism:* The Rite of Christian Initiation. New York: Pueblo Publishing Company, 1978.

Lampe, G.W.H. *The Seal of the Spirit* (2nd ed.). London: S.C.M. Press, 1967.

Louisville Consultation on Baptism. Faith and Order Paper No. 97. Geneva: World Council of Churches, n.d., also published in *Review and Expositor* 78:1 (1980), pp. 1–108.

Made, Not Born: New Perspectives on Christian Initiation and the Catechumenate. Notre Dame, IN: University of Notre Dame Press, 1976.

Maldonado, L. and D. Powers, eds. *Structures of Initiation in Crisis,* Concilium, vol. 122. New York: Seabury Press, 1979.

Marcel, P. *The Biblical Doctrine of Infant Baptism*, trans. P.E. Hughes (2nd impression). Cambridge, England: James Clarke & Co., 1959.

Marsh, H.G. *The Origin and Significance of the New Testament Baptism*. Manchester, England: Manchester University Press, 1941.

Marty, M. *Baptism*. Philadelphia: Fortress Press, 1962.

Mason, A.J. *The Relation of Confirmation to Baptism*. London: Longman, Green and Co., 1891.

Minchin, B., ed. *Becoming a Christian*. London: Faith Press, 1954.

Mitchell, L.L. *Baptismal Anointing*. London: S.P.C.K., 1966.

──── . *Praying Shapes Believing:* A Theological Commentary on the Book of Common Prayer. Minneapolis: Winston Press, 1985.

Moody, D. *Baptism: Foundation for Christian Unity*. Philadelphia: Westminster Press, 1967.

Moss, B.S., ed. *Crisis for Baptism*. London: S.C.M. Press, 1965.

Mueller-Fahrenholz, G., ed. *...and do not hinder them:* An Ecumenical Plea for the Admission of Children to the Eucharist. Faith and Order Paper No. 109. Geneva: World Council of Churches, 1982.

Neunheuser, B. *Baptism and Confirmation*. New York: Herder and Herder, 1964.

Nurturing Children at Communion. Grove Liturgical Study, No. 44. Bramcote, Notts.: Grove Books, 1985.

One Baptism, One Eucharist and a Mutually Recognized Ministry. Faith and Order Paper No. 73, Geneva: World Council of Churches, 1975.

One Lord One Baptism. Faith and Order Report. Minneapolis: Augsburg Publishing House, 1960.

Pocknee, C.E. *Infant Baptism Yesterday and Today*. London: Mowbray, 1966.

──── . *The Rites of Christian Initiation*. London: Mowbray, 1962.

──── . *Water and the Spirit*. London: Darton, Longman and Todd, 1967.

Powers, D. and L. Maldonado, eds. *Liturgy and Human Passage*. Concilium, vol. 122, New York: Seabury Press, 1979.

Price, C. and L. Weil. *Liturgy for Living*. New York: Seabury Press, 1979.

Quinn, Frank C. "Contemporary Liturgical Revision: The Revised Rites of Confirmation in the Roman Catholic Church and in the American Episcopal Church." Unpublished dissertation, University of Notre Dame, 1978.

Rawlinson, A.E.J. *Christian Initiation.* London: S.P.C.K., 1947.

Repp, A.C. *Confirmation in the Lutheran Church.* St. Louis: Concordia, 1964.

Riley, H.M., *Christian Initiation:* A Comparative Study of the Interpretation of the Baptismal Liturgy in the Mystagogical Writings of Cyril of Jerusalem, John Chrysostom, Theodore of Mopsuestia, and Ambrose of Milan. Washington, D.C.: Catholic University of America Press, 1974.

Rite of Baptism for Children. Washington, D.C.: U.S. Catholic Conference, 1969.

Rite of Christian Initiation of Adults. Washington, D.C.: U.S. Catholic Conference, 1974.

Schlink, E. *The Doctrine of Baptism,* trans. H.J.A. Bouman. St. Louis: Concordia Publishing House, 1972.

Schmeiser, J., ed. *Initiation Theology.* Toronto: Anglican Book Center, 1978.

Schmemann, A. *Of Water and the Spirit.* Crestwood, NY: St. Vladimir's Seminary Press, 1974.

Schnackenburg, R. *Baptism in the Thought of St. Paul.* New York: Herder and Herder, 1964.

Searle, Mark *Christening: The Making of Christians.* Collegeville, MN: The Liturgical Press, 1980.

———, ed. *Baptism and Confirmation,* Alternative Futures for Worship, vol. 2. Collegeville, MN: Liturgical Press, 1987.

Shepherd, M.H. *The Paschal Liturgy and the Apocalypse.* Richmond, VA: John Knox Press, 1960.

Stevick, D.B. *Adult Baptism: Getting Back to the Beginning.* Cincinnati, OH: Forward Movement Publications, 1984.

———. "Supplement to *Holy Baptism: together with A Form for the Affirmation of Baptismal Vows...* (*Prayer Book Studies 26*). New York: Church Hymnal Corporation, 1973.

Stookey, L.H. *Baptism: Christ's Act in the Church.* Nashville, TN: Abingdon, 1982.

Strege, Merle D., ed. *Baptism and Church: A Believers' Church Vision.* Grand Rapids, MI: Sagamore Books, 1986.

The Theology of Christian Initiation. Report of a Theological Commission appointed by the Archbishops of Canterbury and York. London: S.P.C.K., 1949.

Thornton, L.S. *Confirmation: Its Place in the Baptismal Mystery.* Westminster, MD: Dacre Press, 1954.

Thurian, M. *Consecration of the Layman: New Approaches to the Sacrament of Confirmation.* Baltimore: Helicon Press, 1963.

————, ed. *Ecumenical Perspectives on Baptism, Eucharist and Ministry.* Faith and Order Paper No. 116, Geneva: World Council of Churches, 1983.

———— and G. Wainwright, eds. *Baptism and Eucharist: Ecumenical Convergence in Celebration.* Geneva: World Council of Churches; Grand Rapids, MI: Eerdmans, 1983.

Van Gennep, A. *The Rites of Passage* (trans. M. Vizedom and G. Caffee). Chicago: University of Chicago Press, 1960. (Originally published in French in 1909.)

Vellian, J., ed. Studies on Syrian Baptismal Rites. The Syrian Churches Series, vol. 6. Kottyam, Kerala: C.M.S. Press, 1973.

Wagner, J., ed. *Adult Baptism and the Catechumenate,* Concilium, vol. 22. New York: Paulist Press, 1967.

Wainwright, G. *Christian Initiation.* Richmond, VA: John Knox Press, 1969.

Weil, L. *Christian Initiation:* A Theological and Pastoral Commentary on the Proposed Rites. Associated Parishes, n.d. [Originally published in the *Nashotah Review* 14:3 (1974), pp. 202–223, and later issued as a booklet.]

Whitaker, E.C. *The Baptismal Liturgy.* London: Faith Press, 1965.

————. *Documents of the Baptismal Liturgy* (2nd ed., revised and supplemented). London: S.P.C.K., 1970.

————. *Sacramental Initiation Complete in Baptism.* Grove Liturgical Study No. 1. Bramcote, Notts.: Grove Books, 1975.

White, R.E.O. *The Biblical Doctrine of Initiation.* Grand Rapids, MI: Eerdmans, 1960.

Wirgman, A.T. *The Doctrine of Confirmation.* London: Longman, Green and Co., 1897.

Yarnold, E. *The Awe-Inspiring Rites of Initiation:* Baptismal Homilies of the Fourth Century. Slough, Bucks.: St. Paul Publications, 1971.

Allen, Horace T. "The Time of Baptism," in *Reformed Liturgy and Music* 19 (1985), pp. 184–187.

Argenti, Cyrille. "Chrismation," in M. Thurian, ed., *Ecumenical Perspectives on BEM*. Geneva: World Council of Churches, 1983, pp. 46–67.

Austin, G. "What Has Happened to Confirmation?" in *Worship* 50 (1976), pp. 420–426.

"Baptism, Confirmation and the Eucharist." Report on a Faith and Order Study in *Studia Liturgica* 8 (1971–72), pp. 81–97.

Beggiani, S. "Christian Initiation in the Eastern Churches," in *The Living Light* 11 (1974), pp. 536–547.

Brand, E.L. "Baptism and Communion of Infants: A Lutheran View," in *Worship* 50 (1976), pp. 29–42.

———. "New Rites of Initiation and their Implications: in the Lutheran Churches," in *Studia Liturgica* 12 (1977), pp. 151–165.

Brock, S. "The Syrian Baptismal Ordines (with special reference to the anointings)," in *Studia Liturgica* 12 (1977), pp. 177–183.

Brown, R.E. "We Profess One Baptism for the Forgiveness of Sins," in *Worship* 40 (1966), pp. 260–271.

"Children and Communion." Report of an International Anglican Consultation in *Anglican Theological Review* 68 (1986), pp. 185–201.

Clark, N. "Christian Initiation," in *Studia Liturgica* 4 (1965), pp. 156–165.

Covino, P.F.X. "The Postconciliar Infant Baptism Debate in the American Catholic Church," in *Worship* 56 (1982), pp. 240–260.

Diekmann, G. "The Laying On of Hands: The Basic Sacramental Rite," in *Proceedings of the Catholic Theological Society of America* 29 (1974), pp. 339–351.

"Documentation and Reflection: Confirmation Today," in *Anglican Theological Review* 54 (1972), pp. 106–119.

"Ecumenical Agreement on Baptism: A Faith and Order Statement," in *Studia Liturgica* 8 (1971–72), pp. 123–128.

Edwards, O.C. "The Exegesis of Acts 8:4–25 and Its Implications for Confirmation and Glossalalia," in *Anglican Theological Review,* Supplementary Series, No. 2 (1973), pp. 100–112.

Erickson, C.D. "The Strong Name of the Trinity," in *Reformed Liturgy and Music* 14:4 (1985), pp. 205–210.

Finn, T.M. "Baptismal Death and Resurrection: A Study in Fourth Century Eastern Baptismal Thought," in *Worship* 43 (1969), pp. 175–179.

Fischer, B. "Baptismal Exorcism in the Catholic Baptismal Rites after Vatican II," in *Studia Liturgica* 10 (1974), pp. 48–55.

Frederick, J.B.M. "The Initiation Crisis in the Church of England," in *Studia Liturgica* 9 (1972), pp. 137–157.

Goodson, M.L. "What About Confirmation by Priest?" in *The St. Luke's Journal* 16 (1972), pp. 72–80.

Grainger, Roger. "The Sacraments as Passage Rites," in *Worship* 58 (1984), pp. 214–222.

Guerette, R.H. "Ecclesiology and Infant Baptism," in *Worship* 44 (1970), pp. 433–437.

Gunn, J. "Bishop Hobart's Emphasis on Confirmation," in *Historical Magazine of the Episcopal Church,* 24 (1955), pp. 293–310.

Gwinnell, M. "The Age—or Stage—for Confirmation," in *The Clergy Review* 55 (1970), pp. 10–26.

Hatchett, M.J. "The Rite of 'Confirmation' in *The Book of Common Prayer* and in *Authorized Services 1973*," in *Anglican Theological Review* 56 (1974), pp. 292–310.

Holeton, D.R. "Christian Initiation in Some Anglican Provinces," in *Studia Liturgica* 12 (1977), pp. 129–150.

———. "Confirmation in the 1980's," in M. Thurian, ed., *Ecumenical Perspectives on BEM*. Geneva: World Council of Churches, 1983, pp. 68–89.

Jagger, P.J. "Christian Unity and Valid Baptism," in *Theology,* No. 615, 74 (1971), pp. 404–413.

Jenson, R. "Infant Baptism," in *Dialog* 8 (1969), pp. 214–217.

———. "The Mandate and Promise of Baptism," in *Interpretation* 30 (1976), pp. 271–287.

Karay, D. "Let the Children Lead the Way: A Case for Baptizing Children," in *Worship* 61 (1987), pp. 336–349.

Kavanagh, A. "Christian Initiation in Post-Conciliar Roman Catholicism: A Brief

Report," in *Studia Liturgica* 12 (1977), pp. 107–115.

———. "Christian Initiation of Adults: The Rites," in *Worship* 48 (1974), pp. 318–335.

———. "Confirmation: A Suggestion from Structure," in *Worship* 58 (1984), pp. 386–395.

———. "Initiation: Baptism and Confirmation," in *Worship.* 46 (1972), pp. 262–276.

———. "The Norm of Baptism: The New Rite of Christian Initiation of Adults," in *Worship,* 48 (1974), pp. 143–152.

Kiesling, C. "Infant Baptism," in *Worship,* 42 (1968), pp. 617–626.

Kretschmar, G. "Recent Research on Christian Initiation," in *Studia Liturgica* 12 (1977), pp. 87–106.

Levesque, J.L. "The Theology of the Postbaptismal Rites in the Seventh and Eighth Century Gallican Church," in *Ephemerides Liturgicae* 95 (1981), pp. 3–43.

McDermott, B. "The Theology of Original Sin: Recent Developments," in *Theological Studies* 38 (1977), pp. 478–512.

Marsh, T. "A Study of Confirmation," in *Irish Theological Quarterly* 39 (1972), pp. 149–163.

Mitchell, L.L. "The Place of Baptismal Anointing in Christian Initiation," in *Anglican Theological Review* 68 (1986), pp. 202–211.

———. "The 'Shape' of the Baptismal Liturgy," in *Anglican Theological Review,* 47 (1965), pp. 410–419.

———. "The Theology of Christian Initiation and *The Proposed Book of Common Prayer,*" in *Anglican Theological Review,* 60 (1978), pp. 399–419.

———. "What Does Confirmation Mean?" in *The Anglican* 4 (1973), pp. 2–6.

Morrison, C. "Baptism and Maturity," in *Interpretation* 17 (1963), pp. 387–401.

Mudge, L.S. "Convergence on Baptism," in M. Thurian, ed., *Ecumenical Perspectives on BEM.* Geneva: World Council of Churches, 1983, pp. 33–45.

Powers, J.M. "Confirmation, the Problem of Meaning," in *Worship* 46 (1972), pp. 22–29.

Price, C.P. "Rites of Initiation," in *The Occasional Papers of the Standing Liturgical Commission,* Collection No. 1, New York: Church Hymnal Corporation, 1987, pp. 24–37.

Rodriguez, A.M. "The Minister of Confirmation," in *The Sacraments in Theology and Canon Law*, eds. N. Edelby, T. Jimenez-Urresti, and P. Huizing. New York: Paulist Press, 1968, pp. 28–36.

Shepherd, M.H. "Confirmation: The Early Church," in *Worship* 46 (1972), pp. 15–21.

Stanley, D.M. "The New Testament Doctrine of Baptism: An Essay in Biblical Theology," in *Theological Studies* 18 (1957), pp. 169–215.

Stauffer, Anita S. "Space for Baptism," in *Reformed Liturgy and Music* 19 (1985), pp. 174–178.

Stevick, D.B. "Confirmation for Today: Reflections on the Rite Proposed for the Episcopal Church," in *Worship* 44 (1970), pp. 541–560.

———. "Types of Baptismal Spirituality," in *Worship* 47 (1973), pp. 11–26.

Stookey, L. "Three New Initiation Rites," in *Worship* 51 (1977), pp. 33–49.

———. "Toward a Spirituality Based in Baptism," in *Reformed Liturgy and Music* 19 (1985), pp. 211–214.

Turner, H.E.W. et al. "One Baptism for the Remission of Sins" (a symposium), in *Theology*, No. 544, Oct. 1965, pp. 455–479.

Verghese, P. "Relation between Baptism, 'Confirmation' and the Eucharist in the Syrian Orthodox Church," in *Studia Liturgica* 4 (1965), pp. 81–93.

Wainwright, G. "The Baptismal Eucharist before Nicaea," in *Studia Liturgica*, 4 (1965), pp. 9–36.

———. "Christian Initiation in the Ecumenical Movement," in *Studia Liturgica* 12 (1977), pp. 67–86.

———. "Images of Baptism," in *Reformed Liturgy and Music* 19 (1985), pp. 171–173.

———. "The Rites and Ceremonies of Christian Initiation," in *Studia Liturgica* 10 (1974), pp. 2–24.

Weil, L. "Christian Initiation in the Anglican Communion: A Response," in *Studia Liturgica* 12 (1977), pp. 126–128.

———. "Confirmation: Some Notes on Its Meaning," in *Anglican Theological Review*, 59 (1977), pp. 220–224.

Werblowsky, R.J. Zwi. "On the Baptismal Rite According to St. Hippolytus," in *Studia Patristica* vol. 2, part II (1957), pp. 93–105.

Wilburn, R.G. "The One Baptism and the Many Baptisms," in *Theology Today* 22 (1965), pp. 59–83.

Wiles, M.F. "One Baptism for the Remission of Sins," in *Church Quarterly Review* 165 (1964), pp. 59–66.

Willimon, W. "A Liberating Word in Water," in *Christian Century*, March 22, 1978, pp. 302–306.

Winkler, G. "Confirmation or Chrismation? A Study in Comparative Liturgy," in *Worship* 58 (1984), pp. 2–17.

———. "The Original Meaning of the Prebaptismal Anointing and Its Implications," in *Worship* 52 (1978), pp. 24–45.

Wright, D.F. "The Origins of Infant Baptism—Child Believers' Baptism," in *Scottish Journal of Theology* 40 (1987), pp. 1–23.

Yarnold, E. "Baptism and the Pagan Mysteries in the Fourth Century," in *The Heythrop Journal* 13 (1972), pp. 247–267.

Index

Creed. *See* Apostles' Creed
Cully, Kendig B., 64
Cyprian, 14, 93
Cyril of Jerusalem, 57

Daily Office, 133
Dalby, J.M.M., 95–96
Davis, Charles, 58
Deacon, baptism by, 150
Deacon, Thomas, 98
Decentius of Gubbio, 15
Devil, renunciation of, 9, 155
Devotions (Deacon), 98
Diaspora, 31
Dickens, Charles, 121
Didache, 92

Easter, 8, 9, 14, 66, 71, 92–93
Easter Vigil, 14, 49, 51, 110, 131, 132, 141
Eastern Churches, 12, 14, 83, 87, 120
Eastman, Bishop, 47
Ecumenical issues, 19, 51–52, 68, 81–84, 110–11
Ephphetha, 65
Epiclesis, 73–75, 140
Episcopal Church, 24, 38, 45–46, 104–105, 105–110, 120–21, 123, 169–72
Episcopal Confirmation, 16–17, 18, 24–25, 58–59, 67, 85–90, 150, 169–72
Erikson, Erik, 77
Evangelical Movement, 24
Exodus, 8
Exorcism, 20, 22, 58, 65, 66

Faith, theology of, 7, 40, 59–61, 62, 100, 165
Family, 7, 9, 39–40
Family Baptism, 7, 9
Feet, washing of, 65
Fisher, Canon, 94
Frederick, J.B.M., 127
Freud, Sigmund, 121
Full, True and Comprehensive View of Christianity, A (Deacon), 98

Gaul, 13, 16
Gelasian Sacramentary, 94
General Convention, 107, 121
Gifts of the Spirit, 21, 57, 58, 67, 69–76, 135, 162
Gilligan, Carol, 77
Gloria in excelsis, 153
Godparents, 20, 154
Goethe, Johann von, 121

Great Thanksgiving, 74
Gregorian Sacramentary, 94
Gregory of Nazianzus, 60
Gregory the Great, 15–16

Hall, G. Stanley, 77–78
Hippolytus, 58, 59, 64, 154, 162
Hobart, John Henry, Bishop, 24–25, 86
Holmes, Urban T., 142
Holy Spirit, 6–7, 9, 17, 20, 21, 23, 57, 66–76, 83–84, 135, 149, 162
Holy Spirit, gifts of. *See* Gifts of the Spirit
Holy Table. *See* Table of the Lord
House of Bishops, 107–08
Huss, Jan, 19, 61, 96

Immersion, 160–61
Indiscriminate baptism, 37, 46
Infant baptism, 7, 12, 18, 33–35, 60, 63, 121, 154
Innocent I, Pope, 15
International Anglican Consultation, 90, 110
Irving, Edward, 98
Italy, 13

Jenson, Robert, 44–45
Jerome, 15
John, 7, 71, 133
John Chrysostom, 9
John the Baptist, 5, 66, 133, 159
Joyce, James, 121
Jung, Carl, 121

Kairos, 32, 33–34
Kavanagh, Aidan, 75, 89, 100
Keniston, Kenneth, 78
Kerygma, 6, 59
Kierkegaard, Soren, 118, 121
Kohlberg, Lawrence, 77
Koinonia, 101

Lambeth Conference, 1968, 106
Lay person, baptism by, 13, 150
Laying on of hands, 9, 15, 21, 22, 57, 68, 168–69
Liber Ordinum, 13, 94
Lord's Table. *See* Table of the Lord
Luke, 69
Luther, Martin, 18, 19
Lutherans, 18, 20, 36–37

Manual, 131
Mass baptism, 100

Matthew, St., 159
Maurice, F.D., 24
Milk and honey, 65–66
Missale Gothicum, 13
Mitchell, L.L., 13
Montaigne, Michel, 121

Nock, A.D., 60
Non-episcopal churches, baptized adults
    from, 81–85
Nudity, at baptism, 9

Oil of Thanksgiving, 58
On Baptism (Tertullian), 66
Ordo Romanus XI, 94
Original sin, 11–12, 39
Oxford Movement, 24, 85

Palmer, William, 85
Paschal Mystery. *See* Easter
Passover, 8, 96
Pastoral Offices, 131, 142
Paul, St., 11, 25, 60, 70–71, 91, 159
Peckham, Archbishop, 17, 82
Pelagius, 11
Pentecost, 6, 71, 132
Peter, 6, 7
Piaget, Jean, 77
"Pocono Statement," 107–08
Postbaptismal sin, 10
Prayer Book Studies 18, 106, 107, 120–21
Prayer Book Studies 26, 109, 136, 146–47
Presbyteral Confirmation, 19, 20, 22, 58–59,
    62, 87, 88–89, 135
Presbyters, 13, 15–16, 21, 58, 135, 151
Prevenience, motif of, 39
Promises at Baptism, 156–58
Proselyte baptism, 5, 7

Rahner, Karl, 31
Reaffirmation of baptismal vows, 18, 21, 59,
    61–62, 135, 144–45, 146, 152, 164,
    166–69, 171, 172
Reception, 81–84, 143, 144–45, 146, 152,
    164, 166–69, 171, 172
Reformation, 18, 19, 20, 25, 55, 59,
    61–62, 96
Reformed churches, 18
Renewal of baptismal vows, 138–46
    See also Reaffirmation of baptismal vows;
    Reception
Renunciations, 9, 22, 155–56, 166, 171

Rite for Christian Initiation of Adults,
    49–50, 88, 89
Rite of Baptism for Children, The, 49
Rites of passage, 115–19, 123–24
Robinson, J.A.T., 84
Roman Catholic Church, 49–50, 62, 104
Rome, early Christians at, 14–16, 58, 94

Salt, giving of, 65
Samaria, 7
Sarum *Manual,* 17, 19, 20, 131
Satan, renunciation of, 9, 155
Schismatics, 14–15
Sealing, 65, 66, 162–64, 167
Service of the Word, 134, 153
Shepherd, Massey H., Jr., 92, 169
Sign of the cross, 15, 20, 21, 22, 65, 135,
    162–63
Sin, baptism and, 10–12
Social Darwinism, 30
Spain, 13
Sphragis, 66
Spirit, gifts of the. *See* Gifts of the Spirit
Sponsors, 154
Standing Liturgical Commission, 106, 107
Summa Theologica (St. Thomas), 95
Syrian Church, 9, 10

Table of the Lord, 68, 93, 96, 105, 107, 172
Taylor, Jeremy, 97–98
Teaching of the Church Regarding Baptism,
    The (Barth), 37
Tertullian, 57–58, 66
Thomas, St., 17, 25, 95–96
Tractarians, 24

Vatican Council II, 49
Vigil of Easter. *See* Easter Vigil

Weil, Louis, 107
White garment, giving of, 20, 22, 65
Wilberforce, Samuel, 24
World Council of Churches, Commission on
    Faith and Order in the World, 111
Wycliffe, John, 61

"Years of discretion," 21, 41–42